BÜLENT SOMAY

A
CASE
FOR
ANOTHER
REGIME
OF
REPRODUCTION,
SEXUALITY
AND
KINSHIP

sublation
press

Beyond Family

First Published by Sublation Media 2023
Copyright © 2023 Bülent Somay

All Rights Reserved
Commissioned and Edited by Douglas Lain
Copy Editor Konrad Jandavs

A Sublation Press Book
Published by Sublation Media LLC

Distributed by Itasca Books

sublation
press

www.sublationmedia.com

Print ISBN: 979-8-9867884-4-9
eBook ISBN: 979-8-9867884-5-6

Edited and typeset by Polifolia in East Germany

Printed in the United States of America

What makes *Beyond Family* so precious is that it combines detailed research of facts with a firm pro-feminist and anti-traditional taking of sides. Somay's starting point is the hypothesis that the time of the family is over: yes, we live in deep crisis, but any kind of return to tradition will just deepen the crisis. However, he is at the same time aware that the disintegration of the traditional family is not a linear progress towards freedom and equality, but a process which brings out new tensions and antagonisms, even new forms of domination. Somay fearlessly articulates all the traps of post-family thinking and acting, and this is what makes his book simply indispensable for everyone who wants to understand the mess we are in... in short, for everyone.

—Slavoj Žižek
Author of *Sex and the Failed Absolute*
and *Surplus-Enjoyment: A Guide for the Non-Perplexed*

With exquisite eloquence and erudition, Bülent Somay shows us why we must move beyond the family, long deteriorating anyway. There are far better ways of satisfying our needs and desires for love, care and sustenance than traditional kin structures have ever offered. This historically grounded, rigorous and compassionate analysis of the complexities of our human hearts and endless needs paves the way for the radical possibilities we can all embrace and work for.

—Lynne Segal
Author of *Radical Happiness: Moments of Collective Joy*
co-author of *The Care Manifesto*

The prolific Bülent Somay's new book is an extraordinarily lively deconstruction of the modern family in the light of the escalation of techno-capitalism and its impact on sexuality and human relationships. *Beyond Family* deploys Freudian and Lacanian psychoanalysis to prize apart family and non-family relations, leading away from recent identity politics towards a new, universal politics of sexual emancipation. This is an exciting, provocative and timely intervention in a crucial domain.

—Stephen Frosh
Author of *Hauntings: Psychoanalysis and Ghostly Transmissions*
and *Those Who Come After: Postmemory, Acknowledgment and Forgiveness*

To the memory of

Shulamith Firestone (1945–2012)

who imagined all this half a century ago.

Contents

Thus, for instance, once the earthly family is discovered to be the secret of the holy family, the former must then itself be destroyed in theory and in practice.

—Marx
Theses on Feuerbach, IV

Preface, Thanks, Etc.

Beyond Family was completed during the COVID-19 lockdown in Berlin (more than a year long and counting), although it is the product of almost twenty years of work, starting with the 2004 publication of "Yasaklanmış Manifesto" in the Turkish journal *Toplum ve Bilim* (Society and Science), a loose translation of my original English text, "The Barred-One Manifesto." At that time it did not look (or read) anything like this at all: it was a series of loosely connected aphorisms and comments on phallocentrism and father domination, an early venture into Lacanian psychoanalysis. It underwent many alterations in style and content throughout the years—I was determined to turn it into a book *sometime*—and I finally abandoned it as a source but went on using it as a reference point, or a road map, for what I later wrote.

In 2012, I wrote two articles, one being "Heterosexuality, Orthosexuality, Idiosexuality" and the other "The Empathic and the Semiotic" (chapters 4 and 8, respectively), which were not published in their original English. I presented the latter as a paper at the X. International Cognitive Neurology Symposium, Istanbul (2013), and it was published (in a Turkish translation) in the journal of psychocultural analysis *Suret* (The Likeness) the same year. The former was also published in the same journal, again as a Turkish translation, in 2014. Both were updated, expanded and almost completely rewritten in 2020–2021.

I wrote "The Queer Family" (chapter 5) in Turkish, and it was published in the book *Cinsellik Muamması* (The Mystery of Sexuality, Metis Publishers, Istanbul, 2012) as "'Bozuk' Aile" (The "Broken" Family), edited by Cüneyt Çakırlar and Serkan Delice. "The Three-Mother Problem" (chapter 2) was first written in Turkish and published in *Suret* in 2016 as "Annelik" (Motherhood). I later translated it into English and, needless to say, greatly updated and expanded it before its publication in *The Journal of Psychosocial Studies* 12, no. 3 in 2019. Likewise, I again rewrote and updated both articles for the present book in 2020–2021.

I presented much shorter Turkish versions of "The Three-Mother Problem" and "The Child's Flesh, the Child's Bones" (chapter 3) in a series of online lectures for the Turkish Association for Psychotherapy and Psychosocial Studies in 2021, which greatly helped me to shape these chapters into their final forms.

The rest of the chapters were written in 2020, during my tenure as an Academy in Exile fellow at the Freie Universität Berlin, and the whole was structured into a book in early 2021.

Writing *A Case for Another Regime of Reproduction, Sexuality and Kinship* in the 2020s was like trying to navigate a minefield of prejudices while driving a car with a half-broken steering wheel; there are people who think that Marxism is hopelessly *passé* and originally sexist regardless. Then there are those who firmly believe that Freud and Lacan are blatant misogynists and that any work based on their *Weltanschauung* is a lost cause from the very start. Then there is the matter of *ad hominem*; some people deem anything written or said by a straight, white male on the issue of the family and male/father domination to necessarily be worthless because… didn't you hear it, he is straight, white and male. And, as if these prejudices are not enough, there is you, yourself, full of your own preconceptions, trying to fight them all the way (as far as you are, and can become, aware of them), and you get very little help from others because you cannot fight prejudices using others' prejudices. In short, the more you try to make your text prejudice-free and prejudice-proof, the more you are caught in the deadly trap of defensiveness and aggressiveness.

There is always the "Le Guin way" out, as I used to console myself in my most desperate moments. She had said in 1989 that she always tried "to subvert as much as possible without hurting anybody's feelings." Although I wholeheartedly agree with her (as with most of the things she said), it does not seem to be a viable option here, when you are trying to catch the bull by the horns; in trying to address the issue at hand point-blank, whatever you do or say will hurt or anger *somebody*, and if you try to hurt nobody at all, you end up saying nothing significant at all. I wish I were a better and wiser person and writer, like Ursula Le Guin, and could manage to avoid offending people with different sensibilities and convictions without backing down on my principles. If I believed this was humanly possible at this particular juncture in history, I would definitely take my time to do so. Unfortunately, we live in a time of the utmost violent upheaval and radical change, as Yevgeny Ivanovic Zamyatin observed almost a century ago in 1923, at a similar juncture:

In a storm, you must have a man aloft. We are in the midst of a storm today, and SOS signals come from every side. Only yesterday a writer could calmly stroll along the deck, clicking his Kodak but who will want to look at landscapes and genre scenes when the world is listing at a forty-five-degree angle, the green maws are gaping, the hull is creaking? Today we can look and think only as men do in the face of death: we are about to die—and what did it all mean? How have we lived? If we could start all over, from the beginning, what would we live by? And for what? What we need in literature today are vast philosophical horizons—horizons seen from mastheads, from airplanes; we need the most ultimate, the most fearsome, the most fearless "Why?" and "What next?"

—Yevgeny Zamyatin
"On Literature, Revolution, Entropy, and Other Matters," 1923

So, I apologize to my readers beforehand if I become too defensive or too aggressive in any of what I say, like Brecht did in 1938:

But we know:
Hate distorts the features
Even if it is the hate for vileness.
And wrath hoarsens the voice
Even if it is wrath against injustice. Alas,
We who wanted to pave the way for friendliness
Couldn't be friendly ourselves.

But you, of a future time,
When people help each other
Be lenient
When you remember us

—Bertolt Brecht
"An die Nachgeborenen," 1934–1938

I cannot, in all fairness, list the names of the people who helped me in this venture without making it look like an old-fashioned phonebook. Even those who most ruthlessly attacked what I was trying to do helped. I will, nevertheless, mention a few of them, starting with the women: I first and foremost thank my mentor, critic and "caregiver," Lynne Segal, who never spared her most severe criticism and praise and who, even as I was trying to complete this book, published *The Care Manifesto* (as a part of The Care Collective), leaving me no option, at the last possible moment, but to change and add to the manuscript something that was seriously lacking. I thank my friend, comrade and long-time editor Müge Gürsoy Sökmen of Metis Publishers, who has inserted her radicalism, her supporting presence and her critical eye in almost everything I have written since the 1990s. I thank Didem Doğan for her work in the Association for Psychotherapy and Psychosocial Studies, as well as for making it possible for me to share parts of this book with a wider audience, allowing for a lot of useful feedback. I thank my former student and now dear friend Aslıhan Niksarlı, the chimp-mother, who helped soften my prejudices about the "red line" between human and animal existences.

I thank Cüneyt Çakırlar and Serkan Delice, who gave me the courage to write "The Queer Family" for their book, something I hadn't felt I was entitled to or even capable of. I thank my fellow editors at *Suret*, Yavuz Erten, Hakan Kızıltan and Özgür Öğütcen, outstanding therapists all, who befriended me, the only non-therapist among them, and taught me, if not the "secrets," then the subtleties of their trade. I thank another former student and now dear friend, Candaş Sert, the "eternal student" (literally) who taught me almost all I know about genetics. I thank my longtime friend and comrade, Hakan Gürvit, not only an exceptionally brilliant neuroscientist but also a fellow Lacanian and Marxist, with whom I spent endless nights throughout the years discussing almost every point in this book.

I thank Academy in Exile, which made possible my stay as a semi-voluntary exile in Berlin from 2019 to 2021.

I thank İskender Savaşır (1955–2018), the best friend with whom I agreed the least but from whom I learned the most once I began writing this book back in 2004. He was a "family man" through and through, although he was "beyond family" all the time. Alas, he is not with his extended family anymore to see the culmination.

Last but not least, I thank my comrade and partner, Ezgi Keskinsoy, *sine qua non*, who was there as my "family which is not a family" at every step of the way once I had the first notions of *Beyond Family* in 2004. She has been my fiercest critic and most meticulous editor, and as usual, she changed the course of my writing many times, defeating my stubborn self-defense in each case with persistent calm.

Familia Delenda Est

Marx was onto something more profound than he knew when he observed that the family contained within itself in embryo all the antagonisms that later develop on a wide scale within the society and the state. For unless revolution uproots the basic social organization, the biological family—the vinculum through which the psychology of power can always be smuggled—the tapeworm of exploitation will never be annihilated. We shall need a sexual revolution much larger than—inclusive of—a socialist one to truly eradicate all class systems.

—Shulamith Firestone
The Dialectic of Sex, 11–12

Convention as Iconoclasm

On March 12, 2012, the Turkish Republic became the first country to ratify the Istanbul Convention (also known as the Council of Europe Convention on preventing and combating violence against women and domestic violence). The convention came into force on August 1, 2014. Almost exactly nine years after ratification, on March 20, 2021, President Recep Tayyip Erdoğan announced Turkey's withdrawal from the treaty with a summary presidential decree, without having sought any domestic or international consensus at all. It was apparent from ongoing discussion in the pro-Erdoğan media (which is now almost *exactly inclusive* of all mainstream media) and political circles close to the government that this move was imminent. All the radical Islamist, nationalist, populist and openly fascist elements either within or supporting his ruling circle had been fiercely inventing and patching up arguments agitating for this action for about a year. While supposedly coming from different ideological positions, the arguments mainly converged on the following five points:

1. The Istanbul Convention is against "local and national" values in the first place, and so it should never have been ratified and/or implemented.
2. It is against the word of the Koran, which openly places women in subservience to men, in the home rather than in the social sphere, and sanctifies their role solely as mother and homemaker, not accepting their role in society as equals.
3. It promotes homosexuality and "LGBTQ+" (although most of the arguments are based on the misconception that the latter is actually an organization), and all that is immoral.
4. It is not working, anyway. In the seven years following its implementation, violence against women and domestic violence skyrocketed rather than diminishing.
5. It undermines the family by giving women the opportunity to exist *outside* the family as individuals.

Those who were surprised by this bold move should not have been, because in June 2011, about six months *before* the signing of the Istanbul Convention, the Ministry of Women and Family Affairs was abolished and transformed into the Ministry of Family and Social Services, dropping the word *women* altogether despite opposition from many women's organizations. The truly surprising aspect was that although the real intentions of the AKP and Erdoğan himself should have been obvious even before the signing of the Istanbul Convention, it stayed in effect for about seven years.

Why this delay? one is bound to ask. Well, it is mainly because populist regimes structurally subsist on the seesaw between people-pleasing and authoritarianism or fascism. When the convention was signed, Erdoğan needed the support of both mildly conservative and somewhat liberal women in addition to his core of fanatic followers, because although he could more or less *govern*, he was still unable to *rule* without such support. However, thanks to the so-called attempted coup of July 2016, the tables were turned: after the violent clampdown that immediately followed, he was able to rule as he pleased but unable to govern. This is because he had extravagantly discarded—that is, forcibly retired, exiled, or imprisoned—nearly all the much-needed, qualified workforce under the pretense that they were involved in the conspiracy. His new allies composed of fascists, ultra-nationalists and elements of the "deep state" had no qualifications to govern other than through brute force or in a "security-oriented" capacity, and support outside his fanatic circle and the nationalist and fascist minorities he was now allied with could no longer increase their numbers. Quite to the contrary, his support since then has been constantly and progressively bleeding out, and is now far below the critical threshold necessary to prolong his presidential position through legitimate elections.

But enough about Turkish politics, which probably sounds to most of you as pathetically boring (while still dreadfully threatening) as it does to me. What I am trying to establish here is that with all five points that the so-called mainstream Turkish media attempted to undermine and invalidate the Istanbul Convention they are absolutely right:

1. It *is* against "local and national" values, because it acknowledges, if only on paper, that women's rights are part and parcel of *universal* human rights and cannot be altered or modified according to what those in power declare to be the local and national values.

2. It *is* against the word of the Koran, because it secularizes women's place in contemporary society without reference to any "sacred" text. It is rather a continuation of or, in some of the countries that are a party to the convention, an *introduction* to the bourgeois revolution that "has drowned the most heavenly ecstasies of religious fervour [...] in the icy water of egotistical calculation" (Marx and Engels 2010, 486–7), by making women subject not to the "word of God" but to the "word of the market," which is ultimately no less patriarchal.

3. It *does* promote (although again only on paper) LGBTQ+ rights and the struggle to exist outside, or contrary to, the moral norms of the patriarchal social order that sanctifies monogamy, straight-sexuality and the subservience of sexuality to reproduction.

4. It *was* not working, anyway. In the seven years since its grudging implementation, the legal system, the security forces and the government did nothing to enforce it in actual practice. But then, violence against women and domestic violence should have stayed about the same, shouldn't they? They *did*, however, skyrocket rather than diminishing or staying the same, because women, emboldened by this mere promise of freedom (even if it was only on paper), started to act accordingly, demanding more independence and breathing space. This transformation

left no other recourse for the already half-emasculated male population—themselves the victims of "fragile masculinity" but desperately clinging to their posture of mastery, like roosters bound for slaughter—than the resort to sheer physical violence in order to preserve their pathetic superiority.

5. It *does* undermine the family by giving women the opportunity to exist *outside* of it as individuals, albeit still subject to the mechanisms of market economy.

This is not to say that the people who drafted, or were parties to, the convention had these specific goals in mind—far from it. They did not even imagine that the convention, drafted with the innocent intention to protect women and children from mostly male violence and molestation, would have ended up weakening the family bond. The parties to the convention rather believed, as Mary Wollstonecraft did more than two centuries before them (which we will see later), that protecting women from arbitrary violence and giving them more token freedoms would have resulted in the *consolidation* of the family bond. They were, however, fatally mistaken: Mary Wollstonecraft, writing predominantly based on liberal principles, was misguided in the first place, because the family as we know it *cannot do* without the coercion of women through the use of violence not only "when necessary" but also often arbitrarily. And second of all, those liberal/libertarian principles were hopelessly outdated anyway; they were already two centuries old and two waves of feminisms behind. Admittedly, however, even token freedoms, supposedly granted to women by "considerate" men, quickly become, albeit unintentionally, constant reminders of alternative modes of sexual and reproductive life, of what could have been and what may yet come to pass. For this reason, every liberal reform implemented to ameliorate women's position in the family, however slightly, is also an unintended harbinger of a much more radical development toward the destruction of the family.

Therefore, because it is still in effect internationally despite Turkey's withdrawal from it, there is no doubt that the Istanbul Convention was and still is undermining the family, however slightly and unintentionally. This is why conservative governments such as those in Poland and Hungary, for example, either refuse to ratify it or struggle to amend it in order to limit and nullify LGBTQ+ and abortion rights. The family in the twenty-first century can only survive by clinging to, or struggling to return to, the pre-bourgeois regime of social and gender structures: keeping women under constant surveillance and the threat of violence, limiting their place in society to the home as mothers and homemakers, and controlling them with "a stick in the back and a foal in the womb," as the old Turkish saying goes. The moral ground for such a gender regime, alas, has mostly eroded during the three centuries in between; morality, and more importantly ethics, have themselves become pluralistic and multivalent. This has occurred not through the goodwill of those in power but by the introduction of cultures with different moralities, the availability of different philosophical approaches to ethics, the universalization of the means of communication (beginning with the increase in literacy and the introduction of the radio, the television, communication satellites and, more recently, the internet and social media), and by the universalization of education. These things were not achieved by the benevolence and moral and ethical flexibility of capitalism but by its boundless drive for profit maximization. Unfortunately for capitalism, however, every step it takes to maximize profits, or even to only keep them from diminishing, is also a step that prepares its ultimate downfall.

"Familia Delenda Est"

Marcus Porcius Cato, the famous Roman politician and orator, is said to have concluded all his speeches during the Punic Wars against Hannibal of Carthage, with the stock phrase, *"Ceterum censeo delendam esse Carthaginem"* (Furthermore, in my opinion, Carthage must be destroyed). In this form I would not have used it, because it is only the manifestation of a wish expressed as an agitative statement. History, however, acts in mysterious ways: the expression was shortened and changed over time to be remembered as *"Carthago delenda est!"* (Carthage is [to be] destroyed!), which makes the statement ambiguous. Is Carthage "destroyed," or is it that it "must be destroyed"? Thanks to this cryptic Latin abridgement, we can now use the "... *delenda est*" pattern for anything that both *must be* abolished *and* is already in the process of disintegration. Using the obligatory form alone only expresses our utopian wish—or an anarchist one (depending on our disposition), which, although sensible enough for manifesting a subjective attitude, does not give us a clue about the objective circumstances.

However, the phrase *delenda est* may perfectly stand for—or, since it was apparently not Cato's intention, could be *exapted* to stand for—Marx's third thesis on Feuerbach: "The coincidence of the changing of circumstances and of human activity or self-change can be conceived and rationally understood only as *revolutionary practice.*" It is not enough for us to wish, however strongly, for something to change radically; the circumstances surrounding it must be changing *already*. The same, needless to say, is true for the reverse: a simple changing of circumstances is never enough for a meaningful transformation of society without the human will and activity to go along with it. Only the *coincidence* (*Zusammenfallen*) of these two can affect real and lasting change.

"*Familia delenda est!*": The family is (to be) destroyed. It is already being changed, disintegrating, decomposing anyway, so, why the effort to destroy it further? Because the disintegration of a structure that had served a necessary function for millennia, that kept human society together through many ordeals, through the savagery of the primordial tribe, through slave and/or despotic societies, through feudalism and autocratic empires and, finally, to bourgeois society, is not a development to be taken lightly. A better regime of living together, a more egalitarian and libertarian structure of not only gregarious but also communal and social existence, will not replace it on its own accord, as if there was a *telos* in history, a predetermined, linear progress toward a specific goal.

The family has now become a hindrance against expanding our horizons, increasing our knowledge, imagining and experimenting with new modes of existence, not only for women, but also for the children who will become men and women, straight and gay persons, transgender and gender fluid people. In short: all of us. Moreover, not only has it become an obstruction due to its sheer presence, but also (and more perilously) due to its thrashing about for survival, which constantly revives older forms, more reactionary, more oppressive and more violent. Once the victims of this violence and oppression start to look for the underlying causes of their victimhood rather than trying to create an *identity* out of it—and unintendedly setting it in stone—they will unerringly find the family there. However strong the ties with (and sympathetic and forgiving the feelings toward) their own families and their own past are, they will upon closer and objective scrutiny find the roots of most of their grievances there. Only then can they discover and start building other networks of kinship, love and reproduction.

However official and formal they may seem, and despite their inherently more conservative and reformist intentions, transnational accords (like the Istanbul Convention) and their guidelines can provide a wider audience for discussions about what the family represents and what might replace it. Even when they are ultimately stricken, as in the case of the Turkish Republic, campaigns for their reinforcement and re-implementation may stir up more radical struggles to counter the increasing violence against women, children, gays and lesbians, and trans and gender fluid people. Whether these struggles originate in response to specific grievances and circumstances or against the underlying regime of sex, reproduction and kinship doesn't really matter. It is always what we do and what we learn through the movement itself rather than our initial motivations that matters. It is the networks of relationships we create, arguments we develop with and sometimes against each other, and forms of action and activity we invent rather than how we start out in our private lives.

Marx's fourth thesis on Feuerbach, which summarily proclaims a death sentence to the institution of the family, both theoretically and practically, was my starting point. It is also a very good preamble to an argument for how a person's life practices rarely overlap their theoretical position(s) unless they also coincide with an actual social movement. The publication history of this thesis is somewhat problematic: Marx supposedly penned the *Theses* sometime around 1845, as a kind of a roadmap for the voluminous *German Ideology* he wrote with Engels. Neither was published in his lifetime. *Theses* was only published posthumously, as an appendix to Engels's 1888 monograph *Ludwig Feuerbach and the End of Classical German Philosophy*. The fourth thesis in this publication, however, was rather heavily edited by Engels. The last sentence in the German manuscript reads:

> Also nachdem z.B. die irdische Familie als das Geheimnis der heiligen Familie entdeckt ist, muß nun erstere selbst theoretisch und praktisch vernichtet werden. (Marx and Engels 1978, 6)

This is later translated into English as:

> Thus, for instance, once the earthly family is discovered to be the secret of the holy family, the former must then itself be *destroyed in theory and in practice*. (Marx and Engels 2010e [1845]; my italics)

More than four decades later, Engels interprets this as

> Thus, for instance, once the earthly family is discovered to be the secret of the holy family, the former must then itself be *criticised in theory and transformed in practice*. (Marx and Engels 2010f [1888]; my italics)

The difference between the two, not only in style but also in content, does not leave room for dispute: Engels softens up Marx's expression, splitting the verb *vernichten*—which is indisputably violent, meaning "destroy," "annihilate" or "obliterate"—into two, "*theoretisch kritisiert*" and "*praktisch umgewälzt.*" Although *umwältzen* roughly reciprocates *vernichten*, it does not convey the overt forcefulness implied in the original. Moreover, the earthly family is only "criticized in theory" in Engels's version, which *may* have the rather reformist implication that the family can stay after undergoing critical scrutiny and alterations.

My intention here is not to "dis" Engels, although he does sometimes have a pronounced propensity toward reformism, especially in his last decades. I would rather point out that Marx—although he had quite a conservative lifestyle as a regular and sometimes unfaithful husband, a despotic father, and a much worse, old-fashioned father-in-law—wrote as a very strong antagonist of the family institution, while Engels—who did not care much about bourgeois morality, never married his lifetime partner Mary Burns, and lived his life in different clandestine homes, most of the time outside the law—appears as a much softer critic. In Marx's case, there was very little resembling a women's liberation movement in his lifetime (he died in 1883), and he was likely unaware of whatever rudimentary organizations and activities existed then, since in his last two decades he was not very much interested in anything other than writing *Capital*—except, perhaps, for his participation in the International Workingmen's Association. Engels, however, died in 1895 and witnessed the beginnings of the first wave of the feminist movement, generally complying with its tenets, which were not against the family as such but mostly about women's right to vote and the demand for equal pay. Both Marx and Engels, despite their apparent differences in style and way of life, thus remained true to their own suggestion in the *Communist Manifesto* that "[the communists] merely express, in general terms, actual relations springing from an existing class struggle, from a historical movement going on under our very eyes," (Marx and Engels 2010d, 498) rather than trying to impose their own principles or utopian demands upon the movement.

No matter how significant and groundbreaking theoretical analyses of future change may be, it is always the real movement that matters. The emancipation struggles of women and LGBTQ+ people are what will count when push comes to shove. Now that there is a much more extensive liberation movement "going on under our very eyes"—indeed a historic movement spearheaded mostly by women and partly by LGBTQ+ people, both in the sense of its conceptual and theoretical scope and of its transnational expanse and impact—maybe it is time to revive Marx's original assertion, which he kept private as a mere note to self at a time (1845) when there was no such movement: the family must be destroyed both in theory and in practice.

Women Resist and Organize

In 1848, when the *Communist Manifesto* was published in Europe, a small group of American women, with the participation of a few men, declared in Seneca Falls, NY, that:

> The history of mankind is a history of repeated injuries and usurpations on the part of man toward woman, having in direct object the establishment of an absolute tyranny over her. (Stanton et al. 1848)

This is from the famous statement that has come to be known as the *Declaration of Sentiments*, most probably penned by Elizabeth Cady Stanton, one of the forerunners of the American Suffragist movement. Fifty-seven years before Stanton, in 1791, Olympe de Gouges had stated in her "Declaration of the Rights of Woman" that:

> Man alone has raised his exceptional circumstances to a principle. Bizarre, blind, bloated with science and degenerated—in a century of enlightenment and wisdom—into the crassest ignorance, he wants to command as a despot a sex which is in full possession of its intellectual faculties; he pretends to enjoy the Revolution and to claim his rights to equality in order to say nothing more about it. (de Gouges 1979, 88)

Only two years later she was sent to the guillotine. At almost the same time as de Gouges, Mary Wollstonecraft published her *A Vindication of the Rights of Woman*.

These three women (born in 1815, 1748, and 1759, respectively) are usually considered to be the forerunners of feminism, for both its suffragist first generation and liberationist second generation. Of these three, Elizabeth Cady Stanton was the one happily married with seven children, an exemplary homemaker and mother as well as an activist. The other two were no homemakers: Olympe de Gouges was forced at the age of seventeen to marry a man she hated and was saved by her husband's early death one year after the marriage. She had one son when she moved to Paris and lived a polyandric, active life until her execution. Mary Wollstonecraft only married her partner William Godwin immediately before the birth of their daughter (also named Mary), who later married the poet Percy Bysshe Shelley, became Mary Shelley, and wrote *Frankenstein*.

Of these three, Mary Wollstonecraft was the only one with a liberal, (proto) modernist bent. She contained her critique of male domination within a more universalist, enlightenment framework, which, rather than consigning her to the gallows or to prison, gained her work a place within the liberal/libertarian canon in a relatively short time. She was an egalitarian and used a rationalist line of argumentation to convince *men*[1] that the institution of the (bourgeois) family would indeed grow stronger once political and everyday equality between the sexes was established:

> Let there be then no coercion established in society, and the common law of gravity prevailing, the sexes will fall into their proper places. And, now that more equitable laws are forming your citizens, marriage may become more sacred: your young men may choose wives from motives of affection, and your maidens allow love to root out vanity.
>
> The father of a family will not then weaken his constitution and debase his sentiments, by visiting the harlot, nor forget, in obeying the call of appetite, the purpose for which it was implanted. And, the mother will not neglect her children to practise the arts of coquetry, when sense and modesty secure her the friendship of her husband. (Wollstonecraft 1796, xii–xiii)

Olympe de Gouges, on the other hand was not as meek. She ended her declaration with an outright attack on the institution of family:

> Marriage is the tomb of confidence and love. A married woman can give bastards to her husband with impunity, and even the family fortune which does not belong to them. An unmarried woman has only a feeble right: ancient and inhuman laws refuse her the right to the name and goods of her children's father; no new laws have been made in this matter. (de Gouges 1996, 128)

---

1   As a matter of fact, Wollstonecraft's *Vindication* was dedicated to Talleyrand-Périgord as a representative of the French Revolution, a man who was in fact one of the most opportunistic figures in history, a true "man for all seasons." He began as a representative of the First Estate in 1789 and went through the periods of revolution, terror, convention, empire and restoration modifying his political position with every change in government, always on top and equally comfortable with Jacobins and Girondins, Napoléon and Louis-Philippe as long as he had his share of power.

What Mary Wollstonecraft practically did was to support the existing family structure, although in "more sacred" or "friendlier" forms, preserving the kernel of male domination upon which this structure was founded. De Gouges, however, was confronting it head on, which may explain the radical difference in their respective destinies, apart from the fact, of course, that one was living in France during the Days of Terror and the other in an already semi-liberalized England.

The same dualistic structure can be observed throughout more than two centuries of feminism(s): the more universalist but conciliatory position represented by Wollstonecraft, which dwelled upon the apparent expressions of inequality between sexes, is still alive in the twenty-first century as the more or less domesticated or liberalized forms of feminism after having been interrupted by the more radical, socialist and/or anarchist feminisms of the 1960s and '70s known as the second wave. When this wave was at its high-water mark, starting with Simone de Beauvoir's *The Second Sex* in 1949 and extending into the radical views and actions of feminists such as Germaine Greer, Betty Friedan, Kate Millett, Shulamith Firestone, Sheila Rowbotham, Lynne Segal, Juliet Mitchell, and Nawal el Saadawi throughout the 1960s and '70s, it became one of the hallmarks of what was later called the spirit of '68.

These two decades witnessed the burgeoning feminist organizations as well as the first splits within them, e.g., between queer and straight feminisms and between black and white feminisms, which initially thwarted the movement but helped broaden its scope and prospects in the long run. Demands for economic equality, while not shelved, were mostly replaced or enhanced by demands for sexual liberation and for freedom from the family and patriarchal morality, representing a certain revival of Olympe de Gouges's radicalism. However, this radical position seems to have come to a standstill after the spirit of '68 faded and a conservative wave emerged, when the Reagan-Thatcher mentality ruled the world. The subsequent two decades represent the heyday of neoliberalism, not only economically but also in the attempt to massively reshape society on the political and cultural levels in order to fit the needs of the so-called free market. Like all antisystemic movements, feminism also succumbed to this drive, being reduced to its early liberal form in the demands for economic equality and a better and fairer family before being revived with new zeal and intensity by the emergent radical feminisms and LGBTQ+ movements of the twenty-first century (and especially after the crisis of 2008). Since then, capitalism has been in a gradually deepening global crisis (also evident as an existential crisis for neoliberalism), its abject failure to reshape society on the political and cultural levels becoming manifest in the past two decades.

During the course of this neoliberal experiment, radical feminism was rather subdued in action but nevertheless quite vigorous theoretically, as can be seen in the works of, e.g., Hélène Cixous, Luce Irigaray and Julia Kristeva. Today's influential feminist figures such as Donna Haraway (*The Cyborg Manifesto*, 1985) and Judith Butler (*Gender Trouble*, 1990) also emerged during this period and became key elements in the last decade's ascent of radical feminism alongside LGBTQ+, decolonialist, antiracist and, indeed, working class movements.

What Next?

My main argument in what follows is simply this: the existing regime of sexuality, reproduction and kinship is not only a political or cultural one but is implicit in the primal split between sexuality and reproduction. Male privilege emerges as a result of this very differentiation and metamorphoses into a cultural, social, and economic hegemony. Any opposition to this hegemony is marked from the very start by whether or not it acknowledges the primal, material, and historic roots of the domination. Any opposition to male domination which aims to overthrow hegemonic male/father supremacy but keep the sexuality/reproduction polarity and the subsequent subservience of sexuality to reproduction—or to use two simple words, *the family*—intact is bound to reproduce the same hegemonic structure. Revolutionary feminists, however, starting with Simone de Beauvoir, insistently included sexual liberation on their agenda. This is not to say that their main priority was free sex unhindered by any rule, law, more or tradition (although this may also have played a minor part). Sexual liberation, albeit not always in this exact formulation, meant the liberation of sexuality from reproduction. This liberation implies not only the emancipation of women from male supremacy but also the emancipation of children from adult hegemony and the emancipation of the physically or mentally "sick," the "old" and the "queer" from the domination of the healthy, the mature, the straight, the (re)productive and the fertile. These concepts have come to define modern—meaning Western—civilization in the last three centuries but are already implicit in the millennia-old structure of male/father domination, which, as Marx and Engels had suggested, is the primal form of the social division of labor, private property and class domination (Marx and Engels 2010c, 46).

The distinction between sexuality and reproduction and the consequent subjection of the former to the latter, however, should not be seen as an *essential* difference, implicit in the nature of things. It is a historical difference in the broader sense of history, coming into being with *gamogenesis*, a fairly recent development from the point of view of natural evolution[2], and took the form of a hegemonic structure only with the advent of humanity, which is but a very small portion of this evolution. There is nothing in this structure to suggest that it is *eternal*, and although it is indeed natural, this does not mean that it is not subject to change, to willful transformation, since the entirety of human history is nothing but the subversion of what is natural. This subversion is most apparent in the all-encompassing and eventually smothering takeover of the entire "Terran ecosystem" by humanity, what is nowadays called the Anthropocene, which is rapidly becoming a fatal threat to the planet itself. It is, however, rooted in something more profound and significant: the struggle to save humanity, and eventually the entire ecosystem of *life itself*, from what neuroscientist Vilayanur Ramachandran calls our "Darwinian shackles" (Ramachandran 2011, 133), from the blind hegemony of so-called natural selection.

If left to its own devices, nature would have let few of us survive. It would have killed off those with genetic disorders (e.g., hemophiliacs) and many people with immune system deficiencies before they reached puberty and were able to reproduce. It would have still-birthed those with numerous other kinds of genetic "defects" and, in one way or another, weeded out the "weak." Under ordinary, billion-year-old circumstances, it would have stopped in its tracks our unchecked dissemination into all kinds of different ecosystems. Human beings, however, played a nasty trick on nature and developed something they would later call consciousness. This new element functioned like an automatic rifle brought to a fistfight and aided humans in their struggle for species survival, which is in perfect accordance with natural selection as such but in time turned into a method for enhancing *individual* survival. It defied so-called natural selection and invented ways to interfere with it, making billions of years of processes and patterns obsolete in mere millennia.

Given enough time, any series of contingencies and coincidences can appear as predestination, becoming the foundation of all kinds of myths and legends, including religion. They can also appear as necessity, becoming understood as the foundation of science, or more precisely, Enlightenment science, making way

---

2   Life on Earth began approximately 4 billion years ago. The history of gamogenesis (sexual reproduction) goes back only 1.2 billion years. The overwhelming majority of all living beings on Earth are still agamogenetic.

for positivistic belief systems. More than two centuries ago, Immanuel Kant had called these contingencies in human existence "a course intended by nature":

> Individual men and even entire nations little imagine that while they are pursuing their own ends, each in his own way and often in opposition to others, they are unwittingly guided in their advance along a course intended by nature. They are unconsciously promoting an end which, even if they knew what it was, would scarcely arouse their interest. (Kant 2001, 41)

More than a century later, Engels repeated (almost) the same thing in his attempt to "briefly define" materialism for Joseph Bloch:

> [H]istory is made in such a way that the final result always arises from conflicts between many individual wills, of which each in turn has been made what it is by a host of particular conditions of life. Thus there are innumerable intersecting forces, an infinite series of parallelograms of forces which give rise to one resultant—the historical event. This may again itself be viewed as the product of a power which works as a whole *unconsciously* and without volition. For what each individual wills is obstructed by everyone else, and what emerges is something that no one willed. Thus history has proceeded hitherto in the manner of a natural process and is essentially subject to the same laws of motion. But from the fact that the wills of individuals—each of whom desires what he is impelled to by his physical constitution and external, in the last resort economic, circumstances (either his own personal circumstances or those of society in general)—do not attain what they want, but are merged into an aggregate mean, a common resultant, it must not be concluded that they are equal to zero. On the contrary, each contributes to the resultant and is to this extent included in it. (Engels 2010, 35)

On closer inspection, however, we can see that they are not talking about the same thing at all. While Kant attributes to *nature* the *function of agency* that people lack, Engels maneuvers away from this naturalistic determinism by using phrases such as "this may again itself be viewed as" and "in the manner of a natural process," which does not suggest a tangible agency but rather a *contingency*, a resultant of free wills acting upon one another, not entirely free in themselves but *interdependent*, constructing necessity in the course of the *event*, including individual free wills in it without assigning them independent agency.

Thus, when natural evolution introduces a new way of propagating life (that of gamogenesis) and humanity—eons later, in its juvenile haste and carelessness in harnessing and transforming nature—takes it and changes it into a form of domination (a haphazard mode of connecting with nature and with each other), humanity eventually ends up enslaving a huge part of itself. The same historical event, however, should also provide us with hope, because in a more mature age, humanity may be able to use the same transforming power to obliterate this domination, again subverting what is deemed natural—this time for the benefit of all humanity (and gradually the entire network of life on Terra), rather than a small minority of (white, male, straight, healthy, mature and productive) humans.

The actual root of the existing male/father domination, therefore, is neither the *natural inferiority of women* nor a *sinister and sly conspiracy by men* but a natural difference: the natural division of labor. This division metamorphosed into a social one during the course of evolution, when human beings as a species were still slaves under the yoke of their "Darwinian shackles." The main problem with this historical sequence is that, although the natural causes of this division of labor have gradually diminished since the Neolithic revolution and almost ceased to exist in the last couple of centuries, the structures and ideologies built upon this foundation still persist and refuse to follow suit. Consequently, most men have also become victimized by the same structure but (as with a much smaller number of women) desperately hold fast to their seeming privileges. The only absolute victims of this entire process are children and those structurally and systematically excluded from this regime of reproduction, sexuality and kinship.

In order to reverse this course of events, of what is deemed natural transforming into a regime of domination, we—women, men and children alike, as well as the LGBTQ+, the elderly, the "sick" and the different, the "usual others" of the male/father dominant order—should first struggle to end the supremacy of reproduction over sexuality, which is the actual material basis for male/father domination. This, however, is not merely a political act: male/father domination is not solely political or ideological but is entrenched in the very language we use, permeating every aspect of our very culture. Male/father domination is organized around a simple linguistic sign: *1*, the *phallus*, the sign of *power as domination*, rather than the penis, which is a simple bodily protrusion. The phallus is the locus, the center of the false promise of power for men, women and children alike: for men if they act as expected of them and *be men*; for women if they take part in this game of power and *be like men*; and for children, regardless of gender, if they are patient and obedient and grow up to *be like their fathers*. The promise of power has only one condition: submission to the function of the phallus (Φ). Unfortunately, everybody who takes part in this game will sooner or later discover that masculinization is nothing but its twin concept, emasculation.

The false promise of the phallus, then, is the promise of our father(s): we assume that they enjoy some kind of power (they must have, since they apparently have power over us), and we are invited to become like them in order to share in this power. The moment, however, we start believing in this promise and heed the siren's call, we only endorse the power of the (Name-of-the-) father over us in any of his incarnations. We try our hands at masculinization and end up emasculated, exactly where we started. The hegemonic power of the father is such that nobody has it: everybody makes a bid for it, and everybody ends up a loser in the process. The father is long dead, his throne torn into pieces and shared. But none of the pieces is good for anything: they are just shapeless, useless pieces of broken stone, wood and gold, over which we have been beating each other up for millennia. This is the very structure that upholds male domination or, to use a more appropriate term, *patriarchy*—father domination.

It is *fatherhood*—that is, the transposition of an insignificant genetic fact into a dominant economic, social, and cultural one—that we must "criticize in theory and transform in practice," because this is where the power of the phallus lies. *The father* as a flesh and blood person has no such power; he is nothing but a name, a symbol. It is our unending struggle with each other over its useless remains that forces us to submit to something that doesn't even exist. Father*hood*, on the other hand, as the bedrock of all male-dominated social structures, implies the coerced monogamy of women (how else are we to know who the actual father is?), the enslavement of children (to somebody who usually does not actually take part in raising them yet still has authority over them), the demonization of homosexuality (why are these people engaging in sex since neither can be a father?) and the degradation of the old, the infirm and the "insane" (what good are they if they cannot become fathers?).

Capitalism, however, tends to upset this structure, especially in its latest, global instalment. It develops technologies which make the biological and material basis of fatherhood obsolete and even comical, revealing in the process that it was ridiculous in the first place. DNA tests make the coerced monogamy of women mostly unnecessary; the changing structure of multinational capitalist corporations and shareholding companies, which leave little need for inheritance (the passage of private property from father to son) makes it completely obsolete. Bourgeois culture makes it necessary to extend childhood indefinitely; this same culture, however, with its gradually relaxing emphasis on sexual morality, transforms more and more children into sexual and sexually active beings. Artificial and extrauterine insemination and more precise tools of birth control tend to separate sexuality and reproduction almost completely. This allows same-sex and gender fluid couples to become parents, domesticating and taming the queer but making a travesty of "sanctified parenthood" at the same time. Some men become single fathers and raise children while other men hold fast to the ancient bond of fatherhood, but both, owing to the immense and still growing network of global communication, are painfully aware of each other.

In short, capitalism itself has already prepared the material conditions for the overthrow of the system of male or father domination, finding its pre-eminent expression in the family. The only problem is that language itself, with its phallic orientation and millennia of male-dominant construction, does not allow for such an overthrow, although the Father is *dead again*. So, we are sentenced once more to live with the ghost of the dead father dominating us, but this time with the stench of its corpse burning our nostrils, since, while the first death was only symbolic or mythical, this second death is material.

The thing to do, then, is to give up our fathers and fatherhood. It is not only a feminist (or rather, pan-feminist) project, however, since men and children have to take an active part in it. They have to denounce their fathers and fatherhood at the same time, give up the already non-existent power they appear to enjoy. It becomes more and more apparent, especially in the recent (and quite profound) crisis of late capitalism, that this power is only make-believe anyway. We should not, however, rejoice in this fact, since the more its falsity becomes apparent, the more arbitrary and violent it becomes rather than going away peacefully of its own accord.

At the same time, the denunciation of fatherhood is not sufficient: motherhood *as we know it* must also be denounced since it is an integral part of the patriarchal structure. The myth that motherhood is natural while fatherhood and its inseparable corollary, patriarchy, are the invention of exploiting males, has already started to shatter along with the foundations of the "modern family." Motherhood (not *maternity*, which remains a biological fact for the time being) is as constructed and performative as fatherhood is, and it too must eventually be sacrificed to make room for trans-generational and non-genetic kinship, friendship, partnership and camaraderie, as free as possible from false promises, unfulfillable desires, and domination over the minds and bodies of the young.

Part I

Three Make
a Family

1.

The Two-Father Dilemma

Luke: [Obi-Wan] told me you killed [my father].
Darth Vader: No, *I* am your father!
—Star Wars V: The Empire Strikes Back

Father, forgive them, for they do not know what they are doing.
—Jesus to God in Luke 23:34

THOSE WHO HAVE WATCHED at least some of the films in the *Star Wars* franchise will immediately know that in the above dialogue, Luke Skywalker and Darth Vader are both right: Vader both *is* Luke's father *and* he killed him. Darth Vader could only come into being by eliminating (killing) Anakin Skywalker, or at least every decent and meaningful thing that was left in him. Let us note, *en passant*, that in the passage from Anakin Skywalker to Darth Vader, the Name-of-the-Father also undergoes a transformation and will do so again, in the opposite direction, at the moment of physical death. It is also important to remember that this dialogue takes place at almost the same moment that Vader severs Luke's hand, one of the most thinly-veiled scenes of symbolic castration by the father in film history. Furthermore, Luke was holding in that hand a lightsaber, both a weapon and a glorified phallus, not only resembling a huge penis but also being a Jedi's connection to The Force. The Force—power, got it?

Anakin Skywalker is the "good" father because he is "dead." Darth Vader is the "bad" father because he is very much alive. It is only after the actual death of Darth Vader himself that these two figures converge and merge, their unification being necessary for the child to stay "sane." When the father is split in two and one half is dead, it befits the needs of the Oedipal children: they can project their unconscious desires onto him and will derive unconditional acknowledgement and affirmation from him since he is unable to object. In the long run, however, the split will cause a corresponding split in their personality and gradually end with psychosis, as we know from the tragic fate of Hamlet, the Prince of Denmark.

The Good Father Is the Dead Father

The similarities and differences between the figures of Hamlet and Oedipus have already been analyzed (meticulously but rather inconsequentially) by Ernest Jones of Freud's first circle of disciples (Jones 1976), so I am not going to repeat his whole series of arguments here. At first glance, Hamlet's relationship with his father is not like that of Oedipus—far from it. The mythical Oedipus (and the protagonist of Sophocles's *Oedipus Tyrannus*) had killed his father, albeit unknowingly; Hamlet, to the contrary, seems to do his father's bidding as an obedient son. Oedipus married his mother; Hamlet strives to save his mother from a killer and usurper. From Freud's interpretation of the myth, however, we learn that this was not a simple accident but corresponded to the satisfaction (or an attempt at the satisfaction) of an unconscious desire. Unfortunately, every ingenious interpretation risks exaggeration, simplification and ignorance. Freud's interpretation of the Oedipus myth was soon made into the story of the *boy* sexually desiring his mother and turning hostile toward his father, wanting him dead in order to escape a rivalry in which he was defeated before it had even begun. At this point we should be reminded of Jim Morrison's lines from the Doors song, "The End"—"Mother, I want to fuck you / Father, I want to kill you"—a rather superficial reading of the Oedipus complex. A more thorough examination of Freud's argument, however, reveals that the psychoanalytic interpretation of the Oedipus myth has nothing to do with gender in this sense (which is not to say sexuality). The actual basis of the Oedipus complex is the fact that children, *regardless of gender*, connect with the mother as their primary object of desire before learning that they must share the mother with the father. In the third, phallic or genital stage of the child's psychosexual development, however, the desires of male and female children will necessarily diverge, and hence their Oedipal identities will take different paths as well.

The father seems to be the primary obstacle to the fulfilment of their desire, placing himself between the child and the mother. No subject can be a subject without at least one inaccessible object, and the father provides this service (supported by the millennia-old incest taboo) by making the mother inaccessible. More precisely, it is the semantic presence of the father, his very *name* (Lacan's *le nom/non-du-père*)[1] rather than his physical existence, that is the obstacle. A father who is dead and lamented, or who abandoned or divorced his wife and is cursed constantly, is as semantically present as any flesh and blood father.

There are two fathers confronting Hamlet. One is the good father who is dead, the other is the bad father who is alive and possesses the mother. The latter is not actually the genetic father but rather the uncle, though he completely fulfils the function of the father, possessing the mother both sexually and socially. The dead father, the specter, calls the living father "that incestuous, that adulterate beast" (*Hamlet* I. V, 42), which is completely wrong on both counts: there is no blood tie between Claudius and Gertrude, so incest is out of the question. There is no adultery either, since the marriage between Claudius and Gertrude takes place after his death. But let us suppose for a moment that the specter of Hamlet (since the father, like his son, is also named Hamlet) is speaking from the position of his son's unconscious. The child, of course, sees the relationship between the father and the mother, whom the child assumes to be in their possession, as adultery, and will consider the relationship between the mother and the father, both of whom are their first-degree blood relatives, as incest. Even if the child does not use these terms consciously, the uneasy connection they will establish between their parents and these acts—both taboo, albeit one less so (adultery) and one more so (incest)—will create the first tension of secrecy within their psyche.

The dead father (good father), is therefore the father onto whom Hamlet reflects his unconscious desires, while the real (living) father can now be freed from ambiguity and put aside as the embodiment of all evil. The healthy (that is, neurotic) Oedipal personality is ambivalent, as it finds the images of the good and the bad father in the same person. This will lead to a neurotic personality and behavioral patterns (mild or severe) later in life, but it is also necessary in order for us to deal with reality. Hamlet moves from neurosis to psychosis by splitting the father imago into two (father and uncle, good father and bad father, dead father and living father). Moreover, he completes this psychotic split by feminizing or emasculating the image of the dead father, merging the images of the good father and the mother. The good father was said to be stung by a serpent (*Hamlet* I. V,

---

1   "Freud constantly emphasizes when he says that the obsessive neurotic always lives in the register of what involves the elements of greatest uncertainty: how long one's life will last, who one's biological father is, and so on. There is no direct perceptual proof of any of that in human reality. Such things are constructed and constructed primitively by certain symbolic relations that can then find confirmation in reality. A [child's] father is effectively its progenitor. But, before we can know who he is with certainty, the name of the father creates the function of the father." (Lacan 2013, 44)

35), but he was actually poisoned through his ear, one of the seven basic holes of the body. In short, the bad father, invoking the phallic imagery of the serpent, "stung" not only the mother but also the good father. Considering that the good father lost his power (that is, his domination over the mother and the state) through an act of penetration (venom through the ear), he was not only killed but at the same time emasculated. This good or "vaginal" father, thus separated from the bad father, then becomes one of the features of the mother. The mother can only be rescued by obtaining approval from this good father, without being asked for *her* opinion or consent (which could easily be procured since the good father is nothing but the projection of the unconscious desire of the Oedipal son). Alas, the mother dies while being rescued, but this, of course, is of no consequence to the males' bargain. Likewise, in the story of Oedipus, when the Oedipal "sin" is revealed, Oedipus gets away with a symbolic act of self-castration (he blinds himself), whereas Iocasta, his wife-mother, has no recourse but to suicide.

The Oedipus complex is not the only instance where the image of the dead father makes an appearance. According to Freud, in prehistoric, mythical times, the alpha male (the "primordial father," *der Urvater*) controlled the entire tribe, and all women were his wives, making all the children his as well. He made the law by himself, without any input from the tribe, but he had no obligation to be bound by his own law. Other men, all hypothetically his sons, either submitted to this law, that is, they agreed to be symbolically castrated and deprived of any kind of (sexual or communal) power, or were driven out of the community. The father's brothers in this order had already been killed or driven away. Freud surmises that one day the brothers/sons came together and plotted a conspiracy (glory be to conspiracy theorists everywhere!) to kill the father:

> One day the brothers who had been driven out came together, killed and devoured their father and so made an end of the patriarchal horde. United, they had the courage to do and succeeded in doing what would have been impossible for them individually. (Some cultural advance, perhaps, command over some new weapon, had given them a sense of superior strength.) Cannibal savages as they were, it goes without saying that they devoured their victim as well as killing him. The violent primal father had doubtless been the feared and envied model of each one of the company of brothers: and in the act of devouring him they accomplished their identification with him, and each one of them acquired a portion of his strength. (Freud 2010f, 2782)

Thus, the power symbolized by the body of the father was supposedly spread among the male members of the tribe. This is the symbolic germinal event of what we now call (Western) civilization. There is no longer the absolute, unchecked power of a single man but rather a shared, oligarchic power (since it still excludes all women and children). Now it is forbidden to covet thy neighbor's wife (whereas the old father could covet all he pleased). That father was destroyed bodily but lived on symbolically and even increased his power since that power was scattered and spread. This act also became the foundation of the incest taboo, owing not to an overpowering moral or natural necessity, but to the simple expediency of being able to co-exist, to continue living together as a community, and later, as a society:

> Though the brothers had banded together in order to overcome their father, they were all one another's rivals in regard to the women. Each of them would have wished, like his father, to have all the women to himself. The new organization would have collapsed in a struggle of all against all, for none of them was of such overmastering strength as to be able to take on his father's part with success. Thus the brothers had no alternative, if they were to live together, but—not, perhaps, until they had passed through many dangerous crises—to institute the law against incest, by which they all alike renounced the women whom they desired and who had been their chief motive for despatching their father. In this way they rescued the organization which had made them strong—and which may have been based on homosexual feelings and acts, originating perhaps during the period of their expulsion from the horde. (Freud 2010f, 2784)

However, just like the Oedipus complex, this tale was also subjected to simplified, reductionist interpretations, and Freud was at one point even accused of having invented some variety of justification for the patriarchal order. Mary O'Brien, for instance, a Marxist-feminist writer and stern critic of second-generation feminists (as well as of Freud), evidently misreads him and confuses the Oedipus myth with the *Urvater* myth:

> It is thus from the standpoint of separated sexuality rather than integrated birth that Freud launches humanity on to the guilty tides of history. He offers us a group of primitive brothers eager to appropriate

their mother as sex-object, the apparent absence of other women being not actual and historical but psychological and Oedipal. Female sexuality remains insignificant in this creation drama, as does reproduction. (O'Brien 1983, 41)

O'Brien seems to have missed Freud's main point by a long shot: the brothers who kill and devour the *Urvater are not after the mother* as such but rather *all women*, to share them alike rather than monopolizing them like the *Urvater* (although it probably is their most profound wish). The tale thus becomes that of a legalized and universalized patriarchal order replacing the rule and *jouissance* of a single alpha male. O'Brien, however, is quite right in her assertion that "female sexuality remains insignificant in this creation drama," since, although there is a radical transformation of the regime of sexuality and reproduction, it is not toward liberating women and female sexuality but rather toward substituting a monarchic patriarchy with an oligarchic one. Although this latter regime had greater potential to develop into a more pluralistic society (and perhaps also prepare the ground for women's liberation eons later), it was at that moment nevertheless more organized and oppressive than the haphazard and arbitrary one-father regime before it.

The murdered primordial father, however, does not simply go away but lives on as a *ghost*, as a *name* which represents a phantasmatic *jouissance*, something denied to all tangible, real-life subjects. Actual fathers, as most (if not all) of the sons will eventually become, are but pale imitations of this dead but supposedly omnipotent father. In dying, the power of the father increases a thousandfold. Life, then, becomes the price you pay for omnipotence, which may sound absurd for individual subjects (*What good is omnipotence if I am not there to enjoy it?*) but is very significant for a concept.

Although Freud's story is an amalgamation of many mythological tales from different time periods, therefore running the risk of being anachronistic, it may best be expressed in the two consecutive "patricides" in the Greek creation myth. Ouranos, the primordial god (which corresponds to Anu in the much earlier Mesopotamian/Hittite mythology), routinely rapes his mother-sister Gaia before being emasculated by his son Kronos (Kumarbi in Mesopotamian/Hittite mythology). Kronos, who becomes a little paranoid due to his own actions (*If I can do it to my father, my children may do the same to me!*), spares his mother but marries his own sister Rhea, the goddess of fertility, systematically devouring his children out of fear that he too will meet his father's destiny. Rhea ultimately tricks him and spares Zeus, who starts a war against his father and finally dethrones him. However, this second "patricide" (neither of which are technically patricides, since both Ouranos and Kronos are supposed to be immortal) is different from the first. It is not the act of a single son but a collective rebellion by the sons and daughters (although the latter are subordinate to the males led by Zeus), almost seamlessly fitting Freud's tale. The father is again castrated and cast out, and power is shared between the victorious children.

These mythical cases also contain two fathers: One is the primordial father who supposedly possesses everything, including an unfettered access to *jouissance*. The other is the sons who dethroned and replaced him. They are potential fathers, each and every one of them, although with their access to *jouissance* severely limited. The former, however, is dead, and we are not likely to encounter him; the latter, although not as *omnipotent*, is very much alive and *omnipresent*, dominating all our lives from the moment we are born. We project our desires (for *jouissance*) onto the dead father, of course, since, being dead, he cannot object. Naturally, by *we* I mean mostly males, since we live in a male- and father-dominated world; but occasionally this license is extended to some females, who are either already privileged—whether through class position, ethnicity, or a position in the extended family (for instance, that of the paternal grandmother in some Eastern cultures)—or else attain this privilege by accepting a station in the phallic hierarchy. Remembering Margaret Thatcher, Condoleezza Rice, Benazir Bhutto, Indira Gandhi, Theresa May, Hillary Clinton, Golda Meir, Tansu Çiller, etc., may be of some help in imagining this privileged female position that is nevertheless phallic.

Where did All These Fathers Come from, Anyway?

It is a mystery to me why anthropologists, evolutionary biologists and psychologists rarely if ever mention the historicity (and hence the transience) of fatherhood and paternity, when this is obviously the elephant in the room. When did human beings start acknowledging—that is, *consciously recognizing*—that males had a part to play in reproduction? Surely they did not *evolve* along with this conscious knowledge. Some may say that the information is God-given, but let's assume (for the time being at least) that, as Laplace said to Napoleon, "[We have] no need of that hypothesis."

Human beings belong to that very rare subset of animals that are constantly in heat, whose females are always receptive to coitus whether ovulating or not and whose males are always ready to hump anything that breathes (and sometimes even that which doesn't).[2] This feature is exactly what makes it so hard to see the connection between copulation and pregnancy or childbirth: humans copulate all year round, and every once in a while the females get pregnant. There is a considerable time lapse (about 3–4 months, a whole season) between the specific coitus that caused the pregnancy and its first visible indications, which makes it next to impossible for the male mind to establish a causal link between them. It takes a fairly sophisticated sense of logic, time awareness (consequentiality), and the ability of foresight to establish this connection, which animals and our early ancestors mostly lack. It is only with Jared Diamond's Great Leap Forward about 50,000 years ago[3] that Homo sapiens achieved all these particular qualities enabling them to, among many other things, detect the connection between coitus and childbirth and *ergo* the reproductive role played by males. It is only then that fatherhood as we know it could have come into existence and acquired its overwhelmingly predominant role in culture and society.

Neuroscientist V. S. Ramachandran connects Diamond's great leap to a genetic mutation, which causes a liberation from genetics itself:

> I suggest that there was indeed a genetic change in the brain, but ironically the change *freed* us from genetics by enhancing our ability to learn from one another. This unique ability liberated our brain from its Darwinian shackles, allowing the rapid spread of unique inventions—such as making cowry-shell necklaces, using fire, constructing tools and shelter, or indeed even inventing new words. After 6 billion years of evolution, culture finally took off, and with culture the seeds of civilization were sown. (Ramachandran 2011, 133)

---

2   "Human ovulation is concealed rather than advertised. That is, women's brief period of fertility around the time of ovulation is difficult to detect for their potential sex partners as well as for most women themselves. A woman's sexual receptivity extends beyond the time of fertility to encompass most or all of the menstrual cycle. Hence, most human copulations occur at a time unsuitable for conception. That is, human sex is mostly for fun, not for insemination." (Diamond 1997, 5)

3   "Human history at last took off around 50,000 years ago, at the time of what I have termed our Great Leap Forward. The earliest definite signs of that leap come from East African sites with standardized stone tools and the first preserved jewelry (ostrich-shell beads). Similar developments soon appear in the Near East and in southeastern Europe, then (some 40,000 years ago) in southwestern Europe, where abundant artifacts are associated with fully modern skeletons of people termed Cro-Magnons. Thereafter, the garbage preserved at archaeological sites rapidly becomes more and more interesting and leaves no doubt that we are dealing with biologically and behaviorally modern humans." (Diamond 1999, 39)

According to Ramachandran, the ability *to learn from one another*, passing information directly to other members of the community and to subsequent generations, a process which would otherwise have taken hundreds of thousands of years if done *genetically* through instincts and accidental mutations, is what makes us what we are today. This is one of the possible solutions to what David Chalmers has termed "the hard problem of consciousness" (Chalmers 1996). Consciousness is (1) "knowing what we know" and hence the ability of both (2) "teaching what we know" and (3) "learning what others know", without the mediation of genetics. In Ramachandran's words, it is the "unique ability" that "liberated our brain from its Darwinian shackles." These three, taken together, are what make a human being a "conscious being" (*bewußte Sein*), which is, according to Marx and Engels (Marx and Engels 1998), identical with consciousness (*Bewußtsein*).

Animals do have the genetic information and instinctual awareness that the act of copulation and reproduction are related, as did human beings prior to the great leap. This information is expressed in the fact that copulating is something pleasurable. Once they become *conscious* of this fact, however, they gain the option to plan ahead, avoid or expedite it: this is how technologies of birth control and planning became available, starting with avoidance (at least 4000–5000 years ago) and developing into in vitro fertilization and surrogate motherhood more recently, with extrauterine fetal development (and consequently, birth) an imminent possibility.

Interestingly enough, the emergence of fatherhood as conscious knowledge was directly addressed as early as 1960 not by anthropologists or evolutionary scientists but by a poet and classicist who studied myths extensively, Robert Graves:

> Fatherhood was not honoured, conception being attributed to the wind, the eating of beans, or the accidental swallowing of an insect; inheritance was matrilineal and snakes were regarded as incarnations of the dead. Eurynome ("wide wandering") was the goddess's title as the visible moon; her Sumerian name was Iahu ("exalted dove"), a title which later passed to Jehovah as the Creator. It was as a dove that Marduk symbolically sliced her in two at the Babylonian Spring Festival, when he inaugurated the new world order. (Graves 1960, 28)

Without the conscious knowledge that fathers (that is, males) were actively involved in reproduction, the realm of fertility belonged to the ancient Kybele (by any other name), the woman without the supposed sex appeal of Aphrodite, signified by her wide hips and oversized breasts. Or maybe Kybele's appeal was precisely in those features emphasizing her fecundity. Much later on, Aphrodite's sex appeal was re-tailored according to the male gaze, even extending into what we call modernity. With the awareness of males' participation in reproduction, however, fertility was taken away from the domain of woman and handed over to the hegemony of the male gods Marduk, Jehovah, and Zeus, and much later the more significant (visually and iconically) minor god of fertility, Priapus (featuring a huge penis and permanent erection).

Then along comes Bronislaw Malinowski, whose incomprehensibly passionate effort to invalidate the Freudian concept of the Oedipus complex introduces a non-genetic hypothesis for fatherhood, grounding it in his observations on the Trobriand Islands. This seems to be a revolutionary idea at a cursory glance, or at least it could have been one if it hadn't been marred by Malinowski's severe functionalism:

> The father's relation to his children is remarkable. Physiological fatherhood is unknown, and no tie of kinship or relationship is supposed to exist between father and child, except that between a mother's husband and the wife's child. Nevertheless, the father is by far the nearest and most affectionate friend of his children. In ever so many cases, I could observe that when a child, a young boy or girl, was in trouble or sick; when there was a question of some one exposing himself to difficulties or danger for the child's sake, it was always the father who worried, who would undergo all the hardships needed, and never the maternal uncle. (Malinowski 2002, 55)

If Melanesians do not know or acknowledge physiological fatherhood, the mother's husband[4] may or may not be the child's genetic father, depending on how strictly the rule of monogamy is enforced. The real question here is *why* the mother's husband should be an "affectionate friend," almost a nurse, for the children. There may or may not be a genetic connection between them, and even if there is, the fact that a man is the provider of half the child's chromosomes does not affect any change in his endocrine system at all (since the insemination took place nine months prior). Malinowski attempts to get out of this impasse by assigning affects

---

4   This, as we will later see, is exactly how a father is defined in the *Digesta Iustiniani* (2.4.5): *Mater semper certa; pater est quem nuptiae demonstrant* (The mother is always certain, the father is the person indicated in the bond of matrimony).

and emotions to a "purely social relation," the evolution and structure of which he again does not try to demonstrate or explain:

> Among the Melanesians "fatherhood," as we know, is a purely social relation. Part of this relation consists in his duty towards his wife's children; he is there "to receive them into his arms," a phrase we have already quoted; he has to carry them about when on the march the mother is tired, and he has to assist in the nursing at home. He tends them in their natural needs, and cleanses them, and there are many stereotyped expressions in the native language referring to fatherhood and its hardships, and to the duty of filial gratitude towards him. A typical Trobriand father is a hard-working and conscientious nurse and in this he obeys the call of duty, expressed in social tradition. The fact is, however, that the father is always interested in the children, sometimes passionately so, and performs all his duties eagerly and fondly. (Malinowski 2001, 20)

Why would a man "perform all his duties [toward children] eagerly and fondly?" Which evolutionary mechanisms (natural and/or cultural) would compel him to do so? Since they would not be his legal or economic descendants (it is the maternal uncle who fulfils this duty) and their genetic descendancy would constantly be in question, why would he submit to the duty of being the children's nurse, affectionate friend, and protector? Is this a conscious decision by the (probable) genetic father not compelled by any natural instinct? Unfortunately, instead of trying to address these fundamental questions, Malinowski proceeds from this potentially significant observation to his favorite hobbyhorse of attempting to prove the non-universality of the Oedipus complex (something that, unbeknownst to Malinowski, Freud had never suggested in this simplified and reductionist way in the first place) and the universality of the family *as we know it*, not structurally (structures may change, he happily admits) but *functionally*. A much later feminist critique catches Malinowski in this little, shall we say, sleight of hand:

> Malinowski's book on Australian aborigines thus gave social scientists a concept of The Family that consisted of a universal function, the nurturance of young children, mapped onto (1) a bounded set of people who recognized one another and who were distinguishable from other like groups; (2) a definite physical space, a hearth and home; and (3)

a particular set of emotions, family love. This concept of The Family as an institution for nurturing young children has been enduring, probably because nurturing children is thought to be the primary function of families in modern industrial societies. The flaw in Malinowski's argument is the flaw common to all functionalist arguments: Because a social institution is observed to perform a necessary function does not mean either that the function would not be performed if the institution did not exist or that the function is responsible for the existence of the institution. (Collier et al. 1997, 72–3)

This critique by Collier, Rosaldo and Yanagisako represents the classic (and almost always valid) argument against the *post hoc ergo propter hoc* fallacy, which is that two phenomena that occur together (*zusammenfallen*) are not necessarily in a causal relationship, *ergo*, the *function* and the *institution* are not inevitably the *raisons d'être* for one another. It also opens up the possibility that under different historical circumstances (transformed or evolved), the function can be undertaken perfectly either by a completely different institution or a non-institution. The existence of the father, then, as either genetic fact or as sociocultural construct, only *seems to be* one of the main pillars of the family. Even when the awareness of genetic/biological paternity was absent, the family was there (as the almost universally accepted axiom goes), as in the case of the Trobriand islanders, through either the legal and economic authority of the maternal uncle or through the constant, affectionate, caring presence of "the mother's husband." We could, however, now question the universal validity of this axiom from the point of view of not only *what may happen in the future* but also from a more rigorous investigation of what exists *here and now*.

There is, for instance, another concept of community still in existence, however rudimentary or residual, that may suggest the non-essentiality of the family as we know it. Cai Hua's research among China's Na people, who live in the Yongning township and only have a population of 30,000, is an example of such a community. The Na still retain their separate language and have preserved a peculiar kinship structure and attitude toward sexuality that do not fit any of the family organizations we have hitherto known:

There is no economic bond between the partners. The children born of this sexual commerce will be a part, invariably, of the mother's *lignée*, whose members see to their upbringing without any intervention whatsoever from the genitor. He is only "identified" by his resemblance to the child. Sometimes, since a woman has different sexual partners, he is not even known. Moreover, I have not found any term that would cover the notion of father in the Na language. Their terminology for kinship is strictly consanguineal and matrilineal. The transmission of inheritance is carried out, from one generation to the next, collectively. (Cai Hua 2001, 20)

Since the Na community is matrilineal and the concept of fatherhood is mostly insignificant (even when it is acknowledged in some cases), the family as we know it has not yet replaced—and cannot replace—the collective presence of the community. The collectivity in kinship, as well as inheritance, also rules out *private property*, which is always co-existent (although not always in a strictly causal connection) with the patriarchal family structure, and as Marx and Engels had commented in the *German Ideology* (which deserves to be quoted in full, since it is one of the most neglected and ignored passages in that manuscript):

The division of labour in which all these contradictions are implicit, and which in its turn is based on the natural division of labour in the family and the separation of society into individual families opposed to one another, simultaneously implies the *distribution*, and indeed the *unequal* distribution, both quantitative and qualitative, of labour and its products, hence property, the nucleus, the first form of which lies in the family, where wife and children are the slaves of the husband. This latent slavery in the family, though still very crude, is the first form of property, but even at this stage it corresponds perfectly to the definition of modern economists, who call it the power of disposing of the labour-power of others. Division of labour and private property are, after all, identical expressions: in the one the same thing is affirmed with reference to activity as is affirmed in the other with reference to the product of the activity. (Marx and Engels 2010c, 46)

Fatherhood, then, apart from being a biological and genetic fact, becomes a sociocultural phenomenon only with the conscious acknowledgement of male lineage, but not as something common for both sexes. With this acknowledgement, matrilineality is replaced, sometimes forcibly, by patrilineality, which is based on the socialization of the natural division of labor, de-historicizing it and making it an absolute, the foundation upon which private property can and will flourish. The need to establish private property as something transhistorical and essential to the human race also makes it necessary to ascertain the essentiality of patrilineality and hence fatherhood. Fatherhood, therefore, ceases to be a simple conscious acknowledgement of a biological fact and is promoted to an axiom for the foundational narratives of all class societies, in which some (mostly males-as-fathers) monopolize "the power of disposing of the labour power of others," not only as a matter of lineage (patrilineality), but also of domination (patriarchy). Even if we concede that a very limited number of women had (and still have) the opportunity to "cross over" to the male side in order to share in this power, class domination is always fundamentally male, although this gender-oriented determination is ideologically passed as an *essential condition,* as inherent in the *nature of things.*

Among many other things, this means that there is no way to get rid of class domination without getting rid of father domination, and the latter act is by no means subservient to the former. An argument can be made that the sequence is not of central significance, but it indicates that these two struggles (against class domination and father domination) are at most co-existent without any hierarchy between them: conscious acknowledgement of fatherhood can only be overturned or trivialized by a *conscious* act. Likewise, the social division of labor (in which private property is always already implicit) can only be left behind by the same conscious act, since almost all the elements and circumstances of the natural division of labor which led to it in the first place have already been nullified (or at least trivialized) by the development of the recent forces and technologies of production and *re*production.

The Good Father *Is* the Bad Father

The dual character of the father often emerges as a profound hypocrisy, or, to choose a kinder expression, as a Janus-like existence. The father is supposed to be both the "nearest and most affectionate friend of his children" (Malinowski) *and* upholder of the strictest discipline and (more often than not) tyranny; both a benevolent supplier of life's necessities *and* a "slaveowner" to the wife and children (Marx and Engels); both an emasculated and motherly ghost *and* an "incestuous, […] adulterate beast" (Shakespeare); both Kumarbi/Kronos/Zeus *and* Anu/Ouranos/Kronos; both the provider of twenty-three chromosomes (including that precious Y) *and* a castrator and occasional rapist; both Laius *and* Oedipus; both the *Urvater* who possesses all women *and* one of the sons who overthrew and devoured him (Freud). Above all, he is both the father *and* a mere child who had been the slave and subject of another father at the dawn of his life—therein lies the root of his dilemma.

On a different note, as I have argued elsewhere (Somay 2014), the father also represents somewhat dissimilar functions in the Occident and in the Orient. In the former, Freud's tale typically holds true for many mythological and literary accounts: the primordial father has a monopoly on the women and produce of the tribe, and at one point the sons come together in a conspiracy and kill him, changing the structure of the tribe radically. This is a transformation symbolized politically in the *Magna Carta* much later, where a "conspiracy" of nobles dictates to the king their rights, especially their right of inheritance. Oriental mythology and literature, on the other hand, has no corresponding tale: although there are some patricides, several filicides and a lot of fratricides, it is the single son (usually the eldest and strongest) that kills the father and takes over his position and function, effecting no radical change in the tribal and political structures. Not surprisingly, there is no political document in the history of Eastern empires resembling the *Magna Carta*. This is one of the reasons why Oriental empires, sultanates and tsardoms did not change much until the eighteenth and nineteenth centuries, when challenges from Western powers sped up development of their economies, technologies and military powers. This was precisely due to the radical change represented by the passage to more pluralistic (oligarchic) but still father-dominant regimes. In the Orient too, therefore, there are two fathers, this time differentiated according to geography and culture. When these two fathers clashed, in precapitalist periods, the Oriental fathers usually had the upper hand due to the autocratic, centralized power they held (witness, for example, the Ottoman Empire's rapid expansion in Southeastern Europe between the fourteenth and seventeenth centuries). With the advent of capitalism, however, the tables were turned, and the Oriental father—in all his glory, with centralized, autocratic rule—started to falter and lose ground until being almost totally invalidated and emasculated by the Western powers.

Considering all of this, we can now safely declare that the "good" father is indeed the "bad" father. To start with the last instance, the fact that the Oriental father was ultimately humiliated and emasculated by the Western powers does not make him "good," it only makes him a victim, which by no means puts one in the right, much less in a morally and ethically superior position. In the millennia-long struggle between the different brands of fathers and tyrants, there had always been victors and losers, and neither of them were ethically superior; they were either "victims of circumstance" when they were defeated or temporary victors when they won the day. In other words, no matter which of the varieties of father has won, it has always been the children who have lost. Those subjects who look down with pity and revulsion upon the Orient from the slightly elevated position of the West, grateful that they have a "better" father, are no less exploited, humiliated and emasculated than the subjects from the rest of the world, who look up to the West with envy and *ressentiment* under their old or emergent fathers, clinging to them in the vain hope that they can bring back the "good old days." Unfortunately for both of them, even in the good old days, the good and bad fathers ruled, sometimes hand-in-glove and sometimes in deadly conflict with each other, but always in tandem, keeping their respective subjects under their thumbs and, more often than not, under their heels.

No father has been an ultimate victim; no father has been the ultimate villain: starting from the archetypal father and son story, Laius/Oedipus, we observe that each father is worse than the other. Laius is the man who, in trying to overturn a prophecy ("Your son will kill you and marry his mother") orders his own infant son killed. He is the bad father, guilty of attempted filicide. Oedipus starts as the victim and acts as the dutiful child, leaving his home and going into voluntary exile when he learns of the prophecy (he believes Polybus and Merope, the King and Queen of Corinth, to be his real mother and father). Then what does he do? He kills an elderly gentleman (who happens to be his genetic father) at a mountain pass after a petty right-of-way altercation! So, even though Oedipus is not guilty of a *conscious* patricide, he a common bully and a murderer after all. He then unknowingly marries his mother, and they have two sons and two daughters together. Eventually his mother-wife commits suicide (he does not!), his son-brothers kill each other, and one of his daughter-sisters is executed, leaving only one daughter-sister in his bloodline. Both fathers are guilty, both fathers are villains, in one way or another, and both fathers are victims.

We observe the same ambiguity in the Ancient Greek cosmogony starting with Kronos. Ouranos, his father, was in fact the father of all that existed. He was father sky with his wife-sister (and, according to some accounts, mother) Gaia, who was the earth mother. His Mesopotamian counterpart, Anu, was almost the same (although a much more significant god within Mesopotamian cosmogony), and in his Sumerian incarnation, he was the husband of Urash, the earth-mother. Both deities monopolized the earth/woman, and both were castrated by their sons (Kronos and Kumarbi, respectively). Both sons took their place as the father god, and Kronos was in turn overthrown through a conspiracy of his children led by Zeus, who also usurped his throne but ruled by consent, albeit almost as arbitrarily. In all of these tales, the primordial deity was first guilty of rape and incest, since the earth-mother was never willing. Secondly, he was also guilty of (attempted) filicide. In all cases the wife, sister, and mother, themselves victims of rape, sided with the sons and aided in the father's emasculation, although the sons later turned into filicides/rapists themselves. In no case is there a father who is innocent. Even Zeus—who castrated and cast out his father Kronos and ruled as the leader of a coalition of deities (the Twelve Olympians)—was a persistent rapist, trying to hump anybody or anything with a pulse, mortal and immortal alike. Likewise, in no case is there a father who was not a victim at some point. The father is killed, or emasculated and/or cast out; at the very least he definitely *had been* at the receiving end of his own father's violence and wickedness at one point in time. The *ghost* of the rapist/filicide/patricide, however, lives on; as in a relay race, the baton of the Name-of-the-Father (*le nom/non-du-père*) is passed on from generation to generation, from culture to culture, and *this* is the father we have to deal with.

Let's examine another tale of the good father/bad father, this time from another Mesopotamian myth, the Old Testament:

> [God] said to him, "Abraham!" And he said, "Here I am." He said, "Take your son, your only son Isaac, whom you love, and go to the land of Moriah, and offer him there as a burnt offering on one of the mountains that I shall show you." [...] Abraham took the wood of the burnt offering and laid it on his son Isaac, and he himself carried the fire and the knife. [...] When they came to the place that God had shown him, Abraham built an altar there and laid the wood in order. He bound his son Isaac, and laid him on the altar, on top of the wood. Then Abraham reached out his hand and took the knife to kill his son. (Genesis 22:1-10)

For all we know, Abraham was a good man: he was the father of all three dominant monotheistic religions that survived to our day (the Abrahamic religions). He was a lawmaker, a good husband and a good father. Still, he raised a knife to kill his son because his God told him to, and he was a pious, God-fearing man. Thanks to a *deus ex machina*, poor Isaac was saved; but imagine the trauma of the child who sees his father looming high above him with a knife in his hand, while he is bound and lying on an altar.[5] Isaac, however, was not the victim of a single father but two. There was Abraham, but there was also God, who gave Abraham the order was the father of Abraham and all faithful, pious people. This gave Abraham all the justification he needed; after all, who could have blamed him for following God's command and slaying Isaac? What if the angel who stopped Abraham's hand was a little bit late? What if there was no suitable ram around?

So, Abraham was also a victim, and one who almost became a murderer, the slayer of his own son. Can we say that he should have rebelled, defying God, and instead of submitting with a meek "*Hineni!*" (translated as "Here I am!" but it could also be "Behold, me!") spoken out for the life of his son? Here we have another case of the two-father dilemma, the irresolvable predicament of the son who cannot save himself from unquestioning submission to his father, and the father who cannot uphold his promise to defend and protect his son. In the end, although the problem is seemingly solved by *deus ex machina*, Abraham is locked in the unforgivable sin of attempted filicide, and although he may be totally justified in the eyes of his unmerciful and arbitrary God, the poets after him will not be as forgiving:

> You who build these altars now
> To sacrifice these children
> You must not do it anymore
> A scheme is not a vision
> And you never have been tempted
> By a demon or a god
> You, who stand above them now
> Your hatchets blunt and bloody
> You were not there before

> —Leonard Cohen
> *Story of Isaac*

---

5 Abraham was also the archetype of the Oriental father, who is *not* killed by his sons and lives on, because he is (according to Genesis) the inventor of circumcision, that is, the symbolic castration of all the males in the tribe. Admittedly, he is also circumcised himself, but *only after* every male in his tribe is already circumcised: "Then Abraham took his son Ishmael and all the slaves born in his house or bought with his money, every male among the men of Abraham's house, and he circumcised the flesh of their foreskins that very day, as God had said to him." (Genesis 17:23)

The two-father dilemma is always resolved through the existence of the third father, in this case, God. If we take the New Testament God as a symbol, however, we can see that it is nothing but the Name-of-the-Father (*le nom/non-du-père*), a mere name that creates the function of the father. Ultimately, however, the Name-of-the-Father does not have a tangible existence outside our belief systems, our moralities, the institutions we establish in his name, our acts that use him as a justification; it does not exist without us doing its dirty work.

To end up where we started: I had suggested that both Darth Vader and Luke Skywalker were correct in the archetypal symbolic castration scene in *The Empire Strikes Back*. Anakin Skywalker is, in fact, Darth Vader, and he is both Luke's father and the entity that killed him. Is it true, however, that Anakin is the good father and Vader is the bad father? Wasn't it also a fact that Anakin started his passage to the dark side (in *Star Wars* terminology) long before he turned into Vader, when he singlehandedly annihilated an entire community of Sand People in an act of revenge for the killing of his mother? With this recognition, we can see that the equally symbolic apparition of the mother reappears to make her presence known, although she was nearly forgotten throughout the rest of the narrative—just as she was throughout all of the narratives we have thus far analyzed to distinguish the good father from the bad (or, conversely, to connect them). In the Oedipus myth, although Iocasta unwittingly marries her son, not out of love or desire but because her community expects her to do so, she was also an accomplice of Laius in the beginning when he attempted filicide. In the Greek cosmogony, both Gaia and Rhea were accomplices to their sons' rebellions (Kronos and Zeus, respectively), although each woman was in cahoots with her husband-brother until that moment. In Freud's *Urvater* myth, as Mary O'Brien justifiably points out, the mothers and sisters are not involved in the narrative at all. And in *Hamlet*, finally, although Gertrude appears to be an innocent victim, to be saved by a son who acts on behalf of her late husband, she had no qualms about marrying her brother-in-law immediately after her husband's death. Even if merely as the seeming accomplice of either side or as an apparition, the mother is always there. Kronos acts not only to save himself from filicide but to end the constant rape of his mother; Hamlet wants to save his mother; the brothers who kill the *Urvater* also act to save their mother(s) from the "incestuous" beast, although she will be taboo for them as well; and Anakin passes to the dark side to avenge his mother.

All the sons act out of some version of the desire of the mother (*la désir de la mère*), which is the unseen, but nevertheless primal, element in the Oedipus complex. Although the Oedipus complex has us believing that we're battling the bad father and trying to make peace with the good father, the mother is the main driving force behind this, and the "desire of the mother" is not a mere object of desire for the son. Her own desire for the child (regardless of gender) is what we should look to. It is the "first signifier introduced into symbolization," which the father will later be a metaphor for.

> What is a father? [...] The question is entirely about what he is in the Oedipus complex.
>
> Well then, there, the father isn't a real object, even if he has to intervene as a real object to embody castration. If he isn't a real object, what is he?
>
> The father's function in the Oedipus complex is to be a signifier substituted for the first signifier introduced into symbolization, the maternal signifier. (Lacan 1998, 158–159)

Once the father replaces the mother in this first act of signification (albeit merely as a metaphor), the mother seems to fade away from the scene of the Oedipal drama, except as an object of desire. We should, however, be careful with Lacan's French: when he says *la désir de la mère*, he means (using the inherent ambiguity of the French language) both "the desire *for* the mother" and "the mother's desire," so the mother is never a passive object; her own desire is always in play, camouflaged by the metaphor of the father.

Let us be forewarned, therefore, by the Freudian (and later, Lacanian) theory of the Oedipus complex that the Oedipal child, regardless of gender, can become anything—anything but free. No matter whether the struggle against the father succeeds or fails, no matter whether the father is killed and replaced or the child unconditionally submits to his authority, the Oedipal child is always the slave to the (desire of the) mother, although the mother herself (in any of her three incarnations) has nothing to do with it. It is not possible to grow up and become an adult, to leave the supposedly protective but in fact severely tyrannical, restrictive and suffocating hearth of the family, to be ultimately liberated, unless the desperate and futile passion for the mother is dealt with—that is, without giving up the desire of the mother.

Whatever happens, we will never get our mother back (except as a case of Hamletian psychosis): all we have is one another.

2.

The
Three-Mother Problem

Mater semper certa; pater est quem nuptiae demonstrant[1]
—Digesta Iustiniani 2.4.5

Mutter eines Kindes ist die Frau, die es geboren hat
—German Civil Code, Paragraph 1591

THE *DIGESTA IUSTINIANI* (the latest inscription of Roman Law, AD 429) is one of the oldest legal documents in existence, and many rules of contemporary law are based on this document. This law tells us that "the mother is always certain," although the position of the father is almost always controversial. Not a surprising precaution, to be sure: the act of the male to become a father takes place in a place of obscurity, almost always hidden from us. And the uncertainty is not limited to this. Even if sexual intercourse was carried out in the public sphere, we would still not know from which man the fertilizing sperm came, since fertilization takes place within the female body (an even more obscure place for the male mind). Thus, at least until the paternity tests of the late twentieth century—that is, until it became possible to compare the child's DNA with the father's—the father was either uncertain, or, as Justinianus's law conceded out of desperation, he was "the person indicated in the bond of matrimony." The only thing to be done in order to create a semblance of certainty, therefore, was to establish indisputable domination over the female body, and to prohibit the woman from having sexual intercourse with anyone other than "the person indicated in the bond of matrimony" preferably by the most oppressive means possible. The boundaries of this oppression are drawn by culture: we can, if we wish, prohibit adultery with the threat of being stoned to death publicly, or we can construct a literary and cultural

---

1 The original expression in the *Digesta* 2.4.5 is "*Quia semper certa est, etiam si volgo conceperit: pater vero is est, quem nuptiae demonstrant,*" although it is commonly referred to as "*Mater semper certa; pater est quem nuptiae demonstrant,*"

edifice that places monogamous and heterosexual love on a pedestal with every possible ideological device, or we can support the hysterical construction of the psyche (that is, the mechanism that substitutes the father's desire for the desire of the subject) with every means possible—the result will not change. We may establish an absolute (or so we would wish to believe) mechanism of oppression over the woman, obliterating her femininity in the process (Lacan's "La femme") (Lacan 1998). Like every tyrant, however, we will become increasingly paranoid in doing so, and we will never be sure of the outcome of our domination: a considerable part of our life will be wasted by the gnawing questions "Who is my (real) father?" and "Is this child really mine?" In short, we will get what we deserve.

Yet, "the mother is always certain." Birth is usually a semi-public event after all: at least one, and usually more than one, person is present at birth. Until the last two centuries, the people present at birth were midwives, usually elderly women. Recently, however, birth has become more of a public event: male gynecologists and the occasional enthusiastic prospective father also observe the moment of birth, and usually record it. There seems to remain, therefore, no possibility of error. Or so we would like to think. But how are we so sure? I will try to discuss now, how we can problematize this certainty, and what this inquiry can teach us about the past, present and future of the concept of the family, or the so-called nuclear family, examining seven narratives spanning almost twenty-eight centuries. These seven narratives are:

1. "The Judgement of Solomon" in I Kings 3: 16–27, The Old Testament. (ca. seventh century BC, Mesopotamia).
10. "Mahaushadha" in The *Maha-Ummagga Jataka,* 546–545 (ca. fourth century BC, India) (The Jataka 1907)
11. Li Qianfu. *The Chalk Circle;* (ca. fourteenth century AD, China) (Qianfu 2001)
12. Bertolt Brecht, "The Augsburg Chalk Circle" (1940, Sweden) (Brecht 2015)
13. Bertolt Brecht, *The Caucasian Chalk Circle* (1944, USA) (Brecht 1966)
14. *Law and Order: SVU,* Season 6, Episode 1, "Birthright" (September 21, 2004, USA).
15. *The Good Wife,* Season 5, Episode 3, "A Precious Commodity" (October 3, 2013, USA).

Who is the "Real" Mother?

I will now summarize the plots of each of these texts briefly:

The parable of the justice of King Solomon (1) is known to most: two prostitutes give birth on the same night, and one of the babies dies. The woman whose baby has died switches the babies and claims that the living one belongs to her. They appear before King Solomon. Solomon cannot make a decision and proposes to divide the baby in half and give a part to each woman. The real mother, rather than abiding by this decision, agrees to give up her claim. Solomon then gives the baby to the real mother, who consented to give her baby to another person rather than letting it die.

In "Mahaushadha" (2), the Future Buddha (also known as the Sage) judges a dispute between a woman and a *yakshini* (a "female genie" in another translation) who tries to steal her baby. His solution is not as bloody as Solomon's: he draws a line on the floor and puts the baby on it, asking the woman and the *yakshini* (disguised as a woman) to hold onto each arm and pull. The real mother sees that her baby will be hurt and releases her arm. The Future Buddha gives the baby to the real mother.

In Li Qianfu's play *The Chalk Circle* (3), the infertile first wife of a rich man fatally poisons him and then blames the murder on his second wife (who has a child by him). After it is proven that the second wife is innocent of the crime, she tries to keep the child, claiming he is hers, in order to possess the inheritance through the first and only male child. The judge now has to answer the question of whose child he is. He draws a chalk circle on the ground and puts the child in the middle, asking the women to hold onto each arm and pull. As in the first two stories, the real mother sees her child being hurt and lets go of his arm, after which the judge gives the child to her.

In these three stories, which span twenty-one centuries between the seventh century BC and the fourteenth century AD, the verity of the mother is not contested at all. There are two claims, one a lie and the other true, and the truth of these claims is decided by either the mother's maternal instinct or her kindness, her inability to let her child be hurt. There are no provisions in the legal system in this regard, *Mater semper certa* being the uncontested principle: whenever there is a glitch (which is exceedingly rare), the decision is completely left to the sense of justice (or fairness) of the judge. He judges accordingly by accepting motherly love and compassion as a given, without question.

After six more centuries, however, things begin to change.

The short story "Augsburg Chalk Circle" (4) and the play *The Caucasian Chalk Circle* (5), both written by Bertolt Brecht (with four years in between), are clearly derivative of Li Qianfu's fourteenth-century play, *The Chalk Circle*.[2] As with every successful literary "theft," however, there is a significant *novum* in Brecht's texts that modifies the gist of the story in a crucial manner, requiring a rethinking of the concept of motherhood. Both of Brecht's stories put forth the same basic argument: the real mother is not the one who gave birth to the child but the one who raises it: *"Die Kinder den Mütterlichen, damit sie gedeihen"* (Children to the motherly, so that they grow and flourish). Brecht names the elephant in the room: motherhood and motherliness, giving birth to a child and raising it, are not always the same thing.

In both stories, the child is abandoned by the real mother in a time of danger (in the first, a Protestant pogrom; in the second, a peasant revolt). In both stories, he is rescued and raised by a servant or nanny. In time, as the danger passes (during which the father dies), the "real" mother wants her child back, even though her maternal instinct was apparently defective when she abandoned her child. Now her only concern seems to be the inheritance (through the male child). In both cases, it falls to the judge to decide the identity of the mother. He solves the problem using the chalk circle method invented by Li Qianfu. This time, however, the woman who cannot tolerate the child's suffering is not the woman who gave birth to her, but the one who raised her. The judge gives the child not to the birth mother but to the mother who raised him.

We have thus split motherhood into two. To be sure, if it were only the matter of a few cases where the mother gave up the offspring deliberately, we would take a passing note and move on, since the dramatic social events that caused the children's abandonment in Brecht's two texts are truly exceptional. However, Brecht's metaphor is meant as more than a simple comment on motherhood as such but also as a broader political comment on owning and possessing versus nurturing, making, and producing. He clearly states his real purpose after he says, "Children to the motherly": *Die Wagen den guten Fahrern, damit gut gefahren wird / Und das Tal den Bewässerern, damit es Frucht bringt* (The carriage to the better driver, so that it will be driven better / And the valley to those who water it, so

---

2   There were earlier German adaptations of Li Qianfu's play, *Die Kreidekreis* (1925), by Klabund (Alfred Henschke), and Alexander von Zemlinsky's opera is based on this adaptation (1933). The first direct translation of the play from Chinese into German was published in 1926 by A. Forke. Brecht was probably aware of all these versions (at least of Klabund's version and the direct translation) and based his interpretations on them.

that it will bring fruit). But, perhaps regardless of the author's intention,[3] what he suggests about motherhood seems to be quite important today, not only as a metaphor but also literally: the mother is not one but two (actually three, but we'll leave this for the time being) different people, which is not in itself a simple matter of law. Above and beyond its legal consequences, this argument brings the concept of the family into question, which we have accepted as self-evident for more than ten millennia. Likewise, what Marx had said in the *Theses on Feuerbach* (also as a metaphor) in 1845 has now become the literal truth.

However, in order for this truth to manifest itself, it is imperative that a development (which is actually not only a development but a significant leap or transformation) in the productive forces takes place. This brings us to the last two texts that belong to the twenty-first century.

Law & Order: Special Victims Unit (6) is still in production after twenty seasons and about 500 episodes. It is one of the most popular series on American television, because it successfully combines two popular genres: courtroom drama and police procedural. It is particularly related to our topic because the term *special victims* refers to victims of rape, domestic violence and child abuse. It is in the first episode of the sixth season of the series (2004) that the concept of motherhood is opened up to discussion in a new light.

A child is abducted from a playground. The SVU detectives, having watched CCTV recordings, find the kidnapper and the child. The kidnapper, a woman, claims that she is the real mother. The child's parentage, however, has never been in doubt: the child does not know the kidnapper at all, and the birth certificate confirms that her parents are the real parents. When the incident is examined in depth, it turns out that things are a bit more complicated than that: the kidnapper had a number of her ova frozen in a birth clinic many years ago and then had a child from one of them who recently died in a car accident. The results of further research are even more confusing: the clinic has used the woman's frozen, healthy ova for various mothers who are infertile (without informing them), violating the law and taking the infertile women's money by convincing them that their own ova were used. The kidnapper turns out to be the genetic ("real") mother after all.

---

3   I am well aware that when dealing with Brecht, it is not a wise move to use generalized phrases like "regardless of the author's intention," because most Brecht narratives consist of multiple layers. It *seems*, for example, that his primary motive in *The Caucasian Chalk Circle* is to comment on the contradiction between possessing and using for the common good, but taken within the totality of his opus, his metaphors are almost always at the same time thinly disguised comments on gender relations (and even on gender-bending, as he offers in *The Good Person of Szechwan*).

However, it is the other woman (whom the child knows as her mother) who gave birth to her and raised her.

Thus, the mother that Brecht had divided in two is now divided into three with this new technology: the genetic mother, the birth mother, and the nurturing mother. The case goes to court, and the child is expected to testify. One of the SVU detectives predicts that the case would solve itself, because it is a matter of Solomon's justice after all: one of the women will give up her claim so that the child will not be exposed to the painful and traumatic process of a trial. And so it happens: the extreme faith in genetics that had swept the American and European cultural atmospheres in late twentieth and early twenty-first centuries has also come into play here. It is the *genetic* mother who withdraws her claim (and thus proves that she is the real mother), as though it was not she herself who traumatized the child by abducting her and telling her she was her real mother, subverting her entire conception of reality. Fortunately, the US Court is not Solomon (or the Future Buddha, or one of the judges of Qianfu or Brecht), and the child remains with the mother who gave birth to her and raised her, although the new ethical and legal problems created by this new technology remain unresolved.

For the next instalment in the problematization of motherhood and family, we need to look at the last item on our list. *The Good Wife* (7), broadcast for seven seasons between 2009 and 2016, is a popular television series combining the genres of political intrigue and courtroom drama. Season 5, episode 3 (2013), features a maternity case similar to those we've discussed. It is a case that carries the motherhood problem to an extreme in its ethical and legal implications, and perhaps represents the last nail in the coffin for family as we know it. A childless couple signs a contract with a surrogate mother because the genetic mother has a physical defect that prevents her from carrying a fetus to term. The woman's ovum and her husband's sperm are combined in an artificial environment, and the zygote is placed in the womb of the carrier mother. However, in the sixth month of pregnancy, it is revealed that the fetus has a fatal disease and will never live a "normal" life; even if it is born alive, it would have a maximum life expectancy of two years under intensive care conditions. The (genetic) mother and father want the surrogate mother to have an abortion, but she refuses, maintaining that the baby is alive (*He kicks!*), and that she is not going to give up a baby growing inside of her. Will she take care of the child after he is born? No, she definitely has no such intention. According to the contract, she must of course give the child to the mother and father, who will then spend a large sum on intensive care treatment only to watch the child they can never have suffer and die. According to Illinois law (since the event takes place in Chicago), abortion is legal, but it is not possible to *force* a woman to have an abortion. On the other hand, the genetic parents argue, it is not a meaningful option for a child who does not have the potential to be a "normal" person (that is, to become a subject with a sense of self) to devastate their lives both materially and emotionally. At the end of the episode, this problem remains unresolved. The ethical dilemma it highlights, however, may help us advance our argument about motherhood.

Three Mothers

I have tried to establish that there are three types of motherhood: genetic, birth and nurturing. Theoretically, these three could be three separate women; nowadays, this has become practically viable as well. Other combinations are also possible: In Brecht's narratives, the genetic mother and birth mother are positioned against the nurturing mother. In *Law & Order: SVU*, birth and nurturing mother is positioned against the genetic mother, whereas it is genetic mother and nurturing mother against the birth mother in *The Good Wife*. In each of these situations, we encounter different ethical and legal problems. Legal issues can be partially solved by adapting the judiciary system (albeit slowly) to new technologies. The ethical problems, however, are not that easily solved.

On the other hand, it is possible in each of these situations to read the stories as metaphors for the contradictory nature of motherhood itself, as personifications of a "splitting in the experience of motherhood." Recalcati (2019, 76) offers an alternative reading of the Judgement of Solomon:

These two mothers are not really two mothers, but demonstrate a splitting in the experience of motherhood, which is itself constituted by the oscillation between the child's enjoyment, appropriation and separation, the gift of loss, recognition of the child as another life, as irreducible otherness; oscillation between the death drive and the life drive, between the urge to possess life, thus condemning it, and the urge to release the life that has been created. Only the intervention of the Name of the Father, embodied by Solomon's ruling and his sword, is capable here of liberating the child from the fatal grasp of its mother.

Following this suggestion, we can read every case we have seen so far as not only exceptions to the rule of *Mater semper certa*, but also as more or less generalized comments on the split nature of motherhood.

Let us start from the last: what could be the origin of the mother's love for her offspring, the empathic relationship she establishes with her child? From a purely biological point of view, we can say that at least one factor is the endocrinal changes—more precisely, the radically increased level of prolactin secretion—the pregnant women experiences. As a matter of fact, it is undisputable that one of the causes of the series of behavioral changes known as the maternal instinct lies in this endocrinal state. On the other hand, human beings are not just instinctual creatures. Thus, for example, postpartum depression, or a child being "unwelcome" (for cultural, social or purely psychological reasons), can radically compromise this love and empathy; conversely, a child may be tasked with saving the relationship, which will disproportionately augment the same emotions. Although the mother's relationship with her child begins biologically, a number of cultural, social, psychic, and even religious and economic factors may have an impact on this relationship; in extreme cases these factors can completely disrupt it, or, inversely, unreasonably amplify it, as can be observed in cases of devouring mother syndrome.

So, in the last example we discussed, the birth (surrogate) mother is biologically equipped with the maternal instinct, but the genetic mother is not: her maternal instinct is not triggered by her endocrine system, and except for a cognitive awareness that the baby is hers, she cannot be expected to have a deep emotional or empathetic connection triggered by her biology. Therefore, the reaction of the surrogate mother (*Feel it, he kicks, he is alive!*) and the reluctance of the genetic mother to accept a fetus who will never grow up to be her child (but only a source of pain and expense) are both perfectly understandable.

What about the situation in *Law & Order: SVU*? How could a woman who had frozen her ova years ago have a maternal instinct as such? This is a woman who lost her own child in a traumatic way and while struggling to make up for this loss later discovered the existence of another (genetic) offspring. The only relationship between the child and the woman is again cognitive: the knowledge that half of the child's chromosomes came from her, and there are no grounds for any emotional, empathic or instinctive relationship to exist. For that reason, the effort of the writers and producers of *Law & Order: SVU* to mimic the Judgement of Solomon parable and make the *genetic mother* the one who cannot tolerate the suffering of the child is seriously problematic, to say the least. Indeed, when we look at American film and television of the past two decades, we will see that in this period of increasing adoptions, sperm donations, frozen ova and artificial insemination, the adolescents of the nineteenth century who were endlessly pondering the question "Who is my father?" are quickly being replaced by a new generation of adolescents morbidly preoccupied by the question "Who are my genetic parents?" In order to determine how real and significant this question is for today's American society, we need another data set from targeted and specific studies. But it is definitely possible to say that this subject has already obtained disproportionate representation in film and on television. This may be because the science of genetics—which gained tremendous popularity in the late twentieth century with the anticipated mapping of the human genome—suggested to some that the secret of humanity would be unveiled, leading to its magnified expression in art and popular culture. In other words, the institution of the family, which was rapidly losing ideological credibility and practical legitimacy, found a new (albeit temporary) semantic framework in genetics. However, the unhappy adolescents looking for their genetic parents would have been no less unhappy had they found them; after the excitement of the newly discovered science is over, we would see that the real source of their unhappiness lay elsewhere.

What do the seven tales we have discussed tell us about this source? We will have to start again from the end: The name of the episode of *The Good Wife* we discussed is "A Precious Commodity." The phrase, "Life is such a precious commodity, isn't it?" is uttered to the surrogate mother by one of the meanest, nastiest and most conniving lawyers in the series, revealing a dirty secret of the family separate from genetic and endocrine structures. But that is not all: The rest of the clue comes in a discussion between the genetic mother and the birth (surrogate) mother. When the surrogate mother tries to defend her position, she says, "Remember what you said, Kathy, after the first sonogram? 'Do everything you can to protect my baby,'" to which the genetic mother answers, "This isn't protecting. This is owning." Perhaps if we take the concept of owning and that of the "precious commodity" together, we can get a little closer to the secret of the family and motherhood.

"A Precious Commodity"

In the first two texts, one written in seventh century BC and one in fourth century BC, the concept of motherhood itself (and therefore the family institution) is not open to discussion. In the first, the rival mothers are prostitutes, so they have already been excluded from the family institution (and indeed from society).

Neither law nor the rest of society is interested in how (or by whom) their children were born, so when a dispute arises, the sentence can easily be left to the wise ruler's sense of justice. In the second text, one of the rival mothers is a *yakshini*, not even a human being but a deceitful *demon*, and her main intention is to eat the child. Here too the problem is not about law or society, and the decision is again left to the sage and then easily forgotten. The real problem begins with Qianfu's *The Chalk Circle*: the matter of inheritance has entered the picture, and although the bigamous structure may not be acceptable to many cultures today, the "unity of the family" (something easily justifiable in every culture) is in dire danger. Li Qianfu solves this problem by borrowing from the two ancient texts at hand (we may safely assume that he knew the *Maha-Ummagga Jataka,* and he may have heard about the Old Testament parables); but this time the mediator is not a supreme and sacred sage but a judge in everyday law practice. Accordingly, the verdict comes at the end of a long and laborious process, and murder and adultery cases are intermingled in the trial. This is because the problem is not to whom the child was born, who actually raised him, nor who his genetic parents were, but rather *whose property he was.* The secret of Justinianus's law is thus solved: what the law actually means is that the child is the common property of the woman who is *publicly seen* to have given birth to it and the man who is *documented* to have inseminated her.

In Li Qianfu's and Brecht's stories, this property is directly linked to an inheritance issue. The other woman's desire to have the child stems not from any maternal instinct but from her desire for the inheritance that comes with him. As a matter of fact, in the stories from the Old Testament[4] and *Maha-Ummagga Jataka,* the gender of the children is insignificant and thus indeterminate, whereas in the next three stories the children are definitely male; they're direct heirs of their fathers. The law that does not involve women in the continuity of property obliges them to be jealously possessive of the sons through whom they will find a place in the property regime.

Is it entirely appropriate, however, to reduce the problem to a matter of inheritance? Does the majority of the population in class societies—people from the working classes who don't have much (if any) property to pass onto their children—have a different type of relationship with their offspring? It appears that

---

4   It is not a coincidence that there is no inheritance dispute in the Solomon parable, because it would scarcely have had any meaning in the matrilineal Jewish society. In any case, there is no father around who will hand down his property, and the women are prostitutes who are already excluded from the property regime.

the ownership of children is not limited to a simple inheritance issue; we should also seek the roots of the problem in the cultural and psychic construction of the family institution that forms the fundamental building block of society.

When we study the source of the family structure of class societies that are based upon patriarchy and women's compulsory monogamy, we must address the necessity of ensuring the continuity of private property (mostly) monopolized by men and, therefore, a radical limitation of female sexuality. However, this finding alone does not shed light on the similar structure in Oriental societies where *individual* private property is extremely limited; nor does it answer the question of why the same psychic structure applies to women. Why do women wish to possess their children, and why do we observe in women jealous, sometimes unhealthy behavior toward their children?

We have already seen the first answer to this question: women's relationships with children are primarily due to a biological (genetic and endocrinal) mechanism which cannot be observed in men and which creates an emotional and empathetic bond between mother and child, beginning prior to birth. If humans were merely biological creatures, this bond would end when women's endocrinal compulsion ceased, and when the children grew up they would be no different for the mother than any other members of the species.

But that's not how things work for human beings. First of all, maturation of the human young continues long after the biological cessation of the maternal instinct. There are cultural and social causes for this that arise later, as well as biological, species-specific causes. As a consequence, there is a fatal gap between cessation of the maternal instinct, the end of the urge to take care of the children, and the point at which the children mature enough to take care of themselves; a gap which could last for years and could have led to the early demise of human beings as a species.

The Helpless Child

This impasse is tempered by two factors, one of them biological and the other cultural. The biological factor is rooted in the fact that the human infant, distinct from other mammalian infants, is born helpless. It is true that as we climb the evolutionary ladder, the time needed for neural (sensory and motor, not to mention the higher mental functions) maturation increases. In human beings, this maturation period reaches such a length as to render the human infant completely helpless and dependent in its first three to four years. As with most mammalians, this dependency is almost always on the mother, and it has to have an instinctual counterpart in mature female human beings.

The foal starts grazing minutes after it is born, the chick is mobile and able to feed itself as soon as it's hatched. Human babies, on the other hand, are born *premature*: as compared to chimpanzees and bonobos, our closest relatives in the animal kingdom, human young spend at least twice the time (in fact almost two-and-a-half times; between eighteen and twenty-one months instead of nine) in the uterus to develop the same neurological and cognitive maturity. Accordingly, they will need much more time under constant care, because they lack not only sensory and motor skills at birth, but also the main skill that gave human beings their only advantage in evolution: the higher mental functions. This premature birth, so to speak, makes human young almost completely dependent on their caregivers for years on end, a stage from which they will begin to emerge only after the mirror stage (almost exclusively a human trait, with a few minor exceptions) and with their introduction to language (Lacan 1997).

The near-absolute dependency of the child on the caregiver, the mother, has an instinctual counterpart in mature female human beings. Without language—that is, as long as the mother communicates with her children mostly on an empathetic level—this dependency does not seem to create any problems. When language intervenes, however, desires emerge and start to claim an ever-increasing share of libidinal energy for their own purposes. Females are not dominated solely by the single-minded urge to nurture and protect their young anymore; they have other desires—from the year-round human urge to copulate to various social and cultural activities and, finally, a career—which compete with this primal instinct. Furthermore, as females are increasingly drawn into a semiotic cosmos chiefly devised and shaped to suit the needs of males' extra-domestic cooperative exploits, they begin to lose their empathic abilities. At this point, evolution intervenes and a series of possible mutations occur to facilitate a genetic difference between the male and female members of *Homo sapiens*.

If, as a result of these mutations, language renders empathic communication practically dysfunctional then communication between mother and infant breaks down as well, desires gain undisputed precedence over the maternal instinct, and, as a result, the offspring do not get the required care. In this case, the helpless human infants almost completely dependent on their mothers have little chance to live on and carry their mothers' genes onto the next generation. Non-empathic women, therefore, who follow men in passing over to the semiotic sphere completely, have very little chance for genetic survival. This was true at least (a) among the lower classes and (b) until the twentieth century. With the emergence of classes, upper-class women attained the option to delegate childcare to lower-class women (as happened with Grusha Vashnadze in Brecht's *Caucasian Chalk Circle*), and in the twentieth century, social organizations took over childcare at least partially for an ever-increasing number of women. In both cases, however, the time span was too short to effect a real genetic change. Even the history of class societies, measured in millennia, is but a moment from the standpoint of evolution. Most women of our day are therefore descendants of the female human beings who somewhat preserved their empathetic skills and secured the survival of their genetic lineage.

The cultural element, on the other hand, is that the extraordinarily long duration of human childcare when compared to that of other mammals keeps females away from other necessary activities of human communities (mainly hunting) and binds them to a "home." This creates an inevitable social division of labor and gives females a different (and hierarchically lower) place in culture and society. Although this interpretation of the (social) division of labor was never very trustworthy in the first place (see Diamond 1997 above), and it eventually loses its functional significance in later stages of cultural development, the patriarchal structure of class societies that subjects women to compulsory monogamy and father domination retains, and even exaggerates, this structure. Women are therefore forced to own their children in order to preserve their place (albeit hierarchically lower) in the social division of labor.

Let us now add the impact of cultural and psychic developments to these two factors: in the gender and age-group hierarchy of class societies, we refer to those human beings whose station is even lower than women as children. As a result of this stratification, we are able to dominate them unconditionally, we can subject them to arbitrary violence, try to shape and mold their minds (although we don't know anything about *how* to do this), harass and even rape them, and despite this, we expect unrequited love, admiration, and even worship from them. From time to time (depending on genetic continuity), they meet our narcissistic needs because they resemble us, or at least glorify our likeness. Since there is no guidebook on how to educate them (parenting is not a certifiable profession), we can convince them of whatever we want and whatever we believe in, at least for a time. We lay the cornerstones of their personality structures (however unconsciously); and even in their adult years, it is we who make the most important decisions in their lives, through emotional and economic pressure and guidance, and sometimes, when these prove to be ineffective, through direct violence. It should not be surprising, then, when we claim to own these children.

Are these children really "precious commodities," as suggested in *The Good Wife*? Excluding the fact that young girls are still bought and sold for a bride token in some cultures, maybe not—not in the popular sense of the commodity as a good bought and sold, anyway. There is, however, another definition of *commodity*: "A commodity is, in the first place, an object outside us, a thing that by its properties satisfies human wants [*Bedürfnisse*] of some sort or another. The nature of such wants, whether, for instance, they spring from the stomach or from fancy, makes no difference" (Marx 1976, 2). In this precise sense, the child is definitely a commodity in capitalism, especially in late capitalism. It satisfies the desires of a number of people in a way no other commodity can. Moreover, this commodity is given to us for free, or at least it seems to be so *prima facie*. To be sure, a child may be extremely costly in the long run, but most parents often ignore this cost, since they regard having a child (the possessive again) to be a human duty, or a debt to the nation, community or religion, as their respective ideologies dictate.

Nevertheless, the psychological yields of possessing a child are almost immeasurable. If you are a man, you hand down your property to your child; if you are property-less, like the majority of society, you hand down your name and, if the genetic circumstances permit, your likeness; if you are an artisan, you hand down your craft. If your child is a girl, she can bring you some money or at least a good (meaning profitable) network of connections through an appropriate marriage. If you can see yourself in your son, you can wait and encourage him to do the things you can't do, or things you could have done but failed to do. In short, you can try to compensate for your own phallic lack through your son (which is also true for women). Needless to say, a child obliged to love you will meet your need to be loved unconditionally, a child obliged to obey you will submit to your irrational desires, and a child who can't hit back will allow you to satisfy your urge to be arbitrarily violent.

If you are a woman, the child frees you from the sexist and misogynic epithet *barren bitch* and raises your social status within the patriarchal order. If you are exposed to domestic violence, it provides you with a secondary object onto which to pass this violence. If you feel unloved, there will be someone in your life who will love you unconditionally, at least for a while. You can establish and assert your power at home (hitherto usurped by men) over your child. And of course, just like men, you can try to compensate for your phallic lack through your child, not because it is a *real* lack, but because throughout millennia the patriarchal order has done its best to convince you that it is. A child becomes a surrogate for anything you wanted to become or do but couldn't.

Do you really love your child? Let's consider the mother in our sixth narrative. Why would a person love a child whom she did not carry to term in her body, nor give birth to or raise, and whom she had not even met prior to abducting her? Because the child is her partial genetic match? This could not be—at least not for biological or conventional reasons. But if she was obsessively seeking a substitute for her own lost child, she could experience the illusion of that overly broadly defined emotion we call love. In the seventh narrative, there is a greater semblance of logic: the genetic mother knows that it is more appropriate, for both parent and child, that a child who would only experience a brief life of suffering without ever becoming a conscious being should not be born at all. The surrogate mother, however, who experiences all the endocrinal and behavioral changes brought about by pregnancy, acts not according to this logic but is instead motivated by a strong compulsion to protect the child. She claims to love the unborn child, but even here there is a limit to this emotion: heightened prolactin levels are not sufficient to support the long, painful and mostly hopeless period that will follow birth, at which point the mother abandons the idea of motherhood and takes refuge in the cold legality of a contract.[5]

The profound problems inherent in the institution of the family, which could have become apparent with even a cursory reading of the first five narratives, become crystal clear in the last two, with the cold and somewhat cruel interposition of new technologies. What we call motherhood, which we believe refers to a single and integral human condition, is actually a mixture of a number of biological, social, cultural, and even economic functions. What we call family, which we assume to have remained more or less the same across all social and cultural formations throughout history, is in fact many different things. The fundamental common element in all these different families is an extremely precarious contract: on the one hand, it is a financial institution (in my homeland, Turkey, marriage certificates were once issued by the Ministry of Finance), and on the other, it is an ongoing crime story, a series of legitimized crimes against women and children (nowadays they are issued by the Ministry of Internal Affairs).

---

5   The pros and cons of surrogate motherhood, as well as the problems arising from the "ownership" of the child, are discussed in detail in Sophie Lewis's book *Full Surrogacy Now*. Lewis is openly pro-surrogacy herself but allocates a considerable part of her book to anti-surrogacy arguments before arriving at the conclusion that although they seemingly speak against the commodification of children supposedly brought about by the mere technology of surrogacy, these arguments do, at the end of the day, advocate for children's *ownership* by their biological parents. Lewis's own suggestion is *communalized full surrogacy*, organized in the network of a sisterhood. (Lewis 2019)

Who is the mother, then? Brecht had the answer when he wrote "The Augsburg Chalk Circle" and *The Caucasian Chalk Circle*, but we need to make it clearer now. The mother is the one who nurtures. Anybody can supply the genetic material. Any being with a uterus can give birth. Moreover, if technology develops just a step further, childbirth with the help of artificial wombs will be possible, liberating women from the much glorified but actually quite traumatic, painful (and sometimes horrifying) event called birth. Donna Haraway's latest book, *Staying with the Trouble* (Haraway 2016), even makes this argument into a slogan: "Make kin, not babies!" This slogan can be read in two ways: the first is the simple either/or reading, suggesting that women should refrain from getting pregnant and giving birth and rather concentrate on "making kin" with all living things, changing the foundation of relatedness from the genetic to the empathetic or affectional. The second ("not only, but also") reading suggests that regardless of whether or not people prefer giving birth, they should stop "having" (or possessing) babies and instead make kin (siblings, friends, relatives) with them, among other living beings, regardless of gender, age group and species.

Even though the genetic mother and the birth mother will gradually lose their significance, we still have to deal with the fact that human infants are born utterly helpless and require a very long time before they can take care of themselves. This will not change, but it has become increasingly intolerable that those who provide them with care also own them, use them as their playthings, and treat them as toys, slaves or modelling clay to be molded and shaped. Children are not our property. We may be their fellow travelers for a while, we may suggest which paths they take, we may shelter and watch over them, but at the same time we will definitely learn something from them if we manage to treat them as equals. In order to do this, we need neither hormone treatment nor (material, emotional or spiritual) compensation.

Is being a mother not this exactly? Brecht's Grusha Vashnadze in *The Caucasian Chalk Circle*, the nurturing mother, who neither had a genetic connection with the child nor had given birth to him, was such a mother. A companion without any expectation of compensation, protecting, watching over, loving the child not because he carries her genes or because hormones so dictate, but because he is a human being and *has the potential to be a good person*. We, who become human as we are gradually freed of the blind enslavement to our biological roots, or at least as we learn to control our subjection to biology through our reason and sense of ethics, may follow Grusha's path and truly become mothers, a special kind of "kin" in Haraway's sense, for a limited period of time, regardless of our gender.

3.

The Child's Flesh,
the Child's Bones

I believe that maturity is not an outgrowing, but a growing up: that
an adult is not a dead child, but a child who survived. I believe that all
the best faculties of a mature human being exist in the child, and that
if these faculties are encouraged in youth they will act well and wisely
in the adult, but if they are repressed and denied in the child they will
stunt and cripple the adult personality.

—Ursula K. Le Guin
"Why are Americans Afraid of Dragons?"

"HIS FLESH IS YOURS, the bones mine!" This is what Turkish fathers used to say
when they delivered their sons to school. Only their sons, not their daughters,
because in those days, girls were not delivered to schools but rather kept at home,
flesh, bone and all. And when they grew up and were delivered to their *husbands*,
they were also given away that way: flesh, bone and all. A barbaric practice, many
will say, but those were the olden days, and it only happened in Turkey, in parts of
the Middle East, and probably in the rest of the Orient. In Turkey, we know otherwise: until the 1960s, in some cases extending into the 1970s, most systematic
beatings happened in Turkey's French schools run by *frères*, where, as in the UK
and most of Europe at the time, the switch was one of the main tools of "education." This was true for centuries, until very recently: the switch in the West and
the *falaka* (another tool of systematic torture usually—but not exclusively—used
on kids) in the East were used by educators throughout the world.

"But We Love Our Children!"

Yet, we all love our children. We all love children in general. As a matter of fact, we
may love them a bit more than is appropriate. Human beings have bred domestic
animals for millennia to look like the infant versions of their adult specimens in

the wild, because the mere look of infancy instinctually creates emotions of love and affection in us, not only toward our own species but toward most mammalian species. This mostly instinctual inclination is a response to what we call *neoteny*:

> Humans generally are more attracted to animals who retain infantile characteristics into adulthood. This is, at bottom, a biological imperative derived from the appearance of human babies, with their proportionately larger heads and eyes and, as they age slightly, their unsteady gait. Human attraction to neotenic animals relates directly to nurturing and species-propagating instincts for our own kind and also explains why, for example, we find a penguin's waddle amusingly endearing. (Estren 2012, 6)

Neotenic attraction or affect is usually defined as an instinctual, rather than cultural or aesthetic, attraction in adults to infantile characteristics, and the corresponding tendency in individuals to retain these characteristics in adulthood. As such, it has to have some genetic and evolutionary foundation, since it is not limited to *Homo sapiens sapiens* but can be observed in most mammalian species. We can speculate that the non-neotenic genetic mutations of most species probably died out because their young did not receive the necessary attention and care when they most needed it, and mutations with the neotenic genetic structures had a better probability of survival. We can further speculate that the longer childhood persists, the greater the need for neoteny, which is also affirmed by the all-encompassing neotenic attraction or affect in *Homo sapiens sapiens*, the species with by far the longest childhood in the entire animal kingdom. Neuroscientist V. S. Ramachandran goes a step further to claim that neoteny is one of the major causes of increased human neuroplasticity, the immense adaptability and mutability of the human brain:

> While other animal brains exhibit plasticity, we are the only species to use it as a central player in brain refinement and evolution. One of the major ways we managed to leverage neuroplasticity to such stratospheric heights is known as neoteny—our almost absurdly prolonged infancy and youth, which leaves us both hyperplastic and hyperdependent on older generations for well over a decade. (Ramachandran 2011, 38)

We love our children, therefore, not only because they are *our* children, but also because their cuteness triggers in us an irresistible feeling of affection and attraction, which usually ends when they reach puberty and become cranky, clumsy, lanky, awkward and uncontrollably irrational creatures. The irrationality was always there, because rationality necessitates a certain degree of grounding in language skills, but even that was cute in infancy and childhood. In adolescence, however, it becomes unbearable, not only because the young become less and less cute (neotenic) as they grow up, but also because the irrationality becomes a product of the tension between an overdemanding superego, a newly discovered (pseudo-)rationality trying to ground itself socially and culturally, and profound endocrinal changes happening suddenly and without warning.

Until that time, however, we feel this attraction toward children, so much so that in some of us it becomes exaggerated and takes improper forms sometimes expressed sexually. Unfortunately, affection cannot usually manifest in any forms other than sexuality, especially for many males of our species who haven't learned any in the first place. Other than the mother's instinctual affection in the first years of postnatal care, all forms of physical contact have been brutally taken over by what we call sexuality.[1] Even when our attraction toward a child is purely due to neoteny, we usually express this in semi-sexual, semi-violent forms, such as "biting the infant" ("eating" becoming an expression of affection), sometimes pinching and squeezing them relentlessly, and sometimes turning this into a public show for relatives and neighbors. "Show your willy to the uncles, son!" is unfortunately still considered a legitimate demand the make of a four-year-old!

In time, as the child grows up, these expressions start to clash with our superego directives, mainly the one prohibiting incest, and therefore we become confused, frustrated and we may eventually become dangerously violent. This confusion extends into the young's adolescence, and violence and affection, sexual desire and rage, kindness and punishment, and love and hate all become mixed up in a tangle ending with what we call the sexual abuse (or molestation) of children. In theory, *all* children are abused (sexually or otherwise) at one point in their lives: no child is free from the unwanted physical contact of the adults around

---

1 Those who complain about Freud's "obsession" with sexuality should read him a second time or, for that matter, for the first time, since many have not bothered to do so before blurting out half-cooked allegations about him. Freud was not obsessed with sexuality; far from it. All he did was to try to unveil the poorly kept secret of our culture's obsession with it, the herd of elephants in the room, something we try to ignore at any cost. He simply called a spade a spade and asked us what we are going to do with this knowledge? This is the question we have all been trying to avoid since the beginning of the last century.

them, no child can control or stop unwanted excess affection from adults, especially as they grow out of infancy and yearn to be left alone as they (try to) develop an inner self, an intimate "room of their own." Furthermore, no adolescent can discern precisely between genuine affection and unwanted sexual attention, since they have not yet (re)constructed the borders between their selves and others, between their bodies and the surrounding world.

Is it possible that our love and affection toward children becomes more and more inappropriate, shall we say, as a result of this neoteny which we cannot understand (it is instinctual, after all, and thus beyond comprehension), and for which we cannot find the proper channels to express? No, research indicates (see Marcus and Cunningham 2003): incarcerated child molesters show no more propensity toward exaggerated neotenic behavior than non-offenders do. Unfortunately, similar studies (and comparisons) have not been made for *pedophiles* and "normal" people, which, we can speculate, will be a little different, but not by much. In 2003, pedophiles were unfortunately included in the umbrella term *child molesters*, so it is not possible to differentiate between these two as regards neotenic attitude. In 2010, Sarah Goode warned us against confusing child sexual abuse with pedophilia:

> There is a clear distinction to be made at the outset between child sexual abuse (adult sexual contact with children below the legal age of consent) and paedophilia (adult sexual attraction to children below the legal age of consent). [...] Paedophilia is, strictly speaking, in a separate conceptual category to child sexual abuse. It is defined as a medical condition similar to other psychosexual disorders or "paraphilias" (disorders of sexual function). The contemporary definition of paedophilia, therefore, is tied up with its medical diagnosis and clinical treatment. Paedophilia, as we currently understand it, is the medical diagnosis of a fixed sexual orientation which may or may not manifest itself in actual behaviour towards a child. (Goode 2010, 10)

Pedophilia pertains to the construction of the neural and endocrine structures, mainly in the brain, and is as such diagnosable and treatable, even if not curable. It is not the same as opportunistic child molestation, and it sometimes may not even be expressed as such. Many pedophiles (probably a large minority of them) do not actively engage in child molestation, and some of them even seek medical help before they become active molesters. Non-pedophilic molesters, however, are those who do not have such an uncontrollable urge but do it anyway, just because they can. Non-pedophilic molestation is more of an act of domination and opportunistic and perfidious violence than a sexual act, and it does not have an excuse. This is not to say that pedophilia proper is excusable: to the contrary, it should be diagnosed and treated from the outset, and if it is left uncontrolled because the perpetrator refuses treatment, they should be held legally responsible, not in order to satisfy our vengeful feelings, but to protect children from them.

Whether by a pedophile or by a non-pedophilic offender, the sexual molestation of children is something culturally and ethically detestable and legally punishable. Here it becomes necessary to define the term sexual molestation in better detail, because the concept of consent should also be included in the argument. Throughout the last few decades, debate over the presence of consent and its precise definition with regard to rape have been re-opened to a wide public debate spearheaded by feminists. We can see from this debate that even between people of legal age, the presence of consent is not as clear-cut an issue as it had seemed when laws regarding rape were written. Many acts and expressions that were hitherto considered to be consensual or to communicate consent are now considered suspect, not only by third parties but also by the very people believed to be giving the consent. The absence or presence of consent after the legal age is the subject of an entirely different discussion; whether children are capable of giving consent, however, is what we must address now.

The legal age or age of majority is defined differently in every culture according to varying circumstances. We can designate it by giving a simple number (recently reduced to fifteen in France, sixteen in the UK, eighteen in a large majority of countries, nineteen, twenty or twenty-one in a handful, including four American states). However, determining the legal age has contradictory implications: the first and positive implication is the protection of teenagers from the sexual attention and acts of adults. Even when there is no actual physical violence in these acts, children and teenagers are much more susceptible to the abuse of authority and to subtle threats, fear of retribution and notoriety, and flattery, although the overwhelming majority will regret succumbing to it later. They should definitely be protected against these acts, and many countries have taken steps to do so: in the US, for instance, even when rape against a minor as such cannot be proven, sex with someone under the legal age is still considered statutory rape and is punished accordingly. On the other hand (and this is the downside of the concept of legal age), many American states have legal loopholes that allow underage teenagers to marry (mostly to their rapists) with the consent of their parents and/or the state. The same thing is true in Turkey, where child brides are quite common, and the same laws and traditions that are supposedly designed to protect children and teenagers pre-emptively deem them unable to express consent.

We should, therefore, question whether the very same laws that are designed to stop the sexual molestation of children subject them to the domination and mercy of their parents and the state (sharing their flesh and bones among them). Depending on the ideological predilections of both the parents and the state, not to mention the moral codes and traditions of the specific communities and societies they live in, the calamity that is supposed to be stopped at the front door may enter from the back door in the form of unwanted underage marriages, where children and teenagers are treated as commodities. Moreover, the very same laws that offer many loopholes for the buying, selling and/or giving away of children against their will (for either material gain or to satisfy sociocultural expectations), still punish innocent and consensual sexual contact between teenagers themselves.

It becomes necessary, then, to turn around and ask ourselves how sincere we are in our exaggerated revulsion, in the disgust we express loudly and publicly whenever we encounter a case of child abuse. Like it or not, the sexual molestation of children creates a disproportionate outrage in most of us, because we feel that it is us who are really being victimized. We feel that children are our property, objects that we possess or, worse still, extensions of ourselves. However, crimes against children—molestation, abuse, rape and turning them into objects of pornography—are atrocious crimes not because children are our property but because these crimes turn something that should be pleasurable, playful and affectionate into hurtful, guilty experiences that will stay with them for the rest of their lives and turn them into neurotic, paranoid, anxious and depressive adults; in other words, make them exactly like us.

This is because, despite all our efforts to pretend otherwise, children are sexual beings. We can turn this statement around and say that sex, freed from the yoke of reproduction (which is actually something different from sex), is basically a childlike act. It is us, especially in the last ten millennia, who have taken sex and made it into a source of shame, revulsion, secrecy and crime. Infants and children who are not yet hampered by our superstitious, horrified and guilty feelings about sex, engage (or at least try to do so) with other people using all five of their senses, just like they did with their mothers, and get an intense pleasure in this. The problems start when they learn that they ought to feel ashamed, disgusted and guilty about this and then keep it a secret.

The acceptance of childhood sexuality without reservation, however, seems to be a problematic concept, to say the least, because under today's circumstances, it is closely related to the phenomena of child sexual molestation (mostly within the family) and child pornography, which have become burning issues. Wouldn't all this talk about childhood sexuality encourage the perverts and at least partially justify their actions? Wouldn't it strengthen their defense strategies in a judicial system already clogged up with temporary insanity and *non compos mentis* pleas? Wouldn't it open sexual molestation charges to questions of mutual consent and (s)he said/(s)he said arguments? If we stop and think for just a moment, we will see that the recognition of childhood sexuality will do exactly the opposite: if children are asexual "things" without a will of their own, then sexual crimes against children are just that: crimes against objects rather than persons. If we accept, however, that children are not passive receivers of molestation, abuse and rape but are emotionally involved in such acts, partially comprehending what is done to them, being physically hurt but also perceiving the peculiar (and definitely confused) pleasure of their molesters (without knowing what to do with it), we may be able to see the true hideousness of the crime. Children sense and distinguish sexual molestation. They are not only physically hurt by it, but they also feel something that they cannot even name. They feel something akin to pleasure, since most have practiced childhood masturbation, but this pleasure is also mixed with intense pain and feels wrong. Adding insult to injury, they will therefore also feel guilty for the rest of their lives due to something done to them, and, because it will contribute to the (mis)formation of their psyche and their later attitude toward sexuality, the psychic trauma they endure may even be worse than that of adult victims of rape and abuse.

"But," some people may still exclaim, "this is what the family and the state are for! To protect the children from pedophiles and molesters!" As we have seen in the discussion about the legal age, this truism is not good enough; if we take a closer look at how and where child abuse happens, at what frequency, and by whom, we can see that it is even dangerously misleading.

Some Facts about Child Abuse
(Warning: Too Many Numbers and Percentages)

Some of the findings of the Abel and Harlow child abuse study conducted between 1994 and 2001 are as follows:

1. In 2001, the number of female children under the age of 13 years who were *current* victims of sexual abuse in the United States was 2,231,372, and the number of male victims in the same age group was 1,004,117 (estimated).

2. As of the same date, the total number of adults who *had been* sexually abused during their childhood was 27,160,752 women and 12,222,388 men (estimated).

3. According to the 2000 census, the total population of the USA was 281,421,906. About 40 million of this population had been sexually abused at one time or another and about 3.5 million were currently being abused.

4. In the study itself, which surveyed 16,109 adults, those who explicitly admitted to having abused a child under the age of 13 number 4007 (25%), of which 3957 are males and only 55 females. The numbers of those who implicitly admit and those who deny but are later proven to be lying are much higher.[2]

5. 47% of the abusers say that they themselves were abused as children.

6. Only 8% of men who abuse boys identify themselves as "homosexual," and 70% proudly declare that they are "heterosexual."

7. 93% of the abusers say they are religious.

8. 68% of the adults who accept that they molested a child under the age of 13 did so within the family under the supposed protection of "home."

9. Abel and Harlow admit that they reach their figures by using the lower end of the estimated ranges for each case. Therefore, the percentage they present for those who have been sexually abused (15.5% in total) is the lowest possible number according to their study. There are also studies that estimate this rate to be as high as 54%, which is probably an inflated number; the truth must be somewhere between these two, but closer to the minimal limit.[3]
    (Abel and Harlow 2001)

---

2   Let us point out that some of these "denials" go like this: "As I was bathing, I stepped on the soap and fell, and my penis accidentally entered my six-year-old daughter's vagina."

3   I have summarized the Abel and Harlow findings to save space, but I advise anyone with more than a passing interest in this matter to read the entire report to get a sense of the sheer horror we are facing.

Since the study was conducted exclusively in the United States, an objection may be raised regarding its universal validity. However, the multi-ethnic nature of the US and the fact that it contains different cultural structures in different geographical regions (e.g., the ultra-conservative southeast, liberal New England and the relatively "free" Northern California) may indicate that it represents a fairly appropriate sampling. Although it is now quite outdated, Abel and Harlow still provide the most extensive American study conducted to this day. A brief inquiry into more recent studies of a similar (albeit more limited) nature indicate that there are no significant variations in its findings: whatever change there is, it is definitely for the worse.[4]

In the EU, the percentage of children who have been (or are currently being) victims of sexual molestation is usually estimated at one in five, or 20%:

> Available data suggest that about 1 in 5 children in Europe are victims of some form of sexual violence. It is estimated that in 70% to 85% of cases, the abuser is somebody the child knows and trusts. Child sexual violence can take many forms: sexual abuse within the family circle, child pornography and prostitution, corruption, solicitation via Internet and sexual assault by peers. (Missing Children Europe)[5]

---

4   More recent US studies offer new figures:

In 2014, the Centers for Disease Control and Prevention (CDC) reported the national rate for the sexual abuse of children and adolescents in all settings to be 25% for girls and 16.6% for boys (20.8% of American children), with an estimated 15 million children being affected (CDC 2014; US Census Bureau 2015). Based on additional studies, a substantial number of these children were sexually abused while in the care of youth-serving organizations.

A US Department of Education study found that on average, nearly 10% of students have been victims of sexual abuse or misconduct by school employees or volunteers (Shakeshaft 2004). The study also reported that at some high schools, as many as 50.3% of the students had been victimized at some point during their education. According to a study by the US Department of Justice (2010), an average of 10.3% of the youth in juvenile detention across all custodial facilities reported having been sexually abused by the staff. The study revealed that many states had facilities with rates of sexual abuse by staff higher than the national rate for sexually abused children and adolescents in all settings, including the familial setting, with as many as 36% of the youth having been sexually abused while in confinement. (Abel et al. 2018, 2–3)

5   There is a sad story behind this quotation. At the time I first included it, it appeared on a Council of Europe website called *The Council of Europe ONE in FIVE Campaign to Stop Sexual Violence against Children*. I used the quotation and didn't feel the need to return to it, since it was too general and did not name any particular study. When my editor told me that the link I provided led nowhere, I checked it and discovered that the site as it was had disappeared. Previously, this passage could be found on the missing Council of Europe website; now it can only be found on

The world, however, is much larger than the US and the EU. What happens in "the rest" (as compared to the West) when it comes to the sexual abuse of children? It's not "much, much worse," as the Orientalists among us would want to believe, since they have no doubt that such problems are endemic only to the Orient and will magically go away as it "Westernizes." In reality it is about the same overall, with some places that are better and some that are definitely worse. But the better instances should not lead us astray either, because they may simply reflect underreporting, especially in family cases where the victim may not have sufficient access to legal protection:

> [A]lthough there are important differences between countries and between genders as regards reported prevalence rates, several relevant findings can be observed. The South African studies report the highest prevalence rates for both men (60.9%) and women (43.7%), whereas the lowest rates correspond to the only study conducted in France, which also concerned both genders (0.6% for males and 0.9% for females). Jordan presents the second-highest prevalence rate for men (27.0%), followed by Tanzania (25.0%). Rates between 10 and 20% are reported for males in Israel (15.7%), Spain (13.4%), Australia (13.0%) and Costa Rica (12.8%), while the remaining countries all have prevalence rates below 10%. In the case of women, Australia (37.8%), Costa Rica (32.2%), Tanzania (31.0%), Israel (30.7%), Sweden (28.1%), the United States (25.3%) and Switzerland (24.2%) all report prevalence rates are above 20%. The figures for New Zealand (18.7%), Spain (18.5%), Great Britain (18.2%), El Salvador and Norway (16.9%), Singapore (15.9%), Canada (15.2%) and China (10.8%) fall between 10 and 20%. The remaining countries have prevalence rates below 10%. (Pereda et al. 2009, 333–334)

---

the above site and on another one about sexual abuse in sports. I was confused and frustrated, so I started checking all Council of Europe websites, only to find that there were no recent (later than 2015) studies on child sexual abuse referenced there. They are now only interested in the criminal and legal aspects, not the actual numbers and causes; most of the current reports are about child cyberpornography and how to prevent it, and most advise the strengthening of family ties as a preventative measure! Not a word about child sexual abuse at home! And, of course, as an inevitable corollary of ever-prevalent neoliberalism, a large portion of them focused upon the material costs of child sexual abuse, how it cost the state a lot of money to deal with the long-term effects of abuse, e.g., the burden on the health system to treat post-traumatic victims. At this point I was speechless and stopped looking.

What we can observe in this multitude of numbers and percentages, therefore, is that we are all in the same boat as a global community, and whatever our economic, political and cultural differences, we all converge in abusing, molesting and mentally and physically crippling children.

We learn from all these studies, whether they employ the terms *harassment*, *abuse* or *molestation*, that children are maltreated and sexually victimized in their homes, in their schools, in youth detention and in care centers *much more* than they are in neutral circumstances in unfamiliar territory. They are victimized by people they know or trust (their fathers, brothers, relatives, teachers, guardians), *much more* than they are by complete strangers. The family, the state, educational institutions and corrections establishments together form a disproportionately great percentage of the cause and habitat of abuse instead of preventing it. So, the question once more becomes, "*Sed quis custodiet ipsos custodes?*" (Juvenalis); who will watch the watchers, who will guard us against our guardians, who will save us from our saviors? Since every new watcher will necessarily need another watcher above them and since this will go on *ad infinitum*, wouldn't it be better to abolish childhood altogether and be done with it rather than settle for petty reforms and half-measures every time the problem raises its ugly head?

Should We Abolish Childhood?

In her 1970 book *The Dialectic of Sex*, Shulamith Firestone established that the biological basis of the inequality between sexes, and therefore of male domination, was the fact that gamogenetic reproduction placed an immensely uneven burden on females:

1. That Women throughout history before the advent of birth control were at the continual mercy of their biology—menstruation, menopause, and "female ills," constant painful childbirth, wet-nursing and care of infants, all of which made them dependent on males (whether brother, father, husband, lover, or clan, government, community-at-large) for physical survival.

2. That human infants take an even longer time to grow up than animals, and thus are helpless and, for some short period at least, dependent on adults for physical survival.

3. That a basic mother/child interdependency has existed in some form in every society, past or present, and thus has shaped the psychology of every mature female and every infant.

4. That the natural reproductive difference between the sexes led directly to the first division of labour at the origins of class, as well as furnishing the paradigm of caste (discrimination based on biological characteristics).[6] (Firestone 1979, 8–9)

Later in the book, Firestone complements the above statements with the radical demand for the "abolition of childhood," which is an inevitable corollary of her historical materialist reasoning, although how this abolition is to come about remains yet to be explained in detail. In her utopian "cybernetic socialism,"

The concept of childhood has been abolished, children having full legal, sexual, and economic rights, their educational/work activities no different from those of adults. During the few years of their infancy we have replaced the psychologically destructive genetic "parenthood" of one or two arbitrary adults with a diffusion of the responsibility for physical welfare over a larger number of people. The child would still form intimate love relationships, but instead of developing close ties with a decreed "mother" and "father," the child might now form those ties with people of his own choosing, of whatever age or sex. (Firestone 1979, 239)

In the passage from statement of facts to the utopian demand, however, the position of the infant also undergoes a change: in the first instance the infant is seen as a physical/biological object, a burden, which is mainly responsible (although not willingly, because it does not yet have a will of its own) for women's subservient position within the male-dominant order, whereas with the demand

6 More than fifty years after publication, we may add that after fifty years of the pill (female-controlled contraception) and decades of artificial and extrauterine insemination, women are still "at the continual mercy of their biology—menstruation, menopause, and 'female ills,' constant painful childbirth, wet-nursing and care of infants." Furthermore, at least a part of the responsibility for this state of affairs should now be assigned to the feminist party, since the political agenda of their representatives hardly included any demands for freedom from the painful childbirth, wet-nursing and care of infants. Some feminists (especially in the 1980s and onwards) even embraced these things as advantages in their political struggle for a much more moderate agenda, especially in the struggle against economic inequality, domestic violence and (child) pornography.

for abolition it becomes a subject, an agent who must be at least partially willfully participant in order to be included in the transformation. This transition from object to subject in Firestone's argument, however, exactly parallels the actual development of the infant who is born an animal, an object from the perspective of the symbolic order, equipped only with instincts (inadequate ones at that when compared to those of an ape or a feline) but through its introduction into the semiotic sphere becomes a subject, complete with desires and a will.[7]

According to Firestone, in a freer and more equal world under what she calls cybernetic socialism, where all people can experience and express their emotions freely and know their bodies as a source of happiness (if such a world will ever exist), childhood, along with child abuse and rape, disappears. Because if children and women exist not only as objects but as also as subjects and sex is no longer an act of domination, not a way to exercise power over other people, how could rape be considered rape and engagement in playful sexuality with people of all ages be considered child molestation? Can you "rape" someone into playing chess or football with you? If the other person refuses to play, there is no "play." If sex is no more (and no less) than play, it always takes at least two to make it happen. For rape to be rape and child molestation to be child molestation, sex must remain a source of shame, revulsion, secrecy and crime, and women and children must remain objects, or "subjects" of male domination. Only in a male-, father-, adult-, white-, straight- (you can add to the list as you please) dominated society can using the bodies of others regardless of their consent give someone pleasure since it will establish and reinforce domination, hierarchy and hegemony. Pleasure in such a society (i.e., ours) comes not from the body but from the relations of domination themselves and does not even deserve to be called pleasure. In Firestone's cybernetic socialism, however, even mutual consent cannot be a question, because without it sex can never happen anyway.

---

7   *Will* is a curious word in English. It means both "volition" and "desire" at the same time, although it is highly class-sensitive: a serf has wants (meaning "lack" and "need") whereas a Lord and a King have a will. To be able to will, therefore, does not only mean that you are able to exercise free will but also that you hold the dominant position in the hierarchical (i.e., phallic) relations of power. In classical Greek philosophy, there was no term for free will. In medieval thought, will belonged to God (and, by way of delegation, to the ruling class). It is only with the Enlightenment and then modernity that *free will* became a household term for the middle classes. As such, the term *free will* has become the ultimate tantalization: it both suggests that you are free to pursue your desires ("the pursuit of happiness" in the American Declaration of Independence) and indicates that *you'd better not,* considering the consequences.

What if some residual narcissists or psycho-/sociopaths, determined not culturally but biologically and delimited by their genetic heritage, still try to make use of child and female bodies as objects, as tools of masturbation or narcissistic self-satisfaction?[8] What if the supposedly benevolent superegos of such a culture prove incompetent against such perpetrators? First of all, since children and women will be under the protection of the entire community rather than the family or the state (institutions which are founded upon and promote gender and age group domination), such occurrences should be extremely rare. Secondly, since sex is not the shameful, revolting, secret and criminal act of the previous culture anymore, this can only harm the victims physically and not psychologically, and thus can be identified, prevented and punished as such, like any other type of physical assault.

Those who feel revolted by such a utopia should check and sincerely question their motivations after examining whether they are equally revolted by the Fritzl affair, which came to light in 2008. Josef Fritzl lived an ordinary life in his "model" home[9] with his wife and sons, occasionally going down to the basement to rape the daughter he kept prisoner for more than two decades. The daughter, Elizabeth, bore seven children; one was killed by Fritzl, three were raised upstairs by his wife, and three remained with their mother. The real uncanny in this situation is not the brutality of the act itself, but the fact that the wife and the sons (and through them, all of us) were his accomplices. Just a friendly reminder: yelling "Such people should be executed—no, first castrated and then executed!" as loud as we can does not cut it, either; it only makes it worse.

---

8   By the same token, we'd better abolish capitalism along with its latest offshoot, the profession of CEOs, because the percentage of psycho-/sociopaths among them is an incredible 20% compared to only 1% in the general population (Fritzon et al 2020).

9   "Does not the very architectural arrangement of the Fritzl household—the 'normal' ground and upper floors supported (literally and libidinally) by the windowless underground space of total domination and unlimited *jouissance*—embody the 'normal' family space redoubled by the secret domain of the obscene 'primordial father'? Fritzl created in his cellar his own Utopia, a private paradise in which, as he told his lawyer, he spent hours on end watching TV and playing with the youngsters while his daughter Elisabeth prepared dinner. In this self-enclosed space, even the language the inhabitants shared was a kind of private language: it is reported that the two sons, Stefan and Felix, communicate in a bizarre dialect, with some of the sounds they utter being 'animal-like.' The Fritzl case thus validates Lacan's pun on perversion as *père-version*—it is crucial to note how the secret underground apartment complex concretizes a very precise ideologic-libidinal fantasy, an extreme version of father-domination-pleasure nexus." (Žižek 2009)

The Child's "Will"

A child is a child so long as it does not have (or cannot exercise) free will. According to Hegel, therefore, it belongs in the same category with the "imbeciles and lunatics," i.e., people with lower than average intelligence or with mental disorders:

> 120. The right of intention is that the universal quality of the act should not only be implicitly present, but should be known by the agent, and be part and parcel of his subjective will. Conversely the right of objectivity of action, as it may be called, is to maintain that it be known and willed by a subject in his character as thinking.
>
> *Note.*—This right to this insight involves that children, imbeciles, and lunatics are completely, or almost completely, irresponsible for their actions. Just as actions on the side of their external reality include accidental results, so also the subjective reality contains an indeterminate element, which depends upon the strength of self-consciousness and prudence. But this uncertain element needs to be reckoned with only in the case of imbecility, lunacy, or childhood. These are the only conditions of mind which supersede thought and free will, and permit us to take an agent otherwise than in accordance with his dignity as free and rational. (Hegel 2001, 105)

Hegel's terms contain significant insights (as always with him) despite being not only "politically incorrect" by today's standards but also displaying inadequate levels of development and conceptualization in the fields of psychology, neurology and psychiatry. It is useful to remember that the term *psychiatry* was first used only twelve years before Hegel published his *Philosophy of Right.* At that time, very little was known about the nature of mental disorders and even less about the nature of so-called intelligence. With the onset of psychoanalytic theory, the self-evident dialectic of normalcy versus "lunacy" became problematized, and throughout the twentieth century the culture- and gender-biased nature of "intelligence" (especially a quantifiable and measurable intelligence) became apparent. What is important to note, however, is that despite all these shortcomings Hegel is essentially correct. After almost two centuries of development, people in these three categories are still treated as *non compos mentis,* as irresponsible for their actions.

The most important difference between these categories themselves regards their permanence: mental retardation is considered as more or less permanent, mental disorders are treated as more or less permanent (in cases of psychoses) or more or less temporary (in cases of treatable neuroses, phobias, etc.), but childhood is completely transitory. Every child is bound to grow up and become an adult. Infants are considered to be little imbeciles and psychotics, the cure for which is mainly the learning of language. Once a child masters language, not only parroting but really *mastering* both syntax and the basic lexicon, it is believed to have been cured, now treatable as a little neurotic with occasional outbursts of mania and/or depression and, since they cannot yet be trusted to know what is good or right for them, moral and ethical values that should be under observation by grown-ups. They should be *taught* these things, first by their parents (who could be "imbeciles" and/or "lunatics" themselves since parenthood is completely arbitrary) and later by the society's schooling system, which is structurally hysterical (in matters of sexuality especially) and ideologically unsound and self-contradictory, trying and constantly failing to reconcile monotheism and rationalism, universalism and nationalism/racism, sexism and egalitarianism, solidarity and vicious competitiveness.

There is one fairly definite line of demarcation between infancy and childhood, and this is the acquisition of language. There are two main (and usually rather blurred) lines of demarcation separating childhood from so-called maturity, the first being related to reproduction and the other being the ability to exercise free will, which is rather arbitrary and uneven depending on the specific historical period, culture and relations of production.

In many cultures and up until modernity in Western civilization, the ability to reproduce was the only condition which marked the end of childhood and the passage into maturity. This is, of course, in the language of all male-dominated cultures, identical with the possibility—or rather the permission—to have sex and to express sexuality. Now that we have categorically separated sexuality from reproduction, we can see that the illusion of childhood can only be maintained by a strict, even jealous perpetuation of the presumed identity shared between these two. Now we can see why more than in any of his other arguments Freud was at his most scandalous in his exposition of childhood sexuality:

> One feature of the popular view of the sexual instinct [*Geschlechtstrieb*][10] is that it is absent in childhood and only awakens in the period

---

10 I do not want to go into detail here, but the translation of Freud's *Geschlechtstrieb* as "sexual instinct" is not entirely correct and is sometimes confusing (although Freud sanctioned this usage himself), and the term "sexual *drive*" is much preferable, as can be seen in more recent

of life described as puberty. This, however, is not merely a simple error but one that has had grave consequences, for it is mainly to this idea that we owe our present ignorance of the fundamental conditions of sexual life. A thorough study of the sexual manifestations of childhood would probably reveal the essential characters of the sexual instinct [*Geschlechtstrieb*] and would show us the course of its development and the way in which it is put together from various sources. (Freud 1953, 173)

The male-dominated "higher" culture and its academic and scientific proponents were almost hysterical in their denouncement of this exposition[11] because it paved the way for the problematization of one of the most fundamental illusions they tried so hard to uphold: the identity between sexuality and reproduction. Although Freud himself did not make this dissociation as such, his arguments on childhood sexuality as well as his definition of the fundamental drives definitely pointed toward it.

The upshot of Firestone's argument on the abolition of childhood, then, is precisely the abolition of all the restrictions on childhood sexuality, bearing in mind, of course, that sexuality is not the same as reproduction or reproductive behavior. In infancy, sexuality is always already prevalent: the pre-linguistic bond between the mother and the infant which involves all of the five senses—almost to the point of the ego's dissolution (or at least a resistance against its formation)—is definitely sexual, although it has nothing to do with reproduction. In the obscure interregnum between infancy and so-called maturity (which we call childhood), however, this bond breaks and the post-infantile and pre-mature entities are deprived of sexual expression, except with themselves, which is the main factor that drives them toward narcissistic behavior. This is the period which prepares them for reproduction, and the central element in such preparation is the absolute submission of the sexual to the reproductive, which means an almost total repression of infantile sexuality. And when they finally reach adolescence, they will need to re-discover sexuality from scratch, but now as a means to complement, justify and promote reproductive behavior. The more the elements of infantile sexuality are erased from the child's psyche, however, the longer it takes

---

translations of his work.

11 This is precisely the reason why, throughout all the schisms in the psychoanalytic movement, almost all the conservative and reactionary dissidents were quick to denounce the concept of childhood sexuality in order to gain acceptance back into the scientific and academic fold.

for such discovery, and this is the precise reason why in the development of modern and postmodern societies, maturity is placed further and further away from adolescence.

Going back to our initial argument, childhood is defined by the inability to make intelligent decisions and to exercise free will (being *non compos mentis* along with people with lower intelligence or mental disorders). Now we can see that it is also defined as the incapability of reproduction and the consequent prohibition of the sexual act. It is impossible, therefore, not to wonder whether there is anything common between these two inabilities.

The presumed inability to exercise free will stems, according to Hegel, from a lack of knowledge, a lack of comprehension of the laws of necessity:

> Necessity is blind only insofar as it is not comprehended, and hence there is nothing more absurd than the reproach of blind fatalism that is levelled against the Philosophy of History because it regards as its proper task the cognition of the necessity of what has happened.[12] (Hegel 1991, 222)

Free will, therefore, becomes, in Hegel's sense, a matter of knowledge. "To know," on the other hand, relates in a roundabout way to the other inability of the child: In Genesis, the Hebrew verb *yada*, meaning "to know" is also a euphemism for the sexual act:

> Now Adam knew Eve his wife, and she conceived and bore Cain, saying, "I have gotten a man with the help of the LORD." (Genesis 4:1)

---

12 Hegel's famous phrase, "*Einsicht in die Notwendigkeit*" (translated as "insight into necessity"), tells us that we are free only if we comprehend the consequences of our acts. This does not mean (as some Marxists thought, following Engels's reference to the phrase in *Anti-Dühring*) that you should know necessity and conform to it, and only then will you be free. What Hegel means is that in order to be free, you should know (insofar as such knowledge is possible) the consequences of your acts, that if you put your hand in a fire, it burns. Only the people who know this are free when putting (or not putting) their hand in a fire. He does not say anything about conforming to "necessity," because necessity does not call for conformity; it does not care, it simply is. Whether you conform or not is a matter of law rather than philosophy. "What is an anarchist?" asks Ursula K. Le Guin: "One who, choosing, accepts the responsibility of choice." (Le Guin 1974, 272)

The connection between knowing and having sex goes back further than this Old Testament statement, because the reason for Adam and Eve's expulsion from the Garden of Eden is related to this fundamental identification: God tells Adam and Eve not to eat from the Tree of the Knowledge of Good and Evil, and when they are seduced by the serpent and do so, what do they discover? Only that they are naked, or rather, that they should feel shame about their nakedness (since they were naked before this, but it felt perfectly normal). Even before the expulsion, therefore, before Adam *knew* Eve, knowledge was about sex and nothing else. In this sense, childhood is presumed to be exactly like Adam and Eve's life in the Garden, devoid of knowledge and sexuality alike.

What Will Happen to our Beloved Family?

The abolition of childhood, then, is nothing but the elimination of the material conditions for the illusory belief that children are asexual and ignorant. In actuality they are neither of these, but their connections to sexuality and knowledge are consistently repressed by, and substituted with, the institutions of family and education respectively. In both instances, however, the substitutions do not work. To start with, the family, especially under the nuclear form it takes in modern, bourgeois societies, is a poor substitute for sexuality (or sexual expression), because it is founded upon an irresolvable contradiction regarding sexuality: it is the main locus which makes (legal, sanctioned) sexuality possible, but at the same time it constantly has to deny that it even exists.[13] Although one of its chief purposes (along with reproduction of the species, consumption and reproduction of labor power) is to convert the primal energy of infantile sexuality into asexual forms of connecting with the world, it nevertheless includes sexuality in perverted forms, either as the inevitable sexuality between parents, very poorly hidden from the children and unavoidably excluding them, or as domestic sexual harassment, even rape. In the former case, it subverts the original sexual drive of the child, which is a burning desire for *inclusion*, into its opposite; in the latter case, it replaces the sexual drive with actual or fantasized violence. In the passage from infancy to childhood,

---

13 It is precisely through this contradiction that the very structuring of the family implicitly affirms the fact that reproduction and sexuality are indeed separate, and although the parents should be involved in the former act (the very reason that children exist), the latter should be completely excluded from the family. Our initial hypothesis, therefore, is nothing but a restatement of what the modern family had been claiming all along. "Ah, but we were only lying to the children," the modern parent will protest, "to safeguard their innocence." Well, one should be very careful what they lie about, because lies have a way of becoming truth, given enough time.

therefore, the sexual drive is substituted with violence and exclusion (actually, *the violence of exclusion*, according to Adam Phillips [Phillips 1996, 113]), which is an inescapable consequence of the modern, Judeo-Christian, nuclear family structure and will later haunt the child in adolescence and mature life.

In so-called postmodernity, on the other hand, with the eventual dissolution of this family structure, the overt exclusion and covert violence implicit in the modern family converge to form a kind of a tragic *peripeteia*, expressed in the increasing number of teenage pregnancies and cases of domestic harassment and rape. The infantile sexuality which has been repressed by the modern family returns, but now with a vengeance, as loss, loneliness and violence. Consequently, the modernizing search for a family so prominent in nineteenth century literature (e.g., Charles Dickens's lost orphans looking for their families) becomes the postmodern search for *biological parents—away from the family*—as can be seen in many examples from popular cinema and television series.

Secondly, the education of the child within the family and later in the society's schooling system does little to obviate its presumed initial lack of knowledge, since its primary objective is to replace the unmediated experience of the external world with the mediation of language, which is structurally flawed in its representation of this externality. Infancy is the transition from an almost total sensory deprivation to the realm of ego-mediated sensations mainly consisting of images. Education, of the other hand, is the coerced passage of the child from this realm into the semiotic, and it strives to either translate these images into symbols (representations which are inadequate at their best) or completely repress them where such translation proves impossible. This passage should take only as long as the child's mastery of language does, but on the contrary gets longer and longer as we go further into modernity. Education becomes a modern article of consumption, like Coca-Cola, tobacco smoking or alcohol, which, rather than satisfying an actual need only creates a need for more of itself: the more you are educated, the more you need education. Needless to say, this education does little to help promote knowledge in any way; it instead dumps a huge pile of information in the child's (or the adolescent or young person's) mind, most of which will become inaccessible and useless in a short while anyway. Whatever children actually learn, they learn it in spite of institutionalized education and in spite of the constant lies or poorly camouflaged ignorance of their parents.

The agency for the cancellation of the phallus, therefore, resides with neither women (as women) nor LGBTQ+ persons (as LGBTQ+ persons) alone but also with children, a group that occupies a near-absolute subaltern position within the male-dominant, phallic order; a group which does not constitute an identity due to its entirely transitory character (and is therefore totally incapable of identity politics) and whose members cannot even imagine sharing in the dominant position as themselves. Of course, in time they grow up and become men or women, straight or LGBTQ+, and assume an identity as befits their gender and sexual preferences and orientations, becoming entrenched in positions made possible for them by the historical period and the social formation in which they live, their social class and their ideology. As children, however, they are not yet any of these things: they will only become them through their families, educational institutions and the state, sometimes in accordance with and sometimes despite the intentions of these institutions.

Children as a social group cannot represent themselves, because of their transitory character; but they also signify an *absolute*. No other social or cultural status or group indicates such an absolute: classes are not absolute, each class is a fraction of the population, and there is always some mobility between them, however tiny. Women are only one half of the population; all ethnic groups are also a fraction, whether in a majority (however great) or a minority (however tiny). Religious groups are the same, and so are sexual orientation groups. None of these are as absolute and as transitory as children. Not even the elderly, because we cannot say that "everyone will belong to the aged one day"; some of them will not live until they reach that status. Every living human being, however, *has without exception been a child*. And *none will remain so*. Even if some *mentally* remain children, their social status will not be the same and they will have to be re-categorized as "special people" rather than as children. Childhood can never be an identity, because it cannot represent itself, and hence cannot be represented by any other social, cultural or political entity *as such* in its entirety, as children, as a separate entity. Individual children can be represented by their parents, the state or any legal guardian for a given period of time, but this is not a permanent situation and can happen only individually.

We may then ask how children can be involved in acts that are primarily political. Infants and younger children may not be able to participate in these acts directly, but the involvement of many adolescents and young adults (and sometimes even pre-teenagers) in the climate rebellion of the late 2010s, even providing the movement a 16-year-old leader in the person of Greta Thunberg,[14]

---

14 Thunberg, who has Asperger's Syndrome (in the autism spectrum) in addition to her being a teenager, is also living proof that contemporary forms of political action go *across* the former boundaries between discursive dimorphisms such as child/adult and infirm/healthy, declaring them invalid.

has demonstrated that they will eventually and inevitably be perfectly capable of doing so. This development alone explicitly demonstrates that childhood is on the way to *abolishing itself* through its own political action: once you stand up for the survival of your entire planet, rather than for any group or identity you belong to, you are not a child anymore, but you are not an adult as such either. You become, in short, like Marx and Engels's proletarians in *The Communist Manifesto*, a social force which can abolish the existing establishment only by abolishing itself.

The abolition of childhood, therefore, which should be the outcome of the acts of children as well as of adults against male and father domination, necessarily involves the ruthless criticism of the two main institutions—family and education—that uphold and maintain the antitheses of sexuality/reproduction, queer/straight, female/male, infirm/healthy and child/adult as the bedrock of modern civilization. The revolutionary critique of the family, however, is not only the criticism of the institution itself but also of its two main pillars, the iconic and sanctified positions of fatherhood and motherhood, and without an *Aufhebung* of these two, the *Aufhebung* of childhood, old age, and of the family as a whole will never be possible.

Part II
Queering

4.

Heterosexuality, Orthosexuality, Idiosexuality

According to this [new] philosophy [of sexuality], sex is no longer a given element of nature, that man has to accept and personally make sense of: it is a social role that we choose for ourselves, while in the past it was chosen for us by society. The profound falsehood of this theory and of the anthropological revolution contained within it is obvious. People dispute the idea that they have a nature, given by their bodily identity, that serves as a defining element of the human being. They deny their nature and decide that it is not something previously given to them, but that they make it for themselves.

—Pope Benedict XVI, formerly Cardinal Ratzinger, 2012

The Invention of Heterosexuality

IT WAS ONLY LESS than a century and a half ago that *homosexuality* as a term was coined, along with its opposite, *heterosexuality*. Ironically, it was not suggested as an "illness" or a pathology as one should expect from the Victorian Era: it was first used in 1869 by Karl-Maria Kertbeny, an Austrian writer of Hungarian origin, in an anonymously published pamphlet opposing Prussia's sodomy law. More than a decade later, it was repeated in a more "respectable" publication, Gustav Jäger's *Die Entdeckung der Seele* (The Discovery of the Soul, 1880). As a matter of fact, Kertbeny was supposed to contribute a chapter on homosexuality to Jäger's book, but Jäger eventually decided against it, deeming it "too controversial." Jäger did, however, use Kertbeny's terminology throughout the book:

Kertbeny first publicly used his new term *homosexuality* in the fall of 1869, in an anonymous leaflet against the adoption of the "unnatural fornication" law throughout a united Germany. The public proclamation of the homosexual's existence preceded the public unveiling of the heterosexual. The first public use of Kertbeny's word *heterosexual* occurred in Germany in 1880, in a published defense of homosexuality, in a book by a zoologist on *The Discovery of the Soul.* (Katz 2007, 53–4)

It was, of course, the infamous *Psychopatia Sexualis*, published by Richard von Krafft-Ebing in 1886, that made *homosexuality* a household term, but this time in a properly Victorian way, i.e., as a form of psychopathology. Havelock Ellis took the term over from him *(Sexual Inversion*, 1897, with J. A. Symonds, and later as the second volume of his six-volume *Studies in the Psychology of Sex)*, and Freud from Ellis. In Ellis and Freud, however, homosexuality appears not as a form of psychopathology (an illness) but rather as an "inversion" or "perversion" or, in later Freud, a "variation" of human sexuality. Also, it appears in Freud and Ellis not as something innate or congenital (as it had in the pamphlet by Kertbeny, the father of the term) but as something acquired or, again in later Freud, as something of an "arrested development":

Homosexuality is assuredly no advantage, but it is nothing to be ashamed of, no vice, no degradation; it cannot be classified as an illness; we consider it to be a variation of the sexual function, produced by a certain arrest of sexual development. Many highly respectable individuals of ancient and modern times have been homosexuals, several of the greatest men among them. (Plato, Michelangelo, Leonardo da Vinci, etc.). It is a great injustice to persecute homosexuality as a crime—and a cruelty, too. If you do not believe me, read the books of Havelock Ellis. (Freud 1951, 787)

Although the kernel of Freud's argument is sound, it is nevertheless marred by the Enlightenment prejudice of *developmentalism*. As in the case of female orgasm, Freud thinks in terms of an unbroken linear progress, from childhood bisexuality to adult heterosexuality, or childhood "clitoral orgasm" to mature "vaginal orgasm" (Freud 1995). If, according to this theory of linear development, a child is "arrested" at the narcissistic stage, it cannot "progress" to heterosexuality, or, in the case of female children, to "vaginal orgasm." This developmentalist approach assumes that copulation between a single man and a single woman is the most "developed" form human sexuality can take and treats homosexuality and clitoral orgasm as, if not pathologies or crimes, then something infantile nevertheless. Due to this Enlightenment vein embedded in his otherwise subversive theoretical framework, Freud now and again falls into the trap of the self-evidentiary, that is, accepting the backbone of the dominant narrative structure of sexuality without question, as something *finally achieved*, the *telos* of everything that preceded it.[1]

What follows is an argument against this widely accepted usage, which indicates a confinement of the homosexuality/heterosexuality dimorphism in a rigid structure of binary opposition, and hence an *essentialization*, making both these concepts seem "essential" or "natural."[2] This essentialization only serves to detach homosexuality from a much wider agenda of freedom of sexual expression. I propose to salvage and re-appropriate the concept of heterosexuality from its present use as the diametrical opposite of homosexuality and a synonym for "straightness" and reinstate the subversive content of the prefix *hetero-* meaning both "other" and "other than the straight path," suggesting that *heterosexuality* may serve as an umbrella phrase for sexual expressions and practices *other than* the orthodox one based on coerced monogamy of women and male/father domination. The opposite of *hetero* in this argument would be either *ortho* (straight) or *idio* (self), rather than *homo*, establishing *orthosexuality* as "straightness" and orthodoxy in sexual expression and acts and *idiosexuality* (self-sexuality) as a narcissistic expression of sexuality which refuses to acknowledge the existence of an other in the sexual act *as such*.

Why, it may be asked, should one rock the boat and create unnecessary confusion as regards "mere" terminology at a time when there are more significant political issues surrounding homosexuality and trans persons (such as homophobia, transphobia, hate crimes against gay and trans people, and the legitimacy of gay marriage, not to mention the criminalization of gay and trans people in many countries) demanding our attention? It is precisely for this reason and precisely

---

1   For a discussion of Freud's relationship with Enlightenment ideas, see Phillips 1995, especially the introduction, 1-17.

2   Branding any trait as essential promotes the trait to being identical with the object or category it characterizes and thus makes it immutable, lest the object or category also change with it and lose its identity. Thus, if we hypothesize that greed and selfishness are essential traits for humanity, for instance, we must accept that non-selfish and non-greedy behavior makes us non-human. By the same token, if we hypothesize heterosexuality as essential to a definite genetic structure, embedded in nature, we must also accept it as immutable and transhistorical. If we accept the historical character of heterosexuality (or homosexuality, its supposed diametrical opposite), however, we also accept its mutability and transformability. Any theoretical approach that expects or calls for a radical transformation of the existing state of affairs must therefore start from a *non-essentialist* axiom, asserting the historicity (and therefore the mutability) of the basic concepts we use to define our existence.

at this time that we should re-examine and re-invent our terminology. Since the political consequences of the homosexual preference or orientation always seemed to be transgressive and subversive, it was usually assumed that homosexuals themselves would also be radicals, endeavoring to transform the structure of normalcy, militating against the existing gender relations, against the accepted standards of sexuality in everyday life, and against the structure of the family, which is the principal mainframe within which all gender, sexual and intergenerational relations are regulated. Thus, today, more than ever, there is a profound need to differentiate between the act itself and its political consequences, and between the act itself and the actor.

The overall structure and discourse of the political struggle for the rights of gays and lesbians to marry, bear or adopt, and raise children during late twentieth and early twenty-first centuries has clearly demonstrated that many (if not most) gays and lesbians were not as subversive as it seemed *prima facie* (D'Emilio 2006): they were mostly vying for *normalcy,* the right to secure a place within the existing social structure and the family and live their lives in peace, however radical and subversive the mere act of homosexuality may initially seem. This is not an unprecedented development, since the former perception was clearly based on a case of mistaken identity, of mistaking the agent for the act. No one should be expected to be a radical, or, worse yet, a revolutionary just because they had an unorthodox sexual orientation. Homosexuality may be an orientation rather than a choice or preference, but being subversive, radical or revolutionary are most definitely not: these are clearly *preferences,* conscious choices, not only in selection of a sexual partner, but also of lifestyle and political position. A homosexual orientation may, in a definite historical period and culture, force one to adopt a certain political stand, an identity politics, so to speak; it does not, however, make one subversive as such. Identity politics is mostly a struggle for the right to exist, acknowledgement and equal rights; unlike subversive or revolutionary politics, it does not strive to transform the existing state of affairs radically.

This does not mean that identity politics is not a tenable political position in and of itself; quite to the contrary, any radical political position usually *starts out* from such politics in the first place and is legitimized so long as it contains and extends its agenda, albeit not limiting itself to the exclusive needs and priorities of this agenda as such, always aware of the fact that at any moment identity politics may (and usually will) be radicalized again by external pressure from the inherently conservative structure of global capitalism. Accordingly, the second decade of the twenty-first century witnessed a growing radicalization in the queer movement, a reaction to a reaction, so to speak, a response to the counterassault of patriarchal sexual orthodoxy. The normalization of homosexuality as well as the renewed radicalization of feminism (as can be observed in the #MeToo movement) caused a rapidly growing precariousness within the formerly self-assured patriarchal structure, creating what is now referred to as fragile masculinity. This wave of counterattack was aimed not only at the legal and cultural existence of gays, lesbians and trans persons as such, but also at the overall existence of any and all choices other than the orthodox path, those which do not succumb to the millennia-old patriarchal dictum that sexuality should be subservient to reproduction, which is expressed in the existing family structure based on monoandric, life-long partnership of two persons of the opposite sex.

This is where the change in terminology I propose becomes necessary: the terms *homosexual, gay* and *lesbian,* as opposed to *heterosexual* and *straight,* have already become insufficient for the entire range of modes of sexual expression in our day. This is why many activists as well as scholars feel the need to add to their palette concepts such as transsexual, transgender, and queer, not to mention the various brands of bisexuality, asexuality and transvestitism. This is why the term *LGBT* (the original one) needed the addendum *Q* (for queer), and when that did not prove sufficient, other addenda became necessary, such as the *I* (for intersex) and *A* (for asexual), used for a while before the all-encompassing + was finally added.

Using an ever-lengthening series of initials as the defining name of a living and growing social movement is never a good idea because it gives the impression of a definite political organization, which is, in this case, a dangerous misconception. LGBTQIA+, or whatever initials we choose, does not represent a political organization but a multitude of political attitudes and movements, differentiated according to not only those initials but also their connections and positions vis-à-vis already existing movements such as feminism, anarchism, socialism, and so on. The re-appropriation of the concept of heterosexuality as an umbrella term denoting all sexual practices *other than the straight one,* will not add to but rather help to solve the conceptual confusion already created around sexual practices, orientations, preferences and expressions. It will also facilitate the differentiation between the act and the agent, and challenge the delimitation of *heterosexual* politics (I now use the term in my proposed sense) within only identity politics as well. The inclusion of *orthosexuality* and *idiosexuality* in this new spectrum may not be essential, but it will definitely help to set the conceptual framework more firmly in place.

The Debate that Never Dies: Nature or Nurture?

The argument about the origin of homosexuality—(either) congenital / (or) acquired—is as old as the term itself. It is important, however, to emphasize that the argument itself is not entirely a scientific one but more often than not, politically motivated: whenever the agenda is about *legitimacy*, be it about decriminalizing homosexuality or (as it has been more recently) about legalizing homosexual marriage, the emphasis shifts to the congenital, to the argument that it is not a conscious choice or preference and therefore cannot be considered a crime or misdemeanor. Neuroscientist Simon LeVay, for instance, who himself professes to be gay, declares that: "[G]ay people told me that my finding validated their own sense of being 'born gay' or being intrinsically different from straight people" (LeVay 2011, x). Although the validation LeVay refers to is a positive step, the attempt at decriminalization also has its price, which is *medicalization*: whenever you try to decriminalize something by claiming that it is natural and intrinsic (and hence unavoidable) in some people with certain genetic and/or hormonal characteristics, you run the risk of *medicalizing* it, and although it is not always the same as *pathologizing*, this act nevertheless places it within the confines of medical discourse. In psychiatric medical discourse, however, the line between a "disorder" and a character trait is usually very fine, and once you submit to medicalization you are never free of the threat of pathologization.

During the political campaign for gay marriage, Kertbeny's original statement—that homosexuality is innate or biologically determined, an orientation rather than a preference—might have been necessary or useful to a certain degree, but it also ran the risk of *essentialization*, something that Gender and Queer Studies have always been on the alert for. After all, nearly all arguments *against* homosexuality have started from the premise that it is *not* natural, that it is against *human nature* since it is not connected to reproduction, and the main (radical) argument to the contrary suggests that there is no such thing as "natural"; that the so-called natural is a construct of the dominant bio-medical discourse. The argument that homosexuality (or any sexual variation other than the "straight" one) is indeed natural represents a return to biologistic essentialism and dispenses with the efforts to problematize what is natural.

Recent neurobiological research implies that there is indeed something ostensibly akin to homosexuality among animals, which may be construed as another argument for the congenital or natural character of homosexuality. The research, however, is in fact just proof for the opposite. That is because these recent findings indeed show that some male animals (some felines and bovines, and more recently [and controversially] sheep) do copulate with each other, but they *fail* to show that (1) there is sexual attraction and performance among females as well; and (2) the males assuming the "female position" (that is, being mounted) are willing and receive some sort of pleasure for doing so.[3]

Bailey and Zuk (2009) warn us against using the term *homosexual* in describing certain animal behavior related to reproduction (and sometimes not even related to it directly):

> Homosexual: in animals, this has been used to refer to same-sex behavior that is not sexual in character (e.g., "homosexual tandem running" in termites), same-sex courtship or copulatory behavior occurring over a short period of time (e.g., "homosexual mounting" in cockroaches and rams) or long-term pair bonds between same-sex partners that might involve any combination of courting, copulating, parenting and affectional behaviors (e.g., "homosexual pair bonds" in gulls). In humans, the term is used to describe individual sexual behaviors as well as long-term relationships, but in some usages connotes a gay or lesbian social identity. Scientific writing would benefit from reserving this anthropomorphic term for humans and not using it to describe behavior in other animals, because of its deeply rooted context in human society. (Bailey and Zuk 2009, 439)

To start with, whether same-sex or opposite-sex, lifelong or temporary, partnering is not readily defined as sexual behavior. It is definitely instinctual and has to do with the care of the young rather than sexuality. To refer to monogamic partnering for care of the young as sexuality is to succumb to nothing less than the self-evidentiary trap of patriarchy, which sets the coercive monogamy of women and the restrictive rules on childhood and same-sex eroticism above all sexual acts in an effort to legitimize homosexuality as normal and/or natural. The so-called

---

3 The findings about bottlenose dolphins and bonobos are significantly different: these animals are genetically and evolutionarily much closer to human beings and represent borderline cases. They have a form of emergent female homosexuality, and in male homosexuality (a rarer occurrence) both partners are involved in the sexual act, suggesting that they do differentiate between the sexual and the reproductive, an almost human trait (for the sexual characteristics of bonobos, see, for instance, De Waal 2005 and De Waal 2009). The observations made of the Laysan albatross (Young et al. 2008) and the zebra finch are both indicative of same-sex lifetime pairing but do not have anything to do with "sexual behavior" at all. (Bailey and Zuk 2009, 440)

homosexual act in some animals, especially in gregarious mammals, can be at least partially explained by, on the one hand, the dominant or violent behavior of alpha males and the submissive behavior of the males being mounted. Neurobiologically, on the other hand, the studies on sheep (or "gay rams" as they have come to be known) show that only 8–10% of the rams—those that have displayed constant "homosexual behavior" or "male-oriented sexual preference"—have pronounced endocrinal and hypothalamic differences from the "normal" ones (see, for example, Roselli and Stormshak 2010). The hypothalamus is, among other things, where olfactory input is translated into instinctual and reproductive behavior: the "homosexual" or "male-oriented" rams have hypothalamic structures and endocrine levels similar to those of female sheep, so, lo and behold, they instinctually show a preference for other rams rather than ewes, which suggests that they are "turned on" by male rather than female odor, and nothing more.

The difference in neural and endocrine structure and the corresponding difference in reproductive behavior definitely suggests a causal link. Causal links in human sciences, however, cannot simply be expressed in mere formulae and equations of pure logical symbols, but require *language*. The problem, therefore, starts here with the *language* these studies use, because when they try to translate their findings from neuroscientific and evolutionary terminology into everyday language, they regularly fall into the trap of the self-evidentiary. In order for sheep, for instance, to be *homosexual*, it must first be demonstrated they are indeed *sexual*. Unfortunately, biology, neuroscience and psychiatry, and especially evolutionary psychology still confuse sexual behavior with reproductive behavior. Animals are not *sexual* beings as such, although they are *sexed*; they only have reproductive instincts that are part of their natural existence. They cannot, therefore, be homosexual or anything-sexual; they merely copulate as their genetic and hormonal constitutions dictate to them through their instincts, and these instincts, especially in mammalians, are usually triggered by the olfactory sense.

Many neurobiological studies, however, insist on using the term *sexual* in interpreting the data obtained by experiments on the mating behaviors of animals, to the extent that they even call mating pairs "sexual partners": "In animals, the choice of *sexual partner* is highly influenced by signals from sex-specific pheromones" (Berglund et al. 2006, 8269; my italics). And, by the same token: "According to animal studies, the choice of *sexual partner* is highly influenced by sex-specific pheromone signals, which are processed by male and female mating centres located in the anterior hypothalamus" (Savic et al. 2005, 7356; my italics).[4] For one thing, referring to mating animals as sexual partners is entirely anthropomorphic, in the sense that it attempts to explain animal behavior using human relational patterns. They fall into the anthropomorphic trap as they strive to escape the *anthropocentric* trap, that is, out of the frying pan, into the fire. Some animals do indeed "partner," a few even for life, but the coincidence in the choice of terms is entirely misleading since their so-called partnering does not entail most of the relational traits involved in *human* partnering. To start with, it does not necessarily entail reproductive mating but only care for the young, and it can be same-sex (usually female-female) but without sexuality. It also lacks gender performance, social status, peer pressure, familial expectations, economic consequences, and, last but not least, love (erotic or otherwise).

The insistence to keep the analogy between human opposite-sex partnering and animal mating is highly suggestive of a (maybe unconscious) biblical frame of mind:

> And the Lord said unto Noah, Come thou and all thy house into the ark; for thee have I seen righteous before me in this generation. Of every clean beast thou shalt take to thee by sevens, the male and his female: and of beasts that *are* not clean by two, the male and his female. Of fowls also of the air by sevens, the male and the female; to keep seed alive upon the face of all the earth. (Genesis 7:1–3)

Although many scientists in the field of genetics and neuroscience are professedly non-religious and some of them even atheists, and although they mostly do not adhere to the orthodox biblical dictum of exclusively heterosexual partnering, they still seem to hold on to the anthropomorphic structure of Noah's Ark, surrendering to the self-evidentiary treatment of "sexual" animal pairing as a model for human sexual partnership—actually, exactly *vice versa*.

Historically, however, human beings have already differentiated sexual behavior from the reproductive, and in doing so have (among other things) differentiated themselves from the animals. This is fairly evident from the millennia-old methods of birth control (sexuality without reproduction) more and more perfected in each historical era, not to mention the recent developments of extrauterine

---

4   I have to point out that these neurobiological studies are mostly repetitive and usually based on the same (or a very similar) data cluster, and their introductory paragraphs use almost the same terminology, as can be observed in the two studies I cite (which, by the way, are written by the same three people with only a difference in the name order).

insemination, fertilization and fetal growth (reproduction without sexuality). In human beings, instincts do not reign supreme; it is not solely our sense of smell or our neurobiological constitution that drive us to select sexual partners; these factors may still play a part, but this dimension has become less and less significant throughout millennia. First of all, the olfactory sense is mostly eclipsed by the visual and auditory senses in human beings, diminishing its significance in sexual behavior[5] and therefore bypassing, at least partially, the hypothalamus. Secondly, none of the senses in human beings have a direct shortcut to behavior anymore; they have to pass through the perception-consciousness (the *pcpt-cs* in Freud's abbreviation) barrier first, to be processed by the prefrontal cortex, a structure substantially more developed in human beings, mostly involved in decision-making, speech and language (Donahue et al. 2018; also cf. Fuster 2008).

The recent attempts at locating the causal structure of *sexual* behavior in nature, then—in the senses, hormones, pheromones or neural clusters—are mostly in vain. We can perhaps find the causal structure of *reproductive* behavior there, which is still in some way related to the sexual, but this is only a rudimentary structure, unable to explain the extensive complexity of human sexual behavior that ranges from envy, violence, and narcissism to gratitude, empathy, and love. The evolutionary psychologists, for example, who insistently refuse to make the distinction not only restrict the concept of sexual behavior to a simple "mating strategy"[6] (thus reducing it to reproductive behavior) but also pointedly ignore the fact of gay and lesbian sexualities, which would either put a sizeable dent in their theories or explain them away by a kind of natural "defect" or an undefined "difference" (the preference between these two terms depending on their degree of political correctness). These psychologists also ignore the fact that human reproductive behavior bears a strongly *negative* relation to their account of evolutionary demands: women having children later in life, having fewer children or none at all, men becoming more monogamous (if a trifle serially), increasing diversities of non-reproductive behavior, etc. John D'Emilio observes in 2006 that, starting in the 1960s,

---

5 Interestingly enough, Gustav Jäger's book *Die Entdeckung der Seele,* which first popularized Kertbeny's dimorphic terminology *homosexual* and *heterosexual,* was insistent on the significance of the olfactory sense in evolution and in sexual behavior, and almost identified the soul with odor. (Jaeger 1884)

6 See, for example, Buss 1995. It is interesting to note that desire (which is an exclusively human, sexual concept) as opposed to instinct (which is only related to reproduction) has been "naturalized" and has become a "mating strategy" in Buss's terminology.

Divorce became increasingly commonplace. Even with greater access to abortion, large numbers of women had children outside of marriage. The number of single-parent households grew. Cohabitation of unmarried men and women became so widespread that the Bureau of the Census began to categorize and count the phenomenon. Women's participation in the paid labor force skyrocketed. Birth rates sank to replacement levels. The living arrangements of heterosexual Americans became bewilderingly varied. Over the course of a lifetime an individual might move in with a partner, break up with that partner and find another, get married, have a child, get divorced, cohabit with someone else who also had a child (or didn't), break up again, cohabit again, marry again, and become a stepparent. Throughout this saga, all the adults involved were working for a living. A succinct way of describing these changes is this: Since the early 1960's, the lives of many, many heterosexuals have become much more like the imagined lives of homosexuals. (D'Emilio 2006)

The question then becomes not a simple choice between (either) congenital / (or) acquired, a version of the ages old (and, as has been demonstrated over and over again, rather pointless) "nature or nurture" debate, but one of "*not only but also*," a properly dialectic one. In some animals, and indeed in some human beings (insofar as they are still animals in one sense), a preference for same-sex copulation may be intrinsic, congenital and instinctual, since many neuro- and evolutionary biologists so insist, providing us with significant data thereof. This fact alone, however, is far from sufficient to explain what we have termed homosexual behavior in human beings, since *sexual* behavior is much more complex and overdetermined than simple, instinctual reproductive behavior.[7]

This line of reasoning has serious implications for the (either) orientation / (or) preference discussion as well: we have already established that homosexuality, transgenderism, and gender fluidity have biological and genetic roots and, as

---

7 Thus, faced with uproar from gay and lesbian communities and the additional accusation (mostly unfair, in my opinion) that he was laying the ground for "human eugenics," Roselli, the leading figure behind the "gay ram" studies, defended himself by saying, "[H]uman sexuality [is] a complex phenomenon that could not be reduced to interactions of brain structure and hormones" (Schwartz 2007). Of course, he does this in a newspaper interview rather than in a scientific article, but it goes to show that the proper use of everyday language, once freed from translation from scientific terminology (which turn it into a kind of pseudo-scientific jargon), brings the scientist closer to truth.

such, are orientations. This does not, however, necessarily mean that everything that follows also constitutes orientations. Whether to stay in the closet or to come out, for instance, is surely a preference, a conscious choice, calculating the risks and ethical implications of either choice. So is the decision to marry or be content with being merely (overt or covert) partners. So is the decision to have or adopt children. In all these cases, there may be some rudimentary underlying biological imperative, but the same is applicable to straight-sexual relationships as well. Having children or not, for instance, is not a decision made solely on biological or genetic grounds. This is doubly true for same-sex partners, since genetic continuity can only be available for one of the partners, if at all. We cannot talk about an instinctual, natural motivation for having children in these cases, but only a cultural and social one, which is not a matter of orientation or any other innate condition but clearly of preference.

In order to understand the extent of the determining congenital and developmental factors that play a part in human sexual behavior and orientations and preferences, then, we must first try to determine the relationship between sexuality and reproduction.

Sexuality or Reproduction?

The "separation of sexuality from procreation" became an important issue, especially in the twentieth century, because it threatens the entire patriarchal order the moment it develops from a mere probability into an actuality. The ideological champions of the patriarchal order, the Catholic Church for instance, do not fail to perceive this imminent threat, as demonstrated in the famous *Ratzinger Report*, prepared by Cardinal Ratzinger:

> The separation of sexuality from procreation has led to the opposite extreme, the nightmare scenario of making procreation independent of sexuality through medico-technical Experimentation.[8] (Ratzinger 1985, 84-5)

---

8   It is interesting to note that the same Cardinal Ratzinger would be elected pope twenty years later, suggesting once again that the subjugation of sexuality by reproduction is indeed high on the agenda of any oppressive order. Ratzinger would follow this up in his papal address of Christmas 2012, demonstrating his awareness of (and alarm over) the new theories of sexuality and gender. After Ratzinger's unexpected resignation, however, the next pope, Francis, would show signs of changing this policy and demonstrating a more tolerant attitude toward homosexuality, birth control and abortion (see the *New York Times* article from September 19, 2013),

It is only fair to add that the leading activists of sexual liberation, at least some of them, were not unaware of this threat and rather considered it an opportunity. John D'Emilio, a gay activist as well as a Gender and Queer Studies scholar, had observed the same fact years before Ratzinger:

[C]apitalism has led to the separation of sexuality from procreation. Human sexual desire need no longer be harnessed to reproductive imperatives, to procreation; its expression has increasingly entered the realm of choice. Lesbians and homosexuals most clearly embody the potential of this split, since our gay relationships stand entirely outside a procreative framework. The acceptance of our erotic choices ultimately depends on the degree to which society is willing to affirm sexual expression as a form of play, positive and life enhancing. Our movement may have begun as the struggle of a "minority," but what we should now be trying to "liberate" is an aspect of the personal lives of all people—sexual expression. (D'Emilio 1983, 110)

As D'Emilio observes, gay and lesbian sexuality is one of the sure-fire indicators of sexuality without reproduction; but then, it is not only gay and lesbian sexuality that stands outside the reproductive matrix: any variety of sexuality that is not related to reproduction, any sexual act that does not submit to the reproductive instinct, should be considered subversive from the point of view of the sexual and reproductive policies of the patriarchal order. Patriarchy has warranted the submission of sexuality to reproduction by designating the structure of the family as the only possible framework of the sexual act.[9] It means that sexual and reproductive performance should predicate its existence on three prohibitions:

---

indicating that the Catholic Church was now more willing to "roll with the blow" than to stand firm on orthodox doctrine. We should be reminded, however, that rolling with the blow is not yielding but rather constitutes a more intelligent way to fight back.

9   Of course, we are talking about the "sublime" version of patriarchy, the one that preaches the sanctity of motherhood and love and respect for the parents as being the pillar of home and family. The other, "deep" version of patriarchy—the "order below" that fills in the gaps, stitches the tears and cleans the gutters of the "order above"—endorsed another institution, prostitution, so that men could have breathing space after having grudgingly given up polygamy in order to ensure female monogamy. While the family was always the legal and sublime institution that regulated sexual relations, prostitution followed it everywhere it went, semilegal and despised but living proof that sexuality without reproduction was an inalienable part of any human society.

(1) the prohibition of polygamy for women, (2) the prohibition of same-gender sexuality, and (3) the prohibition of infantile sexuality.

On closer inspection, it can be observed that all three prohibitions are designed, first and foremost, to make possible and then to ensure the domination of *fatherhood*. The coerced monogamy of women is the only way (short of the very recently developed DNA test) to positively know the identity of the genetic father, and hence it makes possible a communal and social position known as *fatherhood*. The other two prohibitions, on the other hand, dictate the domination of reproduction over sexuality by making non-reproductive sexuality almost impossible. Sexuality is tolerated only insofar as it is a by-product of the reproductive act, and sometimes not even then: the reign of Catholicism and Puritanism in Europe (and later in the Americas) from the middle ages to the twentieth century represents the systematic suppression of female sexuality, as can be observed in instances ranging from the witch-hunts to the prohibition of birth control. All these prohibitions serve to ensure the reign of patriarchy, of *father domination* rather than male domination (Mitchell 2000). It is the specific feature of patriarchy—the law of the hypothesized prehistoric murdered father— that defines the relative places of men and women in human history. This "father" and its representatives—all fathers—are the crucial expression of patriarchal society. It *is* *fathers* not *men* who have the determinate power. And it is a question neither of biology nor of a specific society but of *human* society itself.

Although still patriarchal, Classical Greece (and to an extent, Roman society later on) had a different solution: they radically severed sexuality from reproduction, confined reproduction to the family, to the *oikos*, which was women's only space of existence, and located sexuality (*eros*, or sexual love) outside the "home," that is, in the *polis*, which means it was something strictly between males. Women had no part to play in *eros* since they had no place in the *polis*, and therefore the terms for both *lover* and *beloved* in the Classical Greek language (*erastes* and *eromenos*) were masculine.

To be sure, this arrangement was too appropriate to function faultlessly; there were exceptions and subversions (e.g., Sappho's bid to re-appropriate *eros* for femininity and Socrates's nonchalant dismissal of the family in favor of homoeroticism). Eventually, however, as Classical Greek democracy and early Roman republicanism gave way to empires and kingdoms, it was the subjugation of sexuality by reproduction that won the day. As society became more and more authoritarian, the patriarchal order felt the need to dissolve the free space reserved for male homoeroticism: the order designed to enslave women and children ended up enslaving (at least most of the) men as well.

It is the very identification of reproduction with sexuality (in fact, the subjugation of the latter to the former) that imprisons sexuality in the ritual of a dimorphism. The male/female dichotomy is pertinent only for a natural, pre-human, gamogenetic system of reproduction. As sexuality gradually dissociates itself from reproduction in human culture, however, this dimorphic postulate increasingly loses its validity, and in the twenty-first century, when this separation becomes the rule rather than the exception with the help of new technologies of reproduction, it turns into the shackles of sexuality. This is one of the main reasons why queer and LGBTQ+ liberation movements have started to speak out against the "binary structure of gender," and many people have started to identify themselves as non-binary with regard to gender. The non-binary nature of gender, however, although subversive enough in itself, can be better expressed and defended if firmly grounded in an argument against the subjugation of sexuality to reproduction.

The Need for a New Terminology

The term *homosexuality* would have been meaningless for a Greek citizen of the Classical era because it is bilingual (*homo-* meaning "same" in Greek and *sexus* meaning "being of male or female gender" in Latin). It would have been even more meaningless, almost bizarre, in Latin, since a Latin-speaker would have taken the prefix *homo-* to mean "human" in Latin. Neither would relate the word to sex as we know it, since *sex* came to mean "sexual intercourse" or "sexual attraction" only in the twentieth century.

In any case, if patiently explained to our Classical Greek citizen what *homosexuality* meant (using the term *homoeroticism* would have been a better choice), he (since all citizens were male) would think we were trying to prove the obvious. What else could *eros* have meant anyway? It was something between men; the thing we did with women was mere copulation, something that needed to be done to propagate the species.

On the other hand, eighteenth century Europe wouldn't have been better in comprehending the term. Kant, for instance, wrote in 1797 that:

> This natural union of the sexes [*Geschlechtsgemeinschaft*] proceeds either according to the mere animal Nature (*vaga libido, venus vulgivaga,*

fornicatio [unsettled lust, roving sexuality, fornication]), or according to Law. The latter is Marriage (*matrimonium*), which is the Union of two Persons of different sex [*Geschlechts*] for life-long reciprocal possession of their sexual faculties [*Geschlechtseigenschaften*].—The End of producing and educating children may be regarded as always the End of Nature in implanting mutual desire and inclination in the sexes; but it is not necessary for the rightfulness of marriage that those who marry should set this before themselves as the End of their Union, otherwise the Marriage would be dissolved of itself when the production of children ceased.[10] (Kant 1887, 77)

As is evident from his argument, a "sexual union," or *Geschlechtsgemeinschaft*, is only legitimate for Kant if it is made (1) according to law and (2) according to nature, whose end is producing and educating children, with the stipulation that if a couple *ceases to* produce (but does not consciously refuse to produce) children, their marriage should not be dissolved. However, it is obvious from the use of the term *Geschlecht*, which also means *genus* and *gender,* that Kant is not referring to the *sexual act* as such; for him sexual union can only mean union between different genders, with reproduction as its ultimate aim.

Linguistically, then, we can only differentiate between sexuality and reproduction in the twentieth century, when the word *sex* came to denote the *sexual act* in addition to gender. Originally, the Latin *sexus* comes from *secare*, which means dividing or cutting (in half). *Secare* is also the root of *section* and as such only relates to the fact that the human race (as with animals) is divided or *sectioned* into male and female halves. The connection between these halves can be *genetic* or *erotic*: the former term comes from the Greek root *genos* (race or kind, Lat. *genus*) and/or *gonos* (birth or offspring), and the latter from *eros*, sexual love in twentieth century terms. In the Classical Greek language, there was no unmediated relation between *genos* and *eros*; with the advent of post-Roman/Christian European civilization, however, *eros* became more and more de-sexualized, so to speak, and came to mean a sort of sterile, Platonic heterosexual love which was a source of

---

10 The original text is *Die Metaphysik der Sitten* (The Metaphysics of Morals), which was published in 1797. The translation by William Hastie published in 1887 is the second version. The first translation (by an anonymous translator we now know to be John Richardson) was published only two years after the original's publication, in 1799. Unfortunately, this text has proven to be extremely hard to acquire, so I lack the means to compare how *Geschlecht* was translated into English at the end of the eighteenth century.

suffering rather than pleasure. *Genos* or *genus*, on the other hand, became an ana-tomical or medical term (pertaining to *genitalia*)[11] and came to be used mostly in that context until the advent of the science of genetics in the twentieth century.

When Kertbeny invented the terms *homosexuality* and *heterosexuality* in 1869, then, the concept of sex was already in transition. When Freud took over the terms, the transition was almost complete, and *sex*, while still subservient to reproduction, had expanded in context to include *eros*. In *Beyond the Pleasure Principle* (1920), Freud speaks of "sexual reproduction" (meaning *gamogenesis*, gendered reproduction), but connects this to the rejuvenation process of unicel-lular organisms, which has *nothing to do with reproduction at all*:

> If two of the animalculae, at the moment before they show signs of senescence, are able to coalesce with each other, that is to "conju-gate" (soon after which they once more separate), they are saved from growing old and become "rejuvenated." Conjugation is no doubt the fore-runner of the sexual reproduction of higher creatures; it is as yet unconnected with propagation and is limited to the mixing of the sub-stances of the two individuals. (Freud 1961, 42)

It is fairly obvious that Freud is referring here to *sexuality as we know it*, since the *agamogenetic* (non-gendered) unicellular organisms do not propagate through the "conjugation" process he describes, which is but a reiteration of evolutionary biologist August Weismann's observations. These organisms only "rejuvenate"—replenish their life-energy through temporarily "opening up" to each other in order to mix and exchange their cytoplasm—and then they go their separate ways without any sign of "reproducing," that is, *fission*, since that is how agamogenetic organisms reproduce.[12]

---

11 It is interesting to note that sexually transmitted diseases have always been referred to as "ve-nereal" rather than "erotic" or "genital." Even in Arabic they are *Zührevi* diseases, "*Zühre*" being the Arabic name for Venus. Significantly enough, they are not "Aphroditic" (even though de-sire-inducing substances are *Aphrodisiacs*), referring to the Goddess by her Latin name rather than the Greek one. Aphrodite and Venus may seem to be the names for the same goddess, but the difference between Greek and Roman cultures is at work here as well: Aphrodite was the goddess of love, desire and beauty—as distinct from fertility, which was the domain of ancient Kybele—whereas Venus seems to combine aspects of desire and fertility (sexuality and repro-duction) in her more cosmopolitan and eclectic personage.

12 Freud shouldn't have missed the analogy between this rejuvenation or conjugation and human sexuality, since the opening up of the cell membranes to each other in unicellular organisms

Nevertheless, it is only with the development of more perfected means of birth control (that is, the pill in the 1960s and IUDs) and, conversely, the means of extrauterine insemination and fetal growth that the concepts of sexuality without reproduction and reproduction without sexuality became actual possibilities rather than exceptions. This is why the leading ideologues of the existing patriarchal order were very much alarmed in the 1980s (see *The Ratzinger Report*), and activists of sexual liberation like D'Emilio started to perceive a new possibility, almost a "revolutionary paradigm shift" in the Kuhnian sense, at about the same time.

The strict separation of sexuality from reproduction was already inherent in infantile sexuality and homosexuality. The technological and cultural advances in the second half of the twentieth century made it an actuality for heterosexuality as well. This is why D'Emilio predicted that the liberating content of gay and lesbian movements should expand to embrace all forms of sexual expression, *including* variations hitherto considered to be heterosexual. A decade after D'Emilio, Lynne Segal pointed out the need to redefine and subvert the concept of heterosexuality, in order to bridge the gap between feminist and gay and lesbian movements:

> All feminists could, and strategically should, participate in attempting to subvert the meanings of "heterosexuality," rather than simply trying to abolish or silence its practice. The more familiar and dismissive strategy is not only punitive and unwelcoming—towards women who enjoy straight sex—but misguided, in that it endorses rather than challenges the gendered meanings maintained through normative and oppressive heterosexual discourses and practices. The challenge all feminists face, on top of the need to keep chipping away at men's continuing social power (which gets condensed into "phallic" symbolism), is to acknowledge that there are *many "heterosexualities."* (Segal 1994, 259–60)

In order to comply with Segal's suggestion, we should maybe take a closer look at the self-evidentiary identification of heterosexuality with straightness: it is common practice in gay and lesbian movements as well as in scholarly Queer studies to call heterosexuals "straight." *Straight*, in Classical Greek is the prefix *ortho-*, as in orthodoxy (*ortho-*: straight, true, and *doxa*: thought, belief or teaching). But the opposite of *orthodoxy* is *heterodoxy*, the thought or teaching that varies, strays from

---

and the opening up of the ego barrier in human beings constitutes a very clear parallelism. And again, the opening up of the ego barrier to each other has nothing to do with reproduction, although it is a very apt description of human sexuality.

the straight path, the prefix *hetero-* deriving from *heteros,* meaning *other* or *different.* Heterodoxy in theology is often used for *dissidence.* So why have we given up the subversive content in *hetero* in order to make it a synonym for *straight,* its opposite?

The answer is likely that Kertbeny, thinking in terms of the homogeneity/heterogeneity dualism, invented the term *heterosexuality* as the opposite of same-gender sexual attraction, completely missing its subversive content. With Krafft-Ebing's popularization of both terms, the early twentieth century studies on sexuality had no other choice than accepting it as *self-evident. Hetero-* may have two different meanings, the first, restrictive use being "the other in a dualistic structure," and the second, being simply "other" or different. By accepting the former, restrictive use, the twentieth century has been true to its conservative, Enlightenment heritage, that of contemplating all questions in strictly formulated dualisms, leaving no room for variety and difference.

We may redefine heterosexuality, then, as sexuality that does not conform to the "straight path," that of a monogamous, legalized "union" between a man and a woman with the main purpose of reproduction, in which sexual pleasure and attraction may (or may even *not*) exist only as a by-product. With this attempt at redefinition, we should cease to speak of a singular heterosexuality and, following Segal's suggestion, start to think in terms of heterosexualiti*es.* Heterosexuality cannot be one; it has to be *many.* Straight sexuality, on the other hand, cannot tolerate the existence of many, it has to be *one*: the straight, "right" or "true" path, the path we may now call *orthosexuality*; the path of male/father domination, the path of coerced female monogamy and the suppression of (among many other variations or "perversions") infantile and same-gender sexuality.

There is another possible opposite for *heteros* (other, different) in Classical Greek, which is *idios,* meaning *self* (as in *idiosyncrasy,* "peculiar to one's self"). Heterosexual may also mean "desiring or sexually attracted to an 'other'" (with a lower-case *o,* meaning the *objet petit a,* the object of desire in Lacanian terminology). The opposite of this heterosexual would be *idio*sexual, somebody who exclusively desired themselves, namely, a *narcissist.* I have already referred to Freud's speculation regarding Weismann's "conjugation" being a metaphor for sexuality, and it may be of some help here. It is very easy to think of "the opening up of the ectoderm in order to allow another individual's substance to enter," (Freud 1961, 42) as a metaphor, even a precursor, for sexual intercourse: the female body indeed "opens up" to accept at least a part of the male body inside.[13] If we think of

---

13 Even this simplistic metaphor should not be taken for a partial affirmation of the orthosexual matrix, because the same "conjugation" is also present in oral and anal sex (in their ortho- and

the ectoderm as the precursor of the *central nervous system* ("the grey matter of the cortex remains a derivative of the primitive superficial layer of the organism and may have inherited some of its essential properties," [Freud 1961, 20]), however, the metaphor becomes a lot more complex. If the central nervous system actually originates from the ectoderm, as Freud suggests with reference to embryology, then the psyche, the mind-soul, which is not limited to but certainly is structured around this system, also dates back to the ectoderm. If this is so, then the metaphor of "opening up" becomes an opening up of the mind and the soul to another rather than the opening up of merely the skin or any bodily orifice.

The unicellular organisms in Freud's (actually Weismann's) story opened up their cell membranes to conjugate with others in order to replenish their life energy. We human beings do it in another way: we lower our ego barriers temporarily to conjugate with an other, we *suspend* our egos for a limited period of time and are similarly rejuvenated. There are some of us (if not a majority then definitely a very large minority) who cannot tolerate this suspension of the ego, even temporarily. Although they get married, copulate and have children, they never give up their ego even for a moment, and as a result *they never have sex*, except with themselves. This narcissistic behavior, which prioritizes the preservation of the ego's integrity over conjugation, could be named *idiosexuality*. Idiosexuals challenge our heterosexualities as strongly as the orthosexuals, and in many instances the two may be one and the same in their insistent adherence to the *one* (one being, as always, a sign for the *phallus*), be it the symbolic order, God, or simply their undented, unpierced egos.

---

homosexual forms), and furthermore, the penis is only one of the many bodily protrusions to comply with the invitation generated by this opening up.

5.

The
Queer Family

Mr. Maclay (Tara's father): This is insane. You people have no right to interfere with Tara's affairs. *We* ... are her blood kin! Who the hell are you?

Buffy: We're family.

—*Buffy the Vampire Slayer*
season 5, episode 6

Many a Sign Appeared

Queer, is a "queer" word. In the second half of the twentieth century, it was used as a synonym for the openly hostile and homophobic *faggot* in American slang, and it was eventually taken over (a perfect case of *détournement* in the Situationist sense) by the gay movement and related academic fields of study, eventually becoming the name for one such field. It actually means weird, strange or bizarre. On the other hand, it may also mean uncanny or mysterious. As a verb, to *queer* is to corrupt, to damage or to spoil; but it may also mean "to estrange," that is to say, *queer* may be used to denote something strange or unfamiliar. We can see, therefore, that the word queer has a wide range of associations ranging from Brecht's *Verfremdungseffekt* (estrangement effect) to Freud's *das Unheimliche* (the uncanny). My usage entails both *strange* and *damaged* (but not in a negative or pejorative sense) because it estranges and disrupts the presuppositions of a self-evident, unquestionable conception of sexuality and society, which may even hint (albeit coyly) at the Derridean concept of *deconstruction*. Queer means "out of order," broken: what is *broken* is not only "outside the order (of things)" but it also does not work, does not function properly. I will thus try to point out that *the queer (broken) family* does not function as a family, as a pillar of contemporary social order, and, despite all efforts to the contrary, it does not fulfil the social function expected of it, hence subverting its structural integrity *regardless of intention.*

Marx had said that the secret of the holy family lay in the earthly family. Heidegger, on the other hand, said that we would only start to think when a tool did not function as expected (Heidegger 1962, 102–4). Hence, the secret of the holy family which lies in the earthly family will only be revealed when the earthly family breaks down, does not function, because only then will we really start to contemplate its function, history and existence. In order to understand (and hence critique and transform) the holy family, therefore, we need to look at the queer family, that is, the earthly family broken (probably) beyond repair.

Data on the sexual molestation of children, skyrocketing divorce rates, and the increasing (or at least increasingly visible) instances of abuse, violence, rape and murder directed against women (along with the inevitable reaction: the #MeToo movement) tell us the same thing: the modern family is failing along with the entire halo of sanctity around it. It did not start to fail today. However, the research on the modern family and how it is almost anything other than what it has claimed to be, a space of fear and insecurity rather than an abode of kindness and affection, could only be made today. Even if we did the same research a century ago, however, there probably would not be much change in the results. Even two or three centuries would not make a significant change. The only significant change is that this research could only be done under today's circumstances, because some questions can only be asked and (at least partially) honestly answered today.

We can only now get a glimpse of the truth that lies beneath the modern family, something we could only have predicted before. At this point, we can use the Tom and Jerry story that Žižek has employed countless times: Tom the cat crosses the edge of the cliff while chasing Jerry and, despite being suspended in mid-air, continues to run without falling—*until* he looks down and realizes there is nothing underneath his feet. Only then does he fall. Unless and until we look, we may go on as if nothing has happened (or is happening); but when we look down and see the modern family living in the house of harassment, rape and violence, and not, as advertised for millennia, in the house of love, compassion and solidarity—only then do we start to fall.

The modern family is failing: domestic violence, harassment and rape escalate; divorces increase rapidly; adolescent sexuality, hitherto only held in check by severe (sometimes violent) family supervision, increases after a short pause created by the AIDS scare; teenage pregnancies are at an all-time high, especially in the US and UK, creating a very serious social problem. Abortion causes an important social rift, not only in the United States but also in the EU's Catholic countries. Let it collapse and wither away, we may say, we need not defend it; but do we know what to replace it with? It is not a question of social engineering; I am not suggesting an institutional, universal solution that will replace the modern family in its entirety, something to be imposed on everyone. The question for the time being is whether we have an idea for what to replace this family with *in our own private lives* and, more importantly, whether we have anything to suggest to our friends, comrades, and neighbors? Nazım Hikmet, one of the greatest Turkish poets of all time, had said: "To understand, my love, what a tremendous bliss / To understand what is passing away and what is next." In order to understand what is next, we must understand what is already passing away, so we need to delve a little bit deeper into the basic nature of what we call the modern family.

"Modern Family"

Modern family is not merely the name for the social institution that is collapsing today (or that we have realized only now to be collapsing). It is also the name of a US television series that has been very popular for the past decade. *Modern Family* has been produced for eleven seasons since 2009 and has won one Golden Globe and twenty-two Emmy awards among many others. In this modern family, there are actually three families. The first consists of the well-to-do sexagenarian Jay Pritchett (Ed O'Neill), his wife, the Colombian beauty Gloria Delgado-Pritchett (Sofia Vergara), and Gloria's son from her previous marriage, Manny (Rico Rodriguez). This is the germinal nuclear family of *Modern Family*.

Let us pause here and remember that Ed O'Neill was also Al Bundy, the horrible father of *Married... with Children*, which lasted for eleven seasons between 1987 and 1997. *Married... with Children* showed us for eleven years how the American family was happily disintegrating: a mother (Katey Sagal) who did not think about anything other than petty shopping; the husband, a habitual liar who invented all kinds of excuses to avoid sexual intercourse with his wife, and whose fundamental pleasure in life was taking a crap; the stereotypical "blonde bimbo" daughter (Christina Applegate), who mindlessly bedded every moderately good-looking guy around; and the adolescent son (David Faustino), who was equally obsessed with sex but immeasurably less successful. For eleven seasons, Americans laughed hysterically at the pathetic mirror image of their own family as depicted by the show. The Bundy family consisted of *losers* in all respects (in business, in family, and in their emotional and sexual lives), and being a loser in the US is one of the most pathetic, most pitiable and most unforgivable positions imaginable, the result of having invented an other (*the loser*) and having projected every infirmity that society creates onto it. This time, however, Ed O'Neill is out to save the modern family that he castigated a little more than a decade before.

The other two families featured on the show are those of Pritchett's daughter and son from his first marriage, and both are "married with children." The peculiarity of the modern family of the 2000s begins here: his daughter Claire (Julie Bowen) has a family that is traditional enough: she is married to a real estate broker (Ty Burrell), she is a homemaker, and has two teenage daughters and a son who has recently entered puberty. The internal structure and behavioral patterns of this family are perfectly suited to the classic format we have seen in numerous television series and romantic comedies since the 1950s. Jay's son Mitchell (Jesse Tyler Ferguson), however, is married to a man (Eric Stonestreet), and the pair have adopted a Vietnamese baby girl. These three interconnected nuclear families—the father, his new wife and stepson; the daughter, her husband and three children; and the son, his husband and their adopted daughter; a total of three couples and five grandchildren—make up the new modern American family.

Let us take Claire's classic family as kind of a control group. The other two families violate the American family tradition in various respects: Jay's family is interethnic (white American-Latina) and intergenerational (there is more than thirty years between Jay and Gloria), and the child is from a different ethnic and cultural background as well. On American television, however, the essentials of this change had already been laid out: *Diff 'rent Strokes* (1978–86), for instance, gave us the endearing stories of a white family that adopted two black kids. The other (gay) family is a first on American television. To be sure, gay relationships were previously depicted (in an equally "cute" style). For instance, *Will and Grace* (1998–2006) lasted eight years, but there was no family there: a gay man and a straight woman lived together as roommates. Likewise, the relationship between David and Keith (Michael C. Hall and Matthew St. Patrick) in *Six Feet Under* (2001–2005) might have appeared healthier than many straight relationships in that series; then again, *Six Feet Under* was not a cute sitcom; it was based on black humor, and nothing in it fell into the category of normal. *Modern Family*, therefore, may be considered a first in terms of categorically approving and normalizing a gay family, in the sense of marriage and having children.

It is possible to imagine that this series infuriates many American conservatives, who still believe that homosexuality is a sin and that its removal from the DSM (Diagnostic and Statistical Manual of Mental Disorders) in 1974 is a disgrace (so much so that they continue attempts to invent a similar disorder under a new name, SSAD—Same-Sex Attraction Disorder). The existence of the Tea Party and ex-POTUS Donald Trump (and especially his ex-VP, Mike Pence) alongside *Modern Family* in the same general cultural structure can be seen as an irony of US history and geography. But when we examine this irony a little more carefully, we can see that the contradiction may not be as acute as it seems *prima facie*: *Modern Family* normalizes the sexual relationships between cultures, age groups and people of the same sex. This may have two different implications: on the one hand, it subverts racial and sexual prejudices and may challenge conservatives of both the racist and sexist varieties; on the other hand, however, it familiarizes and domesticates acts that hitherto appeared as subversive and dissident. In other words, it domesticates the queer while queering the familiar.

When we look at *Modern Family* a little more closely, we can observe that all the features that make up the American Dream remain present and that only those who fill these fixed positions have changed race, color, age, gender and sexual orientation. The same houses and house layouts; the same trivial everyday problems, nevertheless experienced as if each one is a latter-day *Medea* or *Antigone*; the same envies and jealousies; the same cars; the same schools; the same problems of adolescence; the same petty (or sometimes serious) lies. Our teenage daughters are of course under strict protection against the menace of sexuality, not by the relatively traditional parents, but also by the gay uncle and brother-in-law. One grandson is Latino, the other white, the former a bit precocious, the latter somehow not too bright, both making cow's eyes at their mothers and admiring their fathers. Abortion should be free, of course, as long as you don't do it. Giving birth is the holiest and most glorious human act. Everything is indexed to winning and being successful. In this modern family (unlike that of *Married…with Children*), there is no room for losers.

Modern Family also tells us that being gay or straight, white or Latinx, old or young, and male or female does not make us automatic losers. From a historical standpoint, things were once different, of course; from a class perspective, they are still different. But we are living at the end of history, aren't we? And it is only the hopelessly dense who insist on mentioning class these days. The decades when it was almost impossible to come out of the closet, or when this could be done only at the cost of excommunication, humiliation, total exclusion or even physical assault are very much vivid in the memory of a significant segment of the public. The same US that salutes the Latina beauty Sofia Vergara was also trying to build a wall at its Mexican border uncannily recently (and to make the Mexicans pay for it). Women can be Secretaries (of State, definitely) and senators, and Supreme

Court members and VPs. Why, an African-American can be the president of the US. The overwhelming majority of those who are still exposed to violence in the family, however, are women; a disproportionally high percentage of those who fill US prisons are African-Americans. But it's all right! Because in the new global order, when you take your skin color, your accent, your gender, and your sexuality and orientation along with you and knock on the door of the modern family, the only thing expected from you will be unquestioning obedience to the social division of labor between gender and age groups, the sanctity of private property, and the ultimate triumph of capitalism. If you fulfil these conditions, you have the chance to be accepted and invited inside among the other winners. Of course, we can't take all of you in; the living room is quite small, and some seats are already booked; but rejoice: you won't ever lose your chance. If not this time, definitely in the next sweepstakes. As long as you agree to dress up for the adult, white, and male position, whose primary function is to maintain the continuity of the species and the integrity of the existing order, you will no longer be pushed out the door. You may, however, need to wait at the threshold for the rest of your life.

A Short Study in Anatomy

The family has been regarded within radical (and most socialist) feminist literature as the main venue of male domination and women's subordination. I propose to make a change in some terms at this point: Family is mainly the locus of *father* domination and *women* and *children's* subordination. Since the father is inevitably a man, and the child will grow up to be either a woman or a man, it may be asked what benefit this change in terminology may bring about. What should be emphasized here is that the father's biological gender is not of fundamental significance. *Father* is the name of a position, a function. The genetic and anatomical properties of the creature that fulfils this function are secondary. To be sure, the father function (what Lacan calls *La fonction du père*) is primarily undertaken by genetic fathers, namely men. In some matrilineal communities, however, the maternal uncle may also fulfil this function.[1] In pre-nuclear extended families, it is often

---

1   In fact, Bronislaw Malinowski believed that when his study on the natives of Trobriand was published, he was also doing away with psychoanalysis and the Oedipus complex as such. As a matter of fact, in psychoanalytic theory (rather than the many popularized versions), fatherhood was already considered to be a sociocultural *position* rather than a genetic one. Therefore, it is not news for psychoanalytic theorists that in a matrilineal community the maternal uncle would play the part of the father. It is the *locus*, the position and the function of the father that matters rather than his genealogy.

observable that sometimes the father's mother assumes the father function. In the absence of everything else, without a viable father imago, the father function can be remitted to an institution (Social Services, boarding school management), even to a concept (Father State, God). Juliet Mitchell suggested in 1975 that the issue was not male domination as such, but patriarchy; not male but father domination:

> It is the specific feature of patriarchy—the law of the hypothesized pre-historic murdered father—that defines the relative places of men and women in human history. This "father" and his representatives—all fathers—are the crucial expression of patriarchal society. It is fathers not men who have the determinate power. And it is a question neither of biology nor of a specific society, but of human society itself. (Mitchell 2000, 408–9)

The "law of the hypothesized prehistoric murdered father" which Mitchell refers to is the story of Freud's mythological patricide in *Totem and Taboo* that we have already discussed (Freud 2001): In savage times, the sons come together in a conspiracy and kill and devour the body of the primordial father, the alpha male who possessed all women and children, and then share the women among themselves. This "new regime" is no less patriarchal than the former one, and even if it represents more freedom, it is more freedom for men: women and children are in the same position vis-à-vis the men with the only difference being they are each now owned by individual male members of the tribe rather than all being owned by a single man, the primordial father. The law of coerced female monogamy replaces the polyandry of the forcible monarchic rule of the father. Needless to say, in the long run it is no less oppressive than the latter, and definitely no less patriarchal, since all these sons will quickly become fathers themselves and enforce a microcosmic model of their father's unrestricted domination (albeit limited to their own families).

One very important point that Freud offers us is often neglected by many of his followers (except for Lacan) and critics: the father's physical presence is not necessary for his domination—his symbolic presence is sufficient. This presence is usually materialized in (1) *the name/no of the father* (Lacan's *le nom/non-du-père*) as a semiotic, linguistic entity; and (2) in the *phallus*, as distinct from the penis (a mere organ), which has been transformed into a universal symbol for any kind of relationship involving privilege and domination. The symbolic power of the father is not only over all women but also over children. It is important to remember that among Freud's findings, the most scandalous one (which virtually led to his excommunication by most of the scientific communities of his time) is *infantile sexuality*. Infantile sexuality is a terrifying concept for a sociocultural structure that posits the concept of sexuality as a by-product of procreation, placing it under the domination of the reproductive act. It is not surprising, therefore, that for a social structure and its smallest unit (the family) which place father domination at the center, the suppression of child sexuality, which has nothing to do with reproduction, should be of primary importance both physically and conceptually.

In this respect, the modern family is a yarn of contradictions, because it is based both on the legitimation of sexuality, which is the inevitable companion of reproduction, and on anathematizing it both outside the family (extramarital sexuality) and inside it (child sexuality). The family, and the nuclear family especially in modern, bourgeois societies, is the locus of an irresolvable contradiction concerning sexuality. In order to avoid the destructive effects of this contradiction, it is obliged to deny systematically and consistently that there is something called sexuality *vis-á-vis* children. This denial, however, leads to a new irresolvable contradiction, because it now has to admit that the functions of reproduction and sexuality are fundamentally different. The family can only legitimize its existence *vis-á-vis* children by excluding sexuality while including reproduction.

To be sure, there is some benefit in defending such blatant nonsense (blatant because no one believes it in the long run) when dealing with children: infantile sexuality must be excluded from our conceptual palette as an oxymoron, because even pronouncing it will be an overt admission of the existence of a sexuality entirely independent from the reproductive function. Children cannot reproduce, but from the moment they are born they have an intimate relationship with sexuality, namely, the pleasures of the body through all the senses. As children grow older, and as these pleasures develop along with them, they will be taken away from them one by one: first, they must be separated from the breast and be deprived of their unmediated relationship with the mother's body; then comes toilet training, and a natural and gratifying function of the body is to be placed under strict social control; and lastly, with the prohibition of childhood masturbation, all connection to the pleasures of the body will be terminated. Alternatively, we could say, "are supposed to be terminated," because this last prohibition (except for some rare cases of sociopathic parenting) can never be fully implemented within the family; children will always find a way. They will, however, indelibly learn during these ordeals to believe that sexuality is essentially an introverted, forbidden and guilty act.

Sexuality within the family is not only inevitable (between parents) but also forbidden and taboo (between mother and child, father and child, and siblings), and children always have to remain on the taboo side. The family thus becomes for children an institution of exclusion, rather than of inclusion. The child is always already excluded from sexuality, which is the main constituent characteristic of the family. Exclusion is the most surefire way to violence:[2] children, who are excluded from the sexual setup of the family in the first five years of their lives, are forced to re-establish a connection with sexuality during adolescence, as proto-grown-ups with a developing ability for procreation. Now, however, burdened with all the guilt, shame and exclusion of these first years, this connection (which is nothing but the "return of the repressed") can only be hysterical and potentially violent. As a result, the adolescent can only relate to sexuality through loss, loneliness and directly physical or fantasized violence.

In the nineteenth century, this problem was "solved" by prohibiting the relationship of the adolescent to sexuality altogether. That is why the second part of that century (the period known as the Victorian era in British-European culture) is literally a hysterical half-century in terms of Western civilization. In the second half of the twentieth century, adolescents started to have a closer relationship with sexuality, not only because the society was more liberal and liberated, but also because the economic and cultural structures dictated so: late capitalism had gone so far in the promotion of unhindered consumption that sexuality had become one of the main avenues for it, and family pressure was no longer sufficient to stop adolescents from exploring this avenue. The first thing to surface after this about-turn was the feeling of loss and loneliness for the adolescent; this period can therefore also be described as a depressed or melancholic half-century. The lost adolescents who desperately searched for their families in the Dickens novels of the nineteenth century disappeared during this period, replaced by the adolescents who desperately searched for their "genetic parents." This showed the influence, no doubt, of the much popularized science of genetics during the last decades of the twentieth century. The adolescent tried to escape from the family as such in order to replace it with another (as yet fantastic) family, a very popular theme in the films and television series of the late twentieth and early twenty-first centuries.

---

2   "There can be no life without violence because all violence is the violence of exclusion. Because everyone has had the experience of being left out—everyone, in other words, has been a child, everyone has an imagination (a provocation is also an invitation)." (Phillips 1996, 113)

Rogue ("Bashi-Bazouk") Sexuality[3]

The fact that reproduction and sexuality are two entirely different activities is so great a problem for patriarchal societies that it must be suppressed under all circumstances and hidden from scrutiny. This is because the domination of the father over women and children is only possible if women are coerced into monogamy, and hence sexuality is subjugated to reproduction. In a world where the coerced monogamy of women is not the absolute law, there would be no such position as fatherhood, because there would be no way to know who the father was. It has recently been possible to identify the genetic father by DNA tests, but only after the fact, when it is already too late anyway. Freud's primordial father had prohibited all males other than himself from copulating with women. The sons who overthrew him invented monogamy, which made their own wives taboo for each other. They created a system of checks and balances over each other's power by monopolizing their wives.

On the other hand, however, it is the same societal structures that develop technologies such as birth control and artificial or extrauterine fertilization that are based on (and promote) the separation between the reproductive act and the sexual act. This ambiguity indicates the severity of the underlying conflict: how can a god, for instance, wipe out an entire city (Sodom) just because sodomy became prevalent there, but tolerate Lot—the exemplary believer whom he has saved from this disaster—sleeping with his daughters? Wasn't incest one of the primal sins? The conservatives who march chanting "God hates gays!" probably know something we don't after all. The father who rapes his daughters[4] is usually ignored and secretly forgiven because he is only an abject relic of a prehistoric age, which does not pose a serious threat to modern-day patriarchy. Of course, the God of this patriarchal world hates gays, because gays, lesbians, and anyone who chooses to walk any path other than the straight one, challenges the supposedly self-evident subjugation of sexuality to reproduction, which is the foundation of the entire father-dominant order.

---

3   We have started with *broken*, so there is no harm in continuing with *rogue*. "Bashi-bazouk" (*Başıbozuk* in Turkish) is the name given to irregular troops in the Ottoman army. "*Bachi-bouzouk*," as it is used in French, is defined as "weak disciplined, not using standard weapons." If we think of *weapon* as a phallic metaphor, it becomes perfectly suitable for our purpose, especially when we consider the non-disciplined and wayward but autonomous character of the rogue or bashi-bazouk.

4   To be fair to Lot, he was not a rapist. It was the daughters who intoxicated him and slipped into his bed so that the prophet's lineage would survive. Even when the father himself is blameless and the agents themselves are female, the reasoning behind the act still belongs to the name of the father.

I suggested above that child sexuality was suppressed because it is independent from reproduction. Another type of sexuality that is suppressed for the same reason is homosexuality.

To be sure, homosexuality did not exactly have the same problems in earlier historical periods, before it was demonized by monotheistic Abrahamic religions. It is, however, necessary to ask ourselves how valid the term *homosexuality* was at those times. Sodomy and pederasty were widely accepted (or at least tolerated) in classical Greek (mostly Athenian) society—but only outside the family. The classical Greeks were less conflicted about it: they assigned the reproductive function to the family and left sexual love (Eros) out of the family, as something between two males, an adult man and an adolescent boy.

On closer inspection, however, it is possible to say that women are still excluded from this equation: as we have already observed, in classical Greek both *lover* and *beloved* (*erastes* and *eromenos*) are masculine terms. Even the language itself does not allow women to have any connection to Eros, that is, sexual love. Sappho, the unforgettable poet of lesbian love, was domesticated and sometimes considered as straight by nineteenth century conservative classicists because she addressed her beloved as *eromenos*. Some earlier historians even claimed that she ended her life by suicide because she fell in love with a man, which is an unsubstantiated fiction. While we have little information about Sappho's life, one thing we are sure of is that she had a daughter named Kleis. We do not, however, know whether Kleis is the product of a forced marriage in her youth, or whether Sappho lived her life in accordance with the masculine model, assigning Eros to her same-sex relationships and procreation to the family. Nevertheless, it is possible to say that Sappho's lesbian love[5] retains its subversive character even after twenty-six centuries because it violated not only the rules of society, which excluded women from the erotic matrix, but also the masculine structure of language.

It is also possible to suggest that Sappho or any "other than straight" people did not live their lives that way just to be radical or different, no matter how. Their sexual preference and/or orientation was an ontological issue rather than epistemological. It was simply a mode of existence, and it still is for most of them. Therefore, the concepts of transgression and subversion that I insistently use for them indicate an objective condition rather than an overt political act. Sappho seems radical to us in her sexuality, due not to an ethical or political attitude but because *as Sappho* she fell in love with women and celebrated Aphrodite. We

---

5   In fact, Sappho is the poet who inspired the term *lesbian love*, because the island of Lesbos in the Aegean Sea is her birth place, and *lesbian* means "from Lesbos."

should not, therefore, hastily assign a political significance to all queer lives; even if there *is* a political meaning present, it is something that is assigned retroactively, as a *surplus meaning*— at least until the second half of the twentieth century, when queerness came to openly *define itself* as an identity politics.

Expecting uncompromising political subversiveness from those with "other than straight" life and sexual choices and/or orientations is downright unfair. As a result, it is not necessary for those people of, let's say, same-sex orientation, to be militating against the modern family as well. In one sense, the gay movement has already played its part in a vast cultural transformation. John D'Emilio argues that:

> The huge steps toward visibility, toward acceptance, toward integration, toward equality—and they have been huge—have come, fundamentally, because the life course of heterosexuals has become more like ours. We've made gains not because we've shown heterosexuals that we are just like them, or because we've persuaded them to respect our "differences," but because many of them have become so much like us that they find us less threatening, less dangerous, less strange. In other words, for the last several decades, our lives have been flowing with the powerful current of social and cultural change. We have been swimming with history, not against it. (D'Emilio 2006)

What comes after this change, however, reverses the trend: as the straight life course absorbs and assimilates the homosexual one within the auspices of the modern family, the latter starts to lose its transgressive dynamics, as D'Emilio argues in the same essay, aptly named "The Marriage Fight is Setting Us Back." Without a doubt, queer people are perfectly entitled to expect acceptance into the modern family by leveraging the possibilities and opportunities which global capitalism provides (albeit involuntarily) in our age. This demand may not make much headway in terms of a radical critique of the family and patriarchy as such; it is, however, a perfectly legitimate demand and deserves support, even if only in the context of civil rights. Gays and lesbians should be free to marry, form partnerships and their rights of common property and inheritance must be under legal protection. This may also have a positive political significance in the long run: the more "other than straight" people penetrate and find a place within the modern family, the more its underlying contradictions and axiomatic assumptions will be under scrutiny. Even though the foundations of this family are gradually collapsing, however, it is still too vigorous to be upset by a few "estrangement effects."

Moreover, the "domestication effect" (*Verhäuslichungseffekt*) embedded in the fundamental structure of this institution is immediately able to engage and assimilate the threatening outside elements, as we can readily observe in the television series *Modern Family*.

Is "Another Family" Possible?

Birdcage (1996), the Hollywood adaptation of the French play *La Cage aux Folles* (Jean Poiret, 1973), begins with the Sister Sledge song "We Are Family." Birdcage, a nightclub famous for its drag shows, is run by a gay couple, Armand and Albert (Robin Williams and Nathan Lane). The drag chorus do their opening number with "We Are Family":

We are family
I got all my sisters with me
We are family
Get up everybody and sing

So, the genetic sisterhood of Sister Sledge's four siblings turns into another kind of sorority in the Birdcage drag show, becoming "broken," *queer*, just like the family in the name of the song. This is not, however, a family in the same sense that Armand and Albert as a gay couple have formed a family. Unlike Armand and Albert—who fuss over inheritance problems, worry about the future of their son, and suffer from frequent bouts of monogamous jealousy not much different from the problems of a classic nuclear family—these sisters are a family of song and dance. What binds them to each other is the "other place" they have created in their "other than straight" identity, vis-à-vis a crowd who applaud them on stage but are openly hostile to them in everyday life, against an ambivalent and confused outside world ready to humiliate and hurt them at any moment.

Michel Foucault called the brothel and the asylum the loci of the "other Victorians"; oases of "other places" in the midst of Victorian sexual conservatism:

The brothel and the mental hospital would be those places of tolerance: the prostitute, the client, and the pimp, together with the psychiatrist and his hysteric—those "other Victorians," as Steven Marcus would say—seem to have surreptitiously transferred the pleasures that are unspoken into the order of things that are counted. (Foucault 1978, 4)

In the same vein, Birdcage becomes the locus of the "other postmodernity": postmodernity is an age of supposed inclusiveness as contrasted to the exclusionism of the Victorian era. The inclusiveness of postmodernity, however, is based on coexistence without any real contact (as in the concept of multiculturalism). Hence, postmodernity is actually composed of many "other postmodernities," the drag club being only one of these venues.

Of course, this "other place" does not create a real alternative to everyday life. It is nothing more than an oasis in the midst of global capitalism, in South Beach, Florida. All the institutions of the external world, the police, journalists and economic obligations are always already waiting just outside the door. Nevertheless, this "other place" is quick to (at least partially) assimilate most transgressions from the external world: when the outside world tries to invade Birdcage in the persona of the ultra-conservative Senator Keeley (Gene Hackman), whose daughter Armand's son wants to marry, it miraculously converts Keeley, albeit for a short while: in an attempt to rid themselves of the Paparazzi, Keeley and his wife (Diane Wiest) dress up in drag and join the sisters in song and dance. Senator Keeley, a conservative Republican, adapts to his new drag identity in such a short time that the script allows him to speak (in my opinion) the most memorable line in the film: "No one will dance with me. I think it's this dress. I told them white would make me look fat." At this point, the film tells us that we all have a transvestite inside (or *outside*, depending on how you look at it), waiting for an opportunity to thrive (as in Keeley's example). Only when it's freed from its fetters can we join in the sisterhood, albeit temporarily. But that's all. *Birdcage* is a Hollywood film after all: in the end, Keeley's daughter Barbara (Calista Flockhart) and Armand's son Val (Dan Futterman) will be married by not one but *two* members of the clergy (a priest and a rabbi) and construct a new, straight modern family. The other family will only be a thing of the past, a long and winding road that eventually ends up in the modern family.

However, although the drag sisterhood in Birdcage is not sustainable in the long run under the existing societal and cultural conditions, it nevertheless indicates another possibility for us through the emotional aura it creates: kinship without blood ties is possible. Moreover, especially in the twenty-first century, when genetic conditions are increasingly easy to manipulate, there is a distinct possibility that it just might be more resilient and meaningful than kinship based on blood.

Let us now review the results of our "study in anatomy" for the classic family model above. The family consists of two adults preferably not connected to each other by blood and who can hence enter into a sexual relationship, and x children connected to the parents and each other by blood and who are hence prohibited from entering into a sexual relationship. The fundamental dynamics of this structure is that within its confines sexual intercourse is *both* mandatory *and* prohibited. It is mandatory because there is no other way to reproduce—or at least there was not until artificial and extrauterine fertilization (and in theory, extrauterine fetal growth) were developed. It is prohibited because everyone in the family is connected to each other by blood except for the parents. By the end of the century, extrauterine fertilization and adoption practices began to increase as an escape from natural birth. And especially as gay and lesbian marriages and adoption practices became widespread, the fundamental dynamic holding the modern family together—the mandatory/prohibited seesaw—also lost its centripetal power, with cracks and splits all along its fabric becoming more visible. As a result, the axiomatic bonds between parents and children and between siblings will also begin to dissolve. Thus, all the conditions for the emergence of a kinship structure independent of blood ties, incest taboo, and hence the underlying mandatory/prohibited seesaw of the family, are almost ripe.

In season 5, episode 6, of *Buffy the Vampire Slayer,* titled "Family," we get a very important clue as to what family is and what it may become. *Buffy the Vampire Slayer* (created by Joss Whedon, 1997–2003), a television series which lasted for seven years, is a combination of high-school comedy-drama, fantasy, and mock-gothic. The protagonists of the series are Buffy, the "Vampire Slayer" with supernatural powers (Sarah Michelle Gellar); Xander (Nicholas Brendon), who has no supernatural powers but is the group's emotional cement; two witches who are also lesbian lovers, Willow and Tara (Alyson Hannigan and Amber Benson); the "impotent vampire" Spike (James Marsters); Buffy's sister Dawn (Michelle Trachtenberg); and mentor and father figure (but not the Name-of-the-Father) for all of them, Giles (Anthony Stewart Head). In the "Family" episode, Tara's father and brother arrive to take her home because, according to family legend, Maclay women are transformed into demons when they turn eighteen and must be kept out of sight and bound to the home. Of course, this legend is pure bullshit, a big patriarchal lie to keep the women at bay as domestic (and maybe sexual) handmaidens. When Tara's friends refuse to let her go, the argument ends in the following altercation:

Mr. Maclay (Tara's father): This is insane. You people have no right to interfere with Tara's affairs. *We* ... are her blood kin! Who the hell are you?

Buffy: We're family.

Joss Whedon thus invents a new (and liberated) meaning for the concept of family, executing a perfect *détournement* in the Situationist sense, and he does that on conservative Fox television to boot.

A kinship is possible outside the traditional patriarchal order. Moreover, this kinship can neither be genetically manipulated, nor are the siblings forced to abide by the prohibitions and obligations of a barbarian class society, by rules invented millennia before they were born, in order to preserve and sustain an unjust, unmerited order based on exploitation. Moreover, this kinship does not have to be subjected to social hierarchy, because it is something freely chosen, not something into which one is born. It can be independent of the straight-sexuality (*orthosexuality*, if I may use the Greek prefix, meaning straight, true or canonic) imposed by the family, and may free sexuality, the vital connection between the body and pleasure, from the oppressive shadow of the reproductive function.

The irresolvable melodramas, uncouth farces, vicious circles of envy and jealousy, lies and backstabbing games of the old family order will still partially exist here, since the new order will not come down from the sky ready-made and will instead carry all the burdens of the past. However, it will not have to repeat the mother-father-child triangle of the old family based on prohibition-necessity-untruth. That is why it deserves the title "queer-rogue family." A mother's love not originating in the endocrine system, instinct and social necessity, and a love of siblings not originating in being accidentally thrown into the same home is what we can expect from this family. The solidarity-cooperation-complicity triangle, formed by siblings in the old family in order to resist its devastating effects, may finally gain a new meaning here.

The important thing is to know that it will not be us who will create this kinship out of thin air. It will not come into existence just because some utopians so desire. "Things fall apart; the centre cannot hold," said Yeats in 1919. The so-called modern family is unable to withstand the centrifugal force created by postmodern, neoliberal capitalism; so, it melts into the air and disperses. It will be up to us to build something new from the broken pieces, the debris we collect. The most important building block we will ever rescue from this debris is the idea and element of a kinship, not of blood but of conscious choice.

Interlude

An Afterthought
on Queering

I got hold of Eliot Schrefer's book *Queer Ducks (and Other Animals): The Natural World of Animal Sexuality* very recently (it was published in May 2022), long after I had already submitted my final draft to Sublation Press. Alas, *Queer Ducks* is a culmination of almost the exact opposite of what I was trying to accomplish in this book (especially in "Part II: Queering"). It is also a near-perfect example of the way in which everything I have been proposing here could be misunderstood, misjudged, misconstrued and, of course, deliberately distorted to fit into a conservative mold, which I have no connection with or sympathy for whatsoever. So, in order to make myself clearer on the issues addressed by Schrefer, I have decided to append this structured and succinct summary of my arguments in "Queering" rather than dispersing my objections throughout the body text. It seems necessary to me to present the reader with a checklist, so to speak, of the problems with the endeavor to naturalize, and therefore normalize, LGBTQ+ movements at the expense of the radicalism they had originally offered (and can hopefully still offer) people seeking different and freer ways to experience and express love, sexuality and life.

For the sake of brevity and concision, I will list my objections to Schrefer using bullet points, something I actually like to do but usually avoid as much as possible to escape accusations of simplicity and shortcutting:

- Schrefer gathers a lot of studies and data on the "natural" occurrence of "queer behavior" in the animal world and telescopes them into a narrative without actual references by translating biological, anthropological and evolutionary terminology into everyday speech. So far, so good. However, he then begins to use this terminology *as though it were natural*; as though there is a consensus that, e.g., *homosexuality* is perfectly applicable to any animal species and *pair-bonding* is incontestably synonymous with *sexual partnering*. His unusual style of endnotes may be interesting for the audience of a popular book, but it fails to direct the more skeptical among us to the sources so we can check for ourselves.

▶ To address the (straight or queer) elephant in the room immediately, I will start by questioning Schrefer's primary hypothesis that queerness is prevalent all over the animal domain and that whoever refuses this "already established" fact is a conservative, homophobe, and transphobe of the worst ilk (rather than engaging further, otherwise sympathetic skeptics may be scared away right from the start, especially in the present age of social media cancellation without a hearing or trial). Schrefer seems to suggest that if we refrain from (or advise restraint in) applying the terms *queer, gay, lesbian* and *homosexual* to any and all animal species, we must be following conservatives throughout history in denying the "naturalness" of queerness and degrading it as an anti-virtue, a sin, and a threat to the natural order of things.

▶ This hypothesis presupposes that naturalness is itself a virtue and completely ignores the fact that there is a serious, if not widespread, theoretical trend in neuroscience, psychoanalysis and in philosophy suggesting that, within the human sphere, naturalness may not be a virtue at all but may merely constitute our succumbing to "our Darwinian shackles" (repeating V. S. Ramachandran's words once again). It necessarily follows from this reasoning that queerness may be important, prevalent and worthy of defense *precisely because (rather than despite) the fact it is not natural.*

▶ So, we may agree to disagree after all, but we must first agree that not everyone who claims that queerness does not necessarily need to be natural must be a card-carrying conservative.

▶ To catch the (queer or straight) bull by the horns: in order to be homosexual, you have to first be sexual, and sexuality is a human construct not applicable to non-human animals. This presupposition stems from the postulate (to which I will return later) that there is or should be a red line, a qualitative break, between human beings and non-human animals. The important point here is that many of the arguments in vogue today regarding the indivisibility of human and non-human existences—enhanced by (but not identical with) much-advertised vegetarian and vegan lifestyles—mostly ignore, neglect or treat as non-existent many basic concepts such as consciousness, theory of mind and culture. I concede that some of these arguments are worthy of respect and should be addressed in full, but this does not mean they are beyond critical inquiry and problematization. The studies and theories that take these arguments as their starting point, meanwhile, must be respectful of opposing arguments, rather than simply dismissing them as being conservative, if they want the same treatment.

▶ My main line of questioning starts from the argument that *anthropomorphism is the evil twin sibling of anthropocentrism* and vice versa. In order to remove humanity from its self-appointed position at the center of the cosmos—something we have been trying to do since Giordano Bruno (or, more precisely, since Hypatia of Alexandria)—we must not assign qualities *imagined by human beings, for human beings,* to the entire cosmos. Some concepts, such as consciousness, society and sexuality, apply exclusively to human beings. This determination does not make human beings more developed, more entitled or more privileged, but merely different, just as the ability to photosynthesize does not make plants automatically superior to rocks and the ability to move at will does not make animals automatically superior to plants. In the greater order of the cosmos (*major ordo saeculorum*), there is no God-given hierarchy or pecking order, and all these surely connect and constitute an integral whole; this does not, however, make them uniform, undifferentiated, and homogeneous.

▶ Nature without human beings is subject to Darwin's survival of the fittest, or natural selection, rule; human beings have changed that, however. They are not subject to natural selection anymore, at least for the last couple of millennia or so, and individual human beings that would have perished (along with their genetic line) according to that rule simply *do not*. They rather live on and propagate their (sometimes defective) genetic material, whereas non-human animals and plants cannot. Human beings do this on their behalf, having learned to control the genetic structures of animals and plants, not for charity or out of the goodness of their hearts but for their own benefit. The suggestion usually attributed to anthropologist Margaret Mead that a healed femur is the first sign of civilization is not applicable to non-human animals: although many animal species are capable of some form of solidarity and cooperation, their instincts urge them to treat another member of their species with a broken femur (i.e., incapable of surviving on their own) as already dead. Human beings, on the other hand, are freed of their Darwinian shackles when they learn to treat a disabled member and care for them.

▸ Furthermore, some of us are willing to make a radical distinction between reproductive behavior based on instincts and sexual behavior based on drives and desires. We have well-developed reasons for doing so and deserve to be heard rather than summarily dismissed as either conservatives or callous enemies of non-human species.

▸ Reproductive behavior is instinctive and is inscribed in the basic genetic structures of all living beings, including human beings, who by definition constitute a sub-species of animals. They do have this instinct and behave accordingly. In addition to this, however, human beings also have desires and drives defined by their *cultural* existence that have nothing to do with this instinct and are often in contradiction with it, as can be observed in their millennia-old (and sometimes ridiculous) attempts at birth control. They strive to have sexual relationships without the (older and more basic) burden of reproduction and, especially in recent decades, vice versa. This separation can only be seen in a human environment (except for some isolated cases such as the bonobo). We may desire a person without the intention of having offspring with them, and we may be driven to have offspring without any sexual desire for the partner we have them with, sometimes not even *knowing* the person who donates the necessary reproductive cells.

▸ Non-human animals, on the other hand, are instinctually driven toward reproductive behavior, and, without the knowledge of the mechanics of this behavior, their males may confuse the gender of the "partner" (contingent upon olfactory and visual disparities). Some may even consistently do so (as shown by the study on "gay rams"), which will, upon further study, owe to a difference in their neurological and endocrine structures. This difference does not in any way indicate that they are homosexual as such since they do not engage in same-sex pseudo-reproductive behavior as a result of their *sexual* desires, but rather as a result of their altered *reproductive* instincts.

▸ Those who ascribe sexuality and desire to these supposedly homosexual acts should be able to show that this is applicable to both (or *all*) genders. Unfortunately, they consistently fail to do so and compensate for this failure by providing "hundreds, even thousands" of examples from the studies made on males, only to proceed with their argument as though the findings are universal, i.e., pertinent for both (or all) genders. However, we do know that there is female homosexuality among only two non-human

species, bonobos and bottlenose dolphins, and that these are almost borderline cases, since these species are the closest genetically to human beings.[1]
In order for female homosexuality to exist among non-human animals, the
presence of a clitoris is almost necessarily a precondition, and even then, an
anatomic blunder of nature may complicate things and lead us to find false
positives, as in the case of the spotted hyena. (Cunha 2014)

▶ Schrefer tries to compensate for the imbalance between male and female
occurrences of queerness in the animal world and ends up assigning sexuality to pair-bonding, which has nothing to do with sexuality at all. We know
that same-sex pair-bonding is prevalent in animals, especially in many species of birds, but is this bonding in any sense sexual? It is usually done for
the care of the young (or eggs), and in some cases it may even be lifelong,
but there is no indication that it is done for pleasure independent of reproduction. For sexuality to exist (especially in the sense of *eros*) there should
be an expectation of physical pleasure, and there are specific organs and/or
nerve clusters in the animal body for this purpose. In pair-bonding (whether
same-sex or other-sex), these organs and/or nerve clusters do not usually
come into play, and although we may observe an increase in oxytocin levels
(which Schrefer claims, but which are usually difficult to measure), this only
indicates a sense of well-being not necessarily related to pleasure.

▶ In human beings, sex is categorically more than mere physical plea-
sure-seeking; it is the opening up of the ego barrier to another person, albeit
temporarily, with a definite opening up of the superego barrier that corresponds. Both acts presuppose the existence of a self, enveloped by the ego
and the superego. In order for sex to exist in non-human animals, we must
postulate for them a self, an ego and a superego. Proving the existence of all
three without distorting, haphazardly redefining or blatantly ignoring most
of the recent theorizing within neuroscience and psychoanalysis (let alone
philosophy) will be a challenge. This does not mean that it is *impossible* to
do so; in this post-truth age of fleeting memory, everything is possible, but it
takes a bit more than *just assuming*.

---

1   For the bottlenose dolphin (*Tursiops truncates*), see, for instance, Brennan, Patricia L.R., Jon-
    athan R. Cowart, Dara N. Orbach (2021). "Evidence of a functional clitoris in dolphins"; in
    Current Biology, Volume 32, Issue 1, PR24-R26, January 10, 2021. For the bonobo, more than
    enough evidence is presented by Frans de Waal (see De Waal 2005 and De Waal 2009).

▸ In the absence of widespread female homosexual behavior, it is understandable that other forms of behavior would quickly be deemed sexual, if for no other reason than to allow one to avoid the criticism of being sexist or patriarchal. But whichever way you cut it, the criticism is there: once finding queer behavior among non-human animals is reduced to finding pseudo-reproductive behavior in males, re-interpreting pair-bonding between females as sexuality becomes unavoidable in order to compensate for this imbalance. Schrefer, however, seems unaware that this comes dangerously close to the very same ages-old male-dominant ideology that ascribes sexual pleasure and behavior to males and homemaking and caring for the young to females, calling both "sex."

▸ Pair-bonding is not sexual partnering; the latter is a cultural (that is, exclusively human) construct. It is not limited to temporary or lifetime bonding between females of the same species. It may also occur between males or between other-sex couples but is not, however, necessarily a sexual relationship; it is an act of solidarity and cooperation for the care of the young, which is directly related to reproduction. This is extremely valuable *as it is* and does not need to be overinterpreted as sex so that female animals can be included in the arguments for homosexuality in nature.

▸ In conclusion, queerness no longer needs to be legitimized by its inscription within common sense, popular or populist, self-evidentiary narratives. It is legitimate and valuable as *queerness*, as a heterodox act, in the sense that it is a deviation from the straight (orthodox) path of class societies which are firmly grounded in straight sexuality, the coerced monogamy of women, and the desexualization of children. Insistently searching for queerness in nature only helps to de-radicalize LGBTQ+ movements and existences, to normalize them, and eventually to *de-queer* them. Rather than *de-queering* LGBTQ+, we should seek to *queer* the so-called normal, the family, and what we call sexuality.

Part III

Desire/Language

6.

Instinct, Desire
and Death

Imagine… imagine a fetishist who becomes infatuated with, let's say, a grubby piece of cloth, and who threatens and entreats and defies every risk in order to acquire this beloved bit of rag. A peculiar idea, isn't it? A man who at one and the same time is ashamed of the object of his desire and cherishes it above everything else, a man who is ready to sacrifice his life for his love, since the feeling he has for it is perhaps as overwhelming as Romeo's feeling for Juliet. Such cases exist, as you know. So, in the same way, there are things, situations, that no one has dared to externalize, but which the mind has produced by accident in a moment of aberration, of madness, call it what you will. At the next stage, the idea becomes flesh and blood. That's all.

—Stanislaw Lem, *Solaris*

THE HISTORY OF HUMANITY is the history of the gradual separation of the sexual act from the reproductive act, or, in other words, of desire from instinct. To be sure, it is many other things at the same time; the history of class struggles, for one thing. Considering, however, that Marx and Engels said in *The German Ideology* that private property and the division of labor were identical expressions, and that the first division of labor occurred in the family, between man and woman, we can allow for the possibility that we are talking about different aspects of one and the same thing. (Marx and Engels 2010b)

The advent of private property is also the precise moment when the sexual act started to be separated from the reproductive act. It is the moment when child bearing and rearing became solely the woman's affair, a conscious choice[1] rather than an instinctual one (as it is for many animals, including many higher mammals and primates), that the division of labor within the family became apparent.

---

1 Not in the sense that it is intelligent and voluntary but that it is done within the parameters of the symbolic order: language.

Consciousness is the acknowledgement of something else beyond the immediate satisfaction of a need. An ape may pick an apple to eat, but when a human being picks apples to trade for a flint knife (i.e., for something else), this is a conscious act. Instinct may drive felines to copulate at defined periods of the year, but when human beings copulate for pleasure (i.e., for something else), they have already become conscious beings. In the same vein, when women are limited to the home and its surroundings not solely as a result of the "maternal instinct" but also for reasons of the *social* division of labor resulting from the dominant relations in society, consciousness is already at work.

Desire Comes to Mind

The reproductive act is instinctual, that is, embedded in the genetic structure, because it is directly linked to the survival of the species as a whole. However, once human beings develop consciousness and consequently have individual wills of their own beyond the collective, instinctual will of the species (itself nothing but an amorphous blob of raw energy, a set of instincts bunched together), the driving force behind their behaviors start to change, and it is not solely instinct anymore. We call this new driving force *desire*. Desire may not (always) be conscious, that is, we may not always *know* that it is guiding our behavior, but it is always co-existent with consciousness. Without a conscious being there is no desire, and consciousness is in fact identical with (a) conscious being: "Consciousness [*das Bewusstsein*] can never be anything else than conscious being [*das bewusste Sein*], and the being of men is their actual life-process…" (Marx and Engels 1998, 42) Only with the development of consciousness can there be an unconscious (what is not yet and not anymore conscious), and only with the interplay of consciousness and the unconscious can we construct a fantasy space in which our desires can have any function.

But this desire should not be taken in the limited, commonplace (i.e., purely sexual) sense of the term. When Marx puts forth the basic definition of the commodity, he also refers to Nicholas Barbon in a footnote:

> A commodity is, in the first place, an object outside us, a thing that by its properties satisfies human wants of some sort or another. The nature of such wants, whether, for instance, they spring from the stomach or from fancy, makes no difference. (Marx 2010, 45)

And:

> Desire implies want, it is the appetite of the mind, and as natural as hunger to the body... (Marx 2010, 45)[2]

According to Barbon, therefore, desire is *natural*, but it is also related to the mind, which is the counterpoint to nature. As we can see, Barbon is thinking within the limits of the Cartesian mind-body dichotomy, as one would expect from a thinker at the end of the seventeenth century. Admittedly, desire springs from the fact that human beings do have a mind, but this does not mean, as Barbon seems to assume, that it only operates within the parameters of the mind. Desire is at the same time of the body, or rather, of psyche and soma just like hunger, which although it springs solely from the body is also operative on the mind. When we are hungry, we consciously seek ways to satisfy our hunger; when we can't, our mental processes are adversely influenced. So, as we become desiring beings (that is, desiring things and each other), instead of only hungering beings, we also become civilized beings, insofar as we do more with each other than teaming up in order to satisfy hunger. It is precisely at this point that hunger ceases to be something only of the body, a mere instinctual urge, and becomes also something of the psyche and soma: our minds start to fabricate hunger as desire, even at times when the body itself is not hungry. Eating becomes an act partially independent of instinct, and we may refuse to eat something that doesn't satisfy our gusto (or snobbery, or sense of propriety, or whatever else) even when we are physically hungry, and, reversely, we may eat when we are not just to satisfy our taste or even our curiosity. This is why it is only humans and those poor domesticated animals which co-habit the human cultural space that have a condition called obesity.

Desire is pointed out by Marx as something directed to not only sexual or emotional objects but also to commodities themselves. Furthermore, a commodity is not something we just need but something we desire. We can easily see this in commodities which are not in themselves objects of need: alcohol and drugs,

---

2   Barbon, Nicholas, "A Discourse Concerning Coining the New Money Lighter. In Answer to Mr. Locke's Considerations, &c.," cited in Marx 2010, 45. This is, in fact, a retranslation of Marx's translation into German. The original passage reads: "ihin8, 3)3)Things that have their Value by being useful to supply the Wants of the Mind, are all such Things that satisfy Desire, (Desire implies Want; it is the Appetite of the Mind, and as natural as Hunger to the Body:) such are all those Things that are any ways useful to satisfy the Mind, by contributing to the Ease, Pleasure, or Pomp of Life" (Barbon 1698, 3).

tobacco, coffee, Coke (in both senses of the word), fetish objects such as shoes and garments not used as garments, guns we don't fire, cars not used for their transportation value; in short, anything that "springs from fancy" with a twist, things that do not satisfy a need but only create a need for more of the same thing.[3] For these commodities desire stands alone. In a Lacanian sense, these commodities are object-causes, rather than objects that are supposed to satisfy a need. For many (if not most) commodities, however, need and desire are intermixed. In the twentieth century, however, as universalized commodity production develops to such a degree that the use value of commodities is completely eclipsed by their value,[4] desire reigns supreme over need, and like everything connected with desire, excess becomes the primary principle. Once, for example, hunger as need is effectively replaced by hunger as desire, obesity establishes itself as one of the life-threatening pathologies (or rather, pseudo-pathologies) of civilized humanity.

Of course, this threat can come into being only when the dominant world order (or the symbolic order) ideologically and practically sanctions the replacement of hunger as need with hunger as desire. Before global capitalism, however, the desire that led to obesity was kept in check by the still partially pre-capitalistic social superego, which condemned such desire as gluttony and made it one of the seven deadly sins. As soon as this superego command (*Do not indulge in eating too much!*) was replaced by a new kind of superego—itself a side effect of a novel mode of nutrition dictated by the high speed of life and covert poverty of late capitalism—obesity became a cultural possibility, even a necessity. The protagonist of this new superego is Žižek's obscene master or obscene father, who sanctions

---

3   Of course, once addiction is established and withdrawal symptoms have become a physical threat, it *seems* like there is a *need* for these commodities too. This assumption is misleading, however, because the difference between need and desire is not merely that the former is physical and material and the latter psychical and spiritual. The only difference is that desire is *insatiable* and remains so even when it becomes a physical addiction.

4   Contrary to widespread usage in popular pseudo-Marxist discourse, the basic dichotomy inherent in commodities is not between use value and exchange value but between use value and value: "The utility of a thing makes it a use value. But this utility is not a thing of air. Being limited by the physical properties of the commodity, it has no existence apart from that commodity. A commodity, such as iron, corn, or a diamond, is therefore, so far as it is a material thing, a use value, something useful. (...) Let us now consider the residue of each of these products; it consists of the same unsubstantial reality in each, a mere congelation of homogeneous human labour, of labour power expended without regard to the mode of its expenditure. All that these things now tell us is that human labour power has been expended in their production, that human labour is embodied in them. When looked at as crystals of this social substance, common to them all, they are—Values." (Marx 2010, 48)

and even encourages and provokes excess enjoyment.[5] There is every possibility in today's world that the command *Enjoy!* will lead to obesity, because this super-ego command turns eating into a compulsive act, something for which there is no satisfaction. To be sure, obesity could not have come into being as a social and socially-approved condition without giving rise to its diametrical opposite: anorexia, the almost total rejection of eating, the total disavowal of hunger as desire, the compulsive drive to wipe away the (fantastic) obese body which, as a result, makes it an absolute presence. The anorexic strives to obliterate desire instead of merely controlling or limiting it (as the pre-capitalist superego would have suggested), because the obscene master does not allow for moderation. Anorexia is the excessive reaction to the excess enjoyment of global capitalism.

Capitalism, however, is an antithetical order, which creates the diametrical opposite of its every action. This is why obesity is at the same time pathologized and fought against. As capitalism creates an endless compulsion toward eating, a hunger as desire (*Eat! Eat junk food! Enjoy Coke!*), it creates at the same time its opposite (*Lose weight! Diet! Exercise!*). Thus, instead of easing the constant pressure toward compulsive eating, capitalism creates a second compulsion toward losing weight. This is why the anorexic is caught in a deadly trap: they are besieged by two contrasting compulsions, which can only end up in a drive toward obliterating the body itself altogether. The same thing is observable with tobacco smoking. The compulsion toward smoking, created throughout the twentieth century, is now reversed by the campaign against smoking, but not in the sense of easing the compulsion. Now capitalism creates another compulsion working against the first, a mass hypochondria which advises that *Smoking Kills!* The more accurate (but more moderate) statement that "smoking may kill the ones who smoke, and may

---

5   The terms *obscene master* and *obscene father* are used by Žižek in various instances to denote the changing of the superego command's character from limiting or prohibiting enjoyment to promoting it. Following a very Žižekian anecdote drawn from his memories of compulsory military service—about a military doctor ordering a young conscript to masturbate in front of everybody in order to produce a semen sample—Žižek goes on to posit the existence of a new kind of master specific to the second half of the twentieth century, one who orders "Enjoy!" rather than "Limit your desire!" The long-running Coca-Cola commercial which used the slogan "Enjoy Coke!" becomes the epitome of this master, since it orders us to enjoy (*jouir*) something which does not satisfy any actual need: Coke only provides us with a lot of useless CO_2 bubbles, a lot of sugar our system does not need, and it does not even quench our thirst, only creating more thirst. The new obscene master orders us to enjoy; this enjoyment, however, is not the satisfaction of a real need but rather an attempt to satisfy a desire completely severed from needs. A later Sprite commercial featuring the slogan "Obey your thirst!" shows us that the Coca-Cola Company was trying almost desperately to prove Žižek's point.

adversely affect the health of non-smokers who are subjected to tobacco smoke," is totally unacceptable for the obscene master. Consequently, a whole literature, indeed a whole legend, is built around the half-truth of secondhand smoking, so that smokers can now be identified as not only "suicides" but also "murderers" who endanger non-smokers, as if with intent aforethought. The final outcome of these two compulsions working together but toward seemingly opposing ends is the creation of a new other, the smoker—akin to the Nazis' Jew, the KKK's Nigger, and McCarthy's Communist—which must be eliminated at any cost.[6]

Desire implies a need (*besoin*), but it is not a need as such in itself; need, in turn, implies a lack (*manque*), but it is a presence in itself. Instincts don't work that way: they start out with a concrete need instead of a lack, which the body puts forth, and then the animal performs a series of behaviors which are always already inherent in their genetic pattern. For animals, even the highest mammals (except for a few higher primates who are already borderline cases), lack is never the starting point; lack presupposes humanity due to it always being a lack in the symbolic order. It is only with language (the symbolic order, consciousness, speech) that lack starts to play a part in animal behavior, which immediately makes the animal human. With lack, there is desire; desire affirms the lack—these two are identical expressions: desire is the insatiable urge to reach for that missing element that would (presumably) have made the symbolic order whole.

The concept of desire can be better comprehended if it is approached multilingually: *Wünsch* in Freud's terminology was translated into English as "wish" by Stratchey (and sanctioned by Freud), which shares the same root and is useful in the sense that it has a childish and semi-fantastic denotation. *Désir* in Lacan's terminology, however, is translated as "desire," this time with a denotation of a sexual nature. Throughout their life's work, these two thinkers tried to ascertain, however, that these denotations were only meaningful with their connotations, that *Wünsch* has its sexual connotations (leading to the concept of childhood sexuality), and *désir* is not limited to sexual desire. Marx translated Barbon's *desire* into German as *Verlangen* (translatable as "desire," "demand," "requirement" and even "longing"). Elsewhere he uses *Bedürfnis* which means "need," "want," "requirement" and even "necessity," which in turn was retranslated into English as "want."

---

6   The same thing was done for heroin in the early twentieth century: drug companies (Bayer in this case) who advertised and marketed heroin as a cough remedy in late nineteenth and early twentieth centuries created a lot of involuntary addicts, and when heroin was outlawed as a narcotic, these addicts created by Bayer were demonized, persecuted and jailed, in the end being pathologized and hospitalized (not to mention some having already ODed).

Now, the English *want* is a curious (and immensely helpful) translation, because it means both "desire" and "lack" at the same time (see the first two entries for *want* in *Roget's New Millennium Thesaurus, First Edition). When an animal eats, it does not do it out of an urge to satisfy a desire; it does not have any (feeling of) lack to be filled. It does so because for its every physical need there is a corresponding instinctual response inscribed in the genetic code.* This is why the overwhelming majority of animals are only periodically in heat, while human beings are constantly sexually active.[7] A need is satisfied and therefore does not turn into an obsession; it is only when there is no (possibility of) satisfaction that a need ceases to be a need and appears as desire, something which creates the urge for endless repetition. We want, because we are wanting.

The animals *are* nature; for them the Real does not exist.[8] The Real comes into being, or hints at its own existence, only through the feeling of a lack in the symbolic order. Human beings are the only beings which can sense (construct, fantasize) the existence of the Real, and this is only through an absence. The Real is that which is not yet (*noch nicht*) symbolized, and which can never be symbolized in its wholeness. The problem lies in the fact that human beings themselves are antithetical creatures who are at the same time nature: they are at the same time a part of the Real, endlessly endeavoring to contain it (including themselves) in the symbolic order they have created, while continuing to make and remake it throughout their history. For human beings, the void they seek to fill is also themselves. It is only this antithetical quality that makes human beings subjects, in both senses of the word: as active, willful agents and at the same time subject to such action.

Human beings may desire things, but as soon as they desire them, these things metamorphize into commodities, that is, things touched and transformed by human labor power. Human beings may also desire other human beings and force them into commodity form through their desire. They have the Midas curse, turning everything they touch into gold and thus draining them of their use value.

---

7 Anthropologist and evolutionary biologist Jared Diamond (quite convincingly) argues that the reason why human beings became sexually active all the time even before they became conscious beings, was because human females (along with 31 other higher primate species) do not show outward signs of ovulation. For a comparison with other higher primates, see Diamond 1997, chapter 4.

8 *The Real* is used here in the Lacanian sense of "*Le réel*," meaning the unintegrated totality of everything that is beyond the symbolic order, namely, language, and that cannot be ascribed meaning. In this sense, it can only be co-existent with the symbolic order, that is, any meaning it *lacks* has to be included in its complement, language.

Desire strips every object of its specific qualities, its uniqueness. When we are bored, we confuse all objects of desire; we don't know whether we want to see a film or a reality show on television, eat a pleasant dinner or merely junk food, drink Coke or smoke a joint, meet our friends or our parents, light a cigarette or have a chat on the net, masturbate or go out cruising. All these objects of desire have been stripped of their use value beyond the abstract value of being an object of desire. They are all reduced to each other, and their specific qualities do not matter when they are designated as objects of desire. There is only one common denominator for all commodities, and that is the fact that they are all purchasable with different amounts of money, the commodity of commodities. The same thing is true for objects of desire too, only here the common denominator is *the phallus*, the signifier of signifiers, the central signifier around which language, that is, the entire symbolic order, is organized.

The Phallus as Universal Currency

Let us consider these passages by Marx, in his *Economic and Philosophical Manuscripts of 1844*:

> *Money* is the procurer between man's need (*Bedürfnis*) and the object, between his life and his means of life. But *that which* mediates my life for me, also *mediates* the existence of other people for me. For me it is the *other* person. (Marx 2010, 323)

> *Money* as the external, universal *medium* and *faculty* (not springing from man as man or from human society as society) for turning an *image into reality and reality into a mere image*, transforms the *real essential powers of man and nature* into what are merely abstract notions and therefore *imperfections* and tormenting chimeras, just as it transforms *real imperfections and chimeras—essential* powers which are really impotent, which exist only in the imagination of the individual—into *real essential powers and faculties*. In the light of this characteristic alone, Money is thus the general distorting of *individualities* which turns them into their opposite and confers contradictory attributes upon their attributes. (Marx 2010, 325)

Let us now substitute *money* with *the phallus* in three instances. While Marx's original meaning is not (completely) lost by this slight tampering, we might gain some insight as to the character of the phallus through looking at the text this way. First of all, like money, the phallus is something *external* and *universal*; this recognition re-establishes the much repeated but little understood fact that the penis and the phallus are completely different concepts. The penis, unlike the phallus, is internal[9] and specific to the body. Second, the phallus, again like money, replaces reality by images, impotence by a false feeling of potency. And third, the phallus mediates the existence of others, the *third* persons which make language and all other forms of social intercourse (*Verkehr*) possible.

The paradigmatic shift from money to the phallus in my little experiment does not only make Marx sound like Lacan but also betrays the fact that, just like money, the phallus (not the penis) does not have a use value of its own. It is not good for anything: you can't eat it, drink it, wear it, or use it for pleasure. It only stands for *everything else* other than itself. Just like money, which started out as a convenient medium for exchange before eventually taking over the entire spheres of production and circulation, the phallus starts out as a convenient but inflated symbol of fertility[10] and then goes on to stand for "the latent slavery in the family," ending up as the universal signifier for all hierarchical relations of power.

As we have briefly seen above, the concept of phallus as money tends to put an end to the confusion between the penis and the phallus: the penis is the paper, and the phallus is the money printed on this paper. But this is not only true for the act of printing, either: those who print money must also be authorized to do so by some higher power; in order for money to become money, we need an entire economic order, an entire set of hierarchies, and an entire state apparatus to proclaim that these essentially worthless bits of printed paper represent value (*This note is legal tender*). In the same vein, the phallus becomes the phallus only when it has several millennia of patriarchy, compulsive female monogamy and a viable threat

---

9   If we want to be specific, it is *borderline*: it resides on the border of the internal and the external, as can be observed from some men's childish and semi-perverted tendency to address their penis in the third person singular and occasionally name them.

10 This symbolism has been quite late to develop, if we consider the entire history of *Homo sapiens* (as opposed to *Homo sapiens sapiens*). Until a certain point in history, the fertility symbol was the entire female body, a complex whole with no phonetic or calligraphic value, signifying only itself and nothing else. Once the male role in reproduction was acknowledged, however, the symbolism shifted from the entire female body to the simple male sexual organ, from Kybele to Priapos, that is, from the bodily whole to the part, and from that to a mere symbol, to a single calligraphic stroke which is simply 1.

of castration to support it. Without the power of money, a one hundred dollar (or euro, pound, etc.) bill is nothing but a piece of paper with dead presidents (or dead or alive monarchs or leaders, in short: images of the Names-of-the-Father)[11] printed on it. Taken separately from the symbolic order that makes it money, it is not even good for writing on, since it is filled with a lot of (now) meaningless symbols. The penis is likewise just an organ which facilitates urination and ejaculation, and without the power of the phallus it is only one of the more expendable parts of the body, since, as is observable in females, urination is perfectly possible without it, and, as recent technological developments have established, male reproductive cells don't need a launcher to fulfil their function, to reach their destination, so to speak.

The phallus is the signifier of a lack; it is at the same time the symbol of having always already been castrated and the constant threat of castration to come. It is both in the past and future tenses, thus dominating the present tense. It is something we all believe to have lost, although not one of us ever had it, and at the same time it is a promise never to be fulfilled. The penis, on the other hand, is a specific material presence, an overblown and overrated one in every patriarchal culture. It is only with the confusion of the concepts of the phallus and the penis that the penis gains a specific predominance over the other organs of the male body and over the sexual organs of women and the entire female body. Men—regardless of their social, cultural, intellectual and class positions—are usually disturbed by any act or statement which challenges this overestimation because it reminds them of something that they can never remember in its entirety: that the phallus and the penis were never the same thing in the first place.

Thus, for example, when Lacan equates "the erectile organ" with $\sqrt{-1}$, the scientist and critic (Alan Sokal in this case) becomes "distressed," and immediately spews out a salvo of arguments in mathematics in order to prove that Lacan didn't know what he was talking about.[12] A genuine resentment for the "abuse"

---

11 The use of the slang term *dead presidents* for money reveals the fact that the Name-of-the-Father must always be the name of the *dead* father, because the actual live father can never stand for the "name" (*nom*) and can never uphold the prohibition (*non*); any live father is too particular (indeed *peculiar*) for such a position. Even the president of the United States between the years 2000 and 2008, George W. Bush, does not represent the Name-of-the-Father as such—despite the fact that he actually carries the name of the/his father (George)—without the power invested in him by millions of paper notes with dead presidents printed on them.

12 This argument can be found on page 27 of Alan Sokal and Jean Bricmont's very self-descriptively named book *Fashionable Nonsense*. It's self-descriptive in the sense that the book immediately became hilariously fashionable among scientific circles and then compassionately forgotten af-

of mathematics in the service of psychoanalysis (if, of course, such abuse indeed existed) would probably lead to a series of arguments to demonstrate the invalidity of the statements or proclamations he makes, or the inadequacy of the mathematical terminology or symbology in question. What we find in Sokal, on the other hand, is a rather extreme attempt to "annihilate" Lacan in the space of a scant twenty pages, in the highly authoritarian style of a fundamentally incompetent high school mathematics instructor who tells us what is right or wrong but does not bother to explain why, probably because we, the readers, are just ignoramuses in the field of mathematics and symbolic logic. If I am permitted to make an observation from psychoanalysis, the field in which I am more knowledgeable (more than mathematics at least), it is fairly safe to assume that Lacan's first negating (the minus sign) and then taking the square root of (and hence disassembling) the phallus was the real cause of Sokal's otherwise inexplicable extreme anger, his "distress," which is not an entirely rational reaction but a retort usually rooted in unconscious processes, probably pointing to *something* which has to do with castration phobia.

Freud's "Instincts" and Drives

As desire is further separated from instinct throughout human history, it becomes increasingly individual-oriented rather than species-oriented. Actually, the sexual act and the reproductive act in human beings are always already distinguished from each other, firstly because human beings as separate, individuated entities are increasingly driven by desires rather than instincts, and they do not have a desire *as such* to propagate the species or their own brand of genes. It is only the instincts and corresponding bodily structures that facilitate reproduction. August Weismann, an evolutionary biologist to whom Freud owes much of his insight into the life and death instincts, states:

---

ter a decade. It took another hoax of the same caliber (the "Grievance Studies" hoax of 2018) to remind us of his work. Building upon his once very revealing and scientifically fruitful victory in proving that postmodernists were very gullible people indeed (see, The Editors of Lingua Franca 2000; Holquist et al. 1996), Sokal marched on to crush Lacan, Kristeva, Irigaray, Latour, Baudrillard, Deleuze and Guattari, and Virilio all in a single blow, a potential case-study in narcissism at large (but this is not the place to argue that). In dealing with Lacan, Sokal triumphantly proved that his mathematics was less than adequate, establishing *en passant* that he himself is a postmodernist after all, since all he managed to do was to literalize a metaphor, something postmodernists are very fond of.

In no case does fertilization correspond to a rejuvenescence or renewal of life, nor is its occurrence necessary in order that life may endure: it is merely an arrangement which renders possible the intermingling of two different hereditary tendencies. (Weismann cited in Freud 2010a, 3757)

Our instincts drive us toward pleasure (*Lust*), but only in the sense of a removal of displeasure (*Unlust*): through filling the stomach to stop acidity, and by sucking, urinating, defecating and ejaculation, that is, rhythmic pressure on the mucous membrane to trigger a release of tension. Desire, on the other hand, actively seeks to *generate* the displeasure itself, and no species-functional benefit is created by the discharge of this self-generated displeasure. This is why (and/or because) human beings are the only mammalians (with the possible exception of a few higher primates) who are constantly in heat. The urge to copulate is always there even when there is no possibility to reproduce. The animal instinct does not know that there is an unmediated causal link between copulation and reproduction. Human desire, on the other hand, is aware of this link, and this is precisely why human beings invented birth control at least as early as 1500 BC,[13] as a means to achieve pleasure without the species-functional outcome.

Human beings' species-universal inclination to separate sexuality and reproduction is apparent not only in their having practiced and later almost perfected methods of birth control, but also in their attempting to devise ways to reproduce without the mediation of sexuality. The invention of artificial insemination dates back to the late nineteenth century, and the developing technologies of artificial and extrauterine insemination that began in the 1960s, and later of extrauterine fetal development, have paved the way for extrauterine *birth*, which will be the ultimate separation of reproduction and sexuality.

This will be the exact moment in human history that is somewhat sardonically anticipated by Aldous Huxley in his *Brave New World*. For Huxley, the perfection and universal practice of extrauterine insemination and birth is synonymous with the elimination of any kind of meaning from sexuality and will pave the way for unhindered and unchallenged totalitarian control, for the state will then have the means to invent and apply built-in mechanisms of mind and body control for all individuals from the moment of insemination onward. Huxley's pessimistic predictions are problematic, to say the least, since he still considers sexuality as a side effect or subset of reproduction. For Huxley, the ultimate separation of sexuality

---

13 That is, this is the date of the first written reference to birth control. It probably started much earlier, but we lack the documentation.

from reproduction and the consequent disappearance of monogamy are indications of the disappearance of love and all the more sublime mental, emotional, and spiritual experiences human beings have invented throughout their history. This point of view, however, is definitely paradoxical, because it sees sexuality as both an experience subservient to something as commonplace, primal and natural as reproduction and at the same time the source of all sublime experiences.

The actual *technological* separation of reproduction from sexuality should not, on the other hand, be mistaken for some kind of a glorious victory for human progress, human science and technology. It is, rather, a return to a much more primitive (or indeed primal, as far as life itself is concerned) state of affairs, since what we may call the primordial forms of sexuality and reproduction are completely unrelated in unicellular organisms:

> If two of the animalculae, at the moment before they show signs of senescence, are able to coalesce with each other, that is to "conjugate" (soon after which they once more separate), they are saved from growing old and become "rejuvenated." Conjugation is no doubt the fore-runner of the sexual reproduction of higher creatures; it is as yet unconnected with propagation and is limited to the mixing of the substances of the two individuals. (Freud 2010a, 3749)

Freud is merely repeating August Weismann's experiments with unicellular organisms here, since (as we'll see later on) these experiments partially confirm his theory of drives,[14] although they also problematize some of his hypotheses. To start with, Weismann suggests that unicellular organisms are *ceteris paribus* immortal, that is, there is no built-in drive toward death within them, and unless they are placed in a stagnant environment (where the only external factor is their own excreta), they do not die:

> [Weismann] considers that unicellular organisms are potentially immortal, and that death only makes its appearance with the

---

14 I am well aware that I'm adding to the confusion created by the mistranslation of Freud's *Trieb* into English as *instinct*. I agree with the critics of Stratchey that *Trieb* should have been translated as *drive*. When speaking about pre-human forms of life, however, there is no discernible difference between instinct and drive, so we must be careful to note that as we start to speak of human beings, as not only biological but also thinking entities, *Trieb* becomes *drive* and *Instinkt* remains *instinct*.

multicellular metazoa. It is true that this death of the higher organisms
is a natural one, a death from internal causes; but it is not founded on
any primal characteristic of living substance and cannot be regarded
as an absolute necessity with its basis in the very nature of life. (Freud
2010a, 3747)

These organisms, however, reproduce by *agamogenesis,* by dividing, which
endlessly repeats the same genetic pattern (which is another kind of "immortality") but at the same time negates the individual cell's existence. When a
unicellular organism divides, we get two cells of the same genetic pattern, two
cells which are genetically identical with (and are actually clones of) the parent
cell. The parent cell, in a manner of speaking, lives on in its posterity, but it also
dies as an "individual" at the precise moment it reproduces. The problem here is
whether we can ascribe individuality to a unicellular organism. If we do this, even
as a metaphor, we genealogically accept the identity of death and reproduction,
because reproduction by division (*agamogenesis*) is the diametrical opposite of
indivisibility ("individuality"). Thus, at the moment an organism divides, it is not
an individual anymore; it is *dead* as an individual.

Concerning death, the difference between gamogenetic and agamogenetic
life forms is that when an agamogenetic cell "dies" (that is, ceases to exist because
it has divided), it leaves behind no dead body to be disposed of. The body, in a
manner of speaking, *has already been disposed of,* and has become the substance of
two new organisms which are genetically identical with the parent cell. Of course,
it is also possible for such an organism to "die" accidentally, due to an unexpected
change in material circumstances, such as environmental stagnation, fatal radia-
tion or acidity, and only then does it leave a dead body behind.

This, however, is not the normal or natural course of events. Normally, an
individual unicellular organism can rejuvenate or divide *ad infinitum,* defying
death either individually or genetically. The unicellular organism, then, has before
it two possibilities for immortality: One is individual immortality, which is possible by *failing* to divide if the organism is placed in a stagnant environment and
the possibility of rejuvenation is provided by the existence of other similar organisms. The other way is genetic immortality, achieved by dividing, which means
the preservation and repetition of the same genetic pattern through consecutive
generations. The first possibility tends toward stagnation, since a given number
of individual cells at a given time may continue to exist practically forever, without any allowance for change. The second possibility, however, tends toward a

different kind of stagnation, that is, the immortality of a given combination of genetic information which, although it allows for a change of individual cells from one generation to another, makes these individual cells simple clones of the ancestral organism, with no genetic change occurring.

The first case, if carried to the extreme, will result in genetic immutability, because the cell nuclei (the receptacles of genetic information) will always be intact, preventing the possibility of a mutation. It is only with reproduction and the dividing of the cell nuclei themselves that the possibility of mutation occurs: every act of reproduction is a trauma for the cell nucleus, because whatever genes it has been keeping inside are forced to split and duplicate themselves. This traumatic event may result in mutations, but only when combined with traumatic changes in environmental factors (through "coincidences"), and this is the only hope for change in the agamogenetic universe. Of course, the incidences of mutation in this universe are severely limited as compared to gamogenetic reproduction, where the genetic structure of the cell is not only forced to split in two but also forced to combine with genes alien to the individual organism. In this second case, mutations are much more likely to occur.

Desire and Immortality

The individual immortality of a unicellular organism, then, is almost exactly similar with that of Adam and Eve before they consume the famous fruit from the tree of knowledge of good and evil. If they had resisted the temptation, they would have lived an eternal life in the Garden of Eden, without reproduction, without toil and without knowledge. They would still have been in the same unchanging, immutable environment, and they would be identical to their own selves at the moment of creation. There would have been no Cain, no Abel, no murder, no reproduction, no children and no death. Death and reproduction occurred only as a result of the acknowledgement of their reproductive capacity (which in biblical discourse is still identical with their sexuality).

What Weismann and Freud call "conjugation"—that is, the union and then separation of two cells, in which process an exchange of cytoplasm takes place—Freud mistakes for "the fore-runner of the *sexual* reproduction of higher creatures." He is only half right: conjugation is in fact the forerunner of sexuality but has nothing to do with reproduction whatsoever. Freud's identification of the ego with death and of sexuality with life instincts stems from this inability to distinguish sexuality from reproduction. This mistake, which is grave but at the same time historically inescapable,[15] leads Freud to actually *hope* that he will be proved mistaken:

> The upshot of our enquiry so far has been the drawing of a sharp distinction between the "ego-instincts" and the sexual instincts, and the view that the former exercise pressure towards death and the latter towards a prolongation of life. But this conclusion is bound to be unsatisfactory in many respects even to ourselves. Moreover, it is actually only of the former group of instincts that we can predicate a conservative, or rather retrograde, character corresponding to a compulsion to repeat. For on our hypothesis the ego-instincts arise from the coming to life of inanimate matter and seek to restore the inanimate state; whereas as regards the sexual instincts, though it is true that they reproduce primitive states of the organism, what they are clearly aiming at by every possible means is the coalescence of two germ-cells which are differentiated in a particular way. If this union is not effected, the germ-cell dies along with all the other elements of the multicellular organism. It is only on this condition that the sexual function can prolong the cell's life and lend it the appearance of immortality. But what is the important event in the development of living substance which is being repeated in sexual reproduction, or in its fore-runner, the conjugation of two protista? We cannot say; and we should consequently feel relieved if the whole structure of our argument turned out to be mistaken. The opposition between the ego or death instincts and the sexual or life instincts would then cease to hold and the compulsion to repeat would no longer possess the importance we have ascribed to it. (Freud 2010a, 3745)

What had happened in the transition to sexual reproduction (we should call it *gamogenesis*, as opposed to *agamogenesis*, from now on in order to be rid of the confusing adjective *sexual*) was that a billion-year-old mechanism, which existed solely for individual enhancement and survival, was recruited for reproduction through *exaptation* (to use the term evolutionary biologists prefer), with which it initially had no relation whatsoever. This transformation, the assimilation of

---

15 We should not forget that Freud published *Beyond the Pleasure Principle* in 1920, before the time of the pill and the application of practical artificial and extrauterine insemination. Lacan, however, who still makes the same identification in 1954 (Lacan 1991), is less easily forgiven.

conjugation (proto-sexuality) by reproduction, may be the "important event" Freud was looking for, and it definitely changes "the whole structure of [his] whole argument," for which he must be relieved. This alternative argument could only have been developed after non-sexual reproduction and non-reproductive sex, which have only existed as sporadic exceptions for thousands of years, became established in the last quarter of the twentieth century as *entities in themselves*. The problem, of course, is that the psychic structures of human beings are still organized around this (now mistaken) identification, and the actual dissociation of sexuality from reproduction will take decades, if not centuries.

Let us see whether "the opposition between the ego or death instincts and the sexual or life instincts" really ceases to hold after we establish this dissociation: First of all, the ego instinct must at once be separated from the death instinct because it is directed toward the survival of the individual organism. The ego is the outer shell of the self, filtering, interpreting and buffering it against the outside and defending it from excess stimuli. Freud believes it to be an analog of the ectoderm and, in human beings, of the skin (Freud 2010a), a metaphor later developed by Didier Anzieu (Anzieu 1995).

Freud further develops this concept in *The Ego and the Id* (Freud 2010b) and places the ego at the borderline between perception and consciousness. It is neither limited to perception nor completely overlaps with consciousness, nor is it itself entirely "conscious." Defined in this way, the ego has nothing to do with death: it resists every attempt, external and internal, to return to a simpler, that is, inanimate, form of existence.[16] It is, at the same time, resistant against the reproductive (not the sexual, because there are not yet sexes) instinct, because reproduction means the disruption of the bodily integrity, hence the dissipation of the ego and the death of the individual. In short, like Woody Allen, the ego says, "I don't want to achieve immortality through my work. I want to achieve it through not dying." Of course, we must substitute *work* here with *offspring*. The sexual instinct Freud is talking about, however, must be decomposed, so to speak: separated into sexual and reproductive instincts. The reproductive instinct is both a life instinct (for the species) and a death instinct (for the individual) at the same time: it strives toward the death of the individual to secure the immortality of the species. This time unlike Woody Allen, it says, "I don't want to achieve immortality through not dying. I want to achieve it through my work [my offspring]." This

---

16 In this sense, the ego is the conscious being's unconscious resistance against the second law of thermodynamics, against *entropy*, which can be interpreted in this context as the tendency to revert to a less complex and more stable state of matter-energy economy.

is probably the reason why Woody Allen never had any children of his own,[17] and also the reason why male ants (and bees) cannot live on after copulation.

The sexual instinct, on the other hand, is extremely individualistic; not in the sense in which Richard Dawkins calls the gene "selfish" but rather the way that Freud calls the germ cells "narcissistic." It does not care whether the species survives and propagates, nor whether a specific genetic line flourishes. Its only concern is with the immortality of the individual ego, with the pleasure to be achieved in the unhindered continuation of *this* individual being. In desperately trying to achieve individual immortality, however, it permanently clashes with the second law of thermodynamics, the law of entropy, and the ultimate result of this clash is not instinctual at all; it is precisely this clash which constitutes what Lacan will call *jouissance,* the fantastic satisfaction of an impossible desire.

In more complex *gamogenetic* life forms, we again observe the correspondence of the reproductive and death instincts. Female (queen) ants have a life expectancy of about five hundred times that of a male ant. The drones that are neuter (but genetically female, that is, bearing no Y chromosome) and play no part in the reproduction process are not quite long-lived, but their life expectancy is still ten times that of a male. The same relationship is also in effect in bees, with less radical ratios: a male bee can live for sixty days (significantly longer than a male ant, who only lives for a few), but the drones live for about 140 days and the queen bees literally for years. All these ratios show us that the male ant or bee is genetically programmed for death once it fulfils its role in reproduction. The longevity of the female, however, is the main concern of all ant and bee communities, because she represents, first, as bearer of the eggs, the continuity of the species, and second, as caregiver for the entire community, the builder of living spaces and the provider of food. Black widow and praying mantis females kill and eat the males after copulation without the male showing any self-defensive behavior. This is because the

---

17 The only child he is assumed to have fathered is Ronan Farrow, who, as his mother Mia Farrow claimed years after her tumultuous separation from Allen, may very well be the biological offspring of Frank Sinatra:

> Farrow discusses her relationship with Frank Sinatra, telling Orth that Sinatra was the great love of her life, and says, "We never really split up." When asked point-blank if her biological son with Woody Allen, Ronan Farrow, may actually be the son of Frank Sinatra, Farrow answers, "Possibly" ("Exclusive: Mia Farrow and Eight of Her Children Speak Out on Their Lives, Frank Sinatra, and the Scandals They've Endured"; in *Vanity Fair,* October 23, 2013).

To be sure, Sinatra was already 71 years old when Ronan Farrow was conceived, and according to his daughter Nancy's account, had had a vasectomy years prior, making the validity of the claim pretty unlikely.

male has no species-function after the reproductive act and becomes a strain on the environment which must be eliminated and (if possible) turned into nourishment for the female (who needs it for the sake of the coming generation).

Going back to Woody Allen, the refusal of the male animal to have (any) offspring is an unmediated outcome of the life (sexual) instinct, because the male animal cannot identify with the offspring. The female germ cell (the ovum) is an integral part of the female body, while male germ cells are excreta to be ejected from the male body as soon as possible. Weismann's (and Freud's) argument is that germ cells in complex gamogenetic life forms take over the initial immortality of the animal, while other bodily tissues become increasingly "mortal" as they become increasingly specialized and hence interdependent:

> The mortal part is the body in the narrower sense—the "soma"—which alone is subject to natural death. The germ-cells, on the other hand, are potentially immortal, in so far as they are able, under certain favourable conditions, to develop into a new individual, or, in other words, to surround themselves with a new soma. (Freud 2010a, 3746)

Freud goes a step further and suggests that these "potentially immortal" germ cells are in fact "narcissistic":

> The germ-cells themselves would behave in a completely "narcissistic" fashion—to use the phrase that we are accustomed to use in the theory of the neuroses to describe a whole individual who retains his libido in his ego and pays none of it out in object-cathexes. The germ-cells require their libido, the activity of their life instincts, for themselves, as a reserve against their later momentous constructive activity. (The cells of the malignant neoplasms which destroy the organism should also perhaps be described as narcissistic in this same sense: pathology is prepared to regard their germs as innate and to ascribe embryonic attributes to them). (Freud 2010a, 3751)

Thus, the "narcissistic" germ cell (as opposed to the other bodily tissues which exist *for* and *in* each other) has only one obsessive goal, and that is its own survival, which in turn means the propagation of the species. Once the male animal "delivers" these narcissistic cells to their destination, it has no species-function left, because it has thrown out all the immortality inherent to it and is left with only the mortal tissues.[18] The female animal, on the other hand, *receives* these narcissistic germ cells and combines them with hers, and can therefore identify herself with this intrinsic immortality, at least for the duration of pregnancy and nurturing of the newborn. This is why (as long as the sexual drive and reproductive instinct are indistinguishable from each other) the female body is able to establish a more peaceful coexistence between its mortal and immortal parts, as opposed to the male body, which is always caught in the deadlock of genetic immortality versus individual mortality.

Contemporary research indicates that removal of the germline precursor cells (but not the entire reproductive system) lengthens the life span of *Caenorhabditis elegans* (a kind of microscopic worm) up to 60%:

> When the germline of *C. elegans* is removed using a laser microbeam or with mutations that block germ-cell proliferation, adult animals live up to 60% longer than intact controls. However, when the entire somatic gonad is removed, the worm has a normal life span. Thus, sterility alone does not lengthen life. These and other findings suggest that *C. elegans'* life span is influenced by counterbalancing cues from the reproductive system: signals from proliferating germ cells reduce longevity, while signals from the somatic gonad promote a longer life. (Berman and Kenyon 2006)[19]

The findings of both sets of researchers, which lead to the same conclusion, seem to support our argument that while giving up the reproductive faculty (blocking germ cell proliferation) results in longer individual life, the same result is not achieved by removing reproductive organs altogether, which would indicate giving up the sexual function as well. Quite on the contrary, blocking reproduction *and* keeping sexuality ("signals from the somatic gonad" without "proliferating germ cells") *together* "promote a longer life."

Freud is well aware that this apparently dualistic structure (death instinct versus life instinct, mortality versus immortality) is just a part of a broader and

---

18 Now we can begin to see the "immortal wisdom" inherent in Daoist sexual techniques, which advise the male to delay ejaculation as long as possible and eventually do away with it altogether. Not giving in to the reproductive instinct results, in Daoist philosophy, in a transcendental immortality of the psyche.

19 The same argument is found originally in Arantes-Oliveira et al. 2002.

more profound cosmological problem, and he therefore refers to a philosopher who has extensively reflected upon the nature of death:

> We may pause for a moment over this pre-eminently dualistic view of instinctual life. According to E. Hering's theory, two kinds of processes are constantly at work in living substance, operating in contrary directions, one constructive or assimilatory and the other destructive or dissimilatory. May we venture to recognize in these two directions taken by the vital processes the activity of our two instinctual impulses, the life instincts and the death instincts? There is something else, at any rate, that we cannot remain blind to. We have unwittingly steered our course into the harbour of Schopenhauer's philosophy. For him death is the "true result and to that extent the purpose of life" while the sexual instinct is the embodiment of the will to live. (Freud 2010a, 3750)

He returns to the problem of death versus life instincts in a later study (*The Ego and the Id*) and once more affirms its cosmological nature:

> On the basis of theoretical considerations, supported by biology, we put forward the hypothesis of a death instinct, the task of which is to lead organic life back into the inanimate state; on the other hand, we supposed that Eros, by bringing about a more and more far-reaching combination of the particles into which living substance is dispersed, aims at complicating life and at the same time, of course, at preserving it. Acting in this way, both the instincts would be conservative in the strictest sense of the word, since both would be endeavouring to re-establish a state of things that was disturbed by the emergence of life. The emergence of life would thus be the cause of the continuance of life and also at the same time of the striving towards death; and life itself would be a conflict and compromise between these two trends. The problem of the origin of life would remain a cosmological one; and the problem of the goal and purpose of life would be answered dualistically. (Freud 2010b, 3974)

Once the sexual drive is conceptually separated from the reproductive instinct, it appears much more complicated, because it is now supposed to stand on its own feet, so to speak, rather than being a mere by-product or function. Just like the ego instinct, it strives, in the most basic, *agamogenetic* forms of life, to ascertain the immortality of the individual. But in order to achieve this, it expects the ego, the representative of the individual vis-à-vis any externality, to sacrifice or suspend its integrity by opening up the ectoderm to allow another individual's substance to enter, albeit for a temporary period. The coalescence of two individual cells means that they give up their respective individualities to a certain extent; they experience a temporary death in order to prolong life in the long run. This function of rejuvenation through the partial denial of individual bodily integrity, and hence acceptance of mortality, may be called *the second immortality*.

I use the term *second immortality* as a kind of synthesis of Bakhtin's "second life" (Bakhtin 1984) and Lacan's "second death" (Lacan 1997). If we try to read Bakhtin with Lacan, the carnivalesque discourse that points to a second life outside the official discourse of the ruling classes emerges as an attempt to re-symbolize through the cracks in the symbolic order. It is only in this second life that the tragic hero's brief transcending of limits can be repeated by the people, by the governed. The carnival, a specific and very temporary state, is a kind of human intercourse (*Verkehr*) that challenges the limits imposed by the symbolic order, some kind of a collective *hubris* without the corresponding *atè*. The second immortality is something that goes beyond the individual immortality of the unicellular organism and the genetic immortality of the species and strives to find immortality in the specific (carnivalesque) relation between individuals, an immortality which results from a brief denial of their respective individualities.

Lacan differs from Freud in this matter of individuality versus immortality, for although they are both rooted in Weismann's findings, he takes the opposite side, that of the species against the individual:

[I]ndividuals are, if one can put it this way, already dead. An individual is worth nothing alongside the immortal substance hidden deep inside it, which is the only thing to be perpetuated and which authentically and substantially represents such life as there is. (Lacan 1991, 121)

Taking her cue from this statement, Marcia Ian goes on to argue that Lacan "sees the individual as dead vermin hiding in the entrails of species, the undead" (Ian 1997, 136). Once we establish that the sexual and the reproductive are separate entities, however, we may see a way out of the deadlock of the individuality/immortality binary opposition: the individual may in fact be "dead vermin hiding in the entrails of species," but we do not have to think solely within the parameters of the individual versus the species. There is another level, which is the *inter-individual,* made possible by Weismann's coalescence, and it will lend a second immortality to the individual once it is willing to temporarily sacrifice (or suspend) its individuality. In other words, the "immortal substance hidden deep inside" the individual does not only represent the species, which is itself a closed system and hence subject to the law of entropy, but also the open system which includes it. We have an immortal core, not only because we are a part of something larger—that is, our species—but also because we are a part of something even larger—that is, life itself. If we take this hypothesis as something viable, we may even go on to suggest that Weismann's coalescence need not be limited to individuals of the same species, and that there is no reason why it shouldn't cross inter-species barriers, allowing for non-genetic, inter-individual hybridization.

As we move on to *gamogenetic* life forms, however, the sexual instinct toward individual immortality through inter-individual intercourse gradually loses its independence and becomes a sub-function in the service of reproduction. In return, reproduction ceases to be *immediately* fatal to the individual, but again with a twist: now all individuals are decidedly mortal, whether they choose to reproduce or not, because the death instinct (along with the reproductive instinct) is imprinted in their genetic structures. Now every individual must die in both senses: they must die individually, and even after that, their genetic structures will live on only in conjunction with another's. However, no genetic structure can endlessly repeat itself, and this development paves the way for genetic diversity, more and faster mutations, and better and faster adaptation to environmental conditions. The suspension of individual immortality is not only for the benefit of a single species but for the dissemination and propagation of life itself, again, an affirmation of the larger open system and of life in general vis-à-vis a single species.

Desire and Entropy

What Freud (and in a sense Schopenhauer) is referring to is known in physics as the second law of thermodynamics, or the law of entropy: every closed thermodynamic system tends toward a simpler, less complex, less ordered and more *chaotic* mode of existence.[20] This is inevitable because any closed system constantly loses energy and matter to its environment, and since a constant supply of energy is needed to hold together complex organizations of matter and energy, the system tends toward simpler, less organized structures. Freud's death instinct

---

20 In Ovid, chaos stands against the ordered nature of the cosmos, as the primeval emptiness before the cosmos came into being.

"endeavouring to re-establish a state of things that was disturbed by the emergence of life" fits this definition of entropy insofar as it is related to life.[21] Every living being has an innate tendency toward death, that is, toward an inanimate state of existence which is simpler, less ordered, less organized and more chaotic. If we consider that every living being also has a tendency toward the preservation of (a) its individual existence and (b) its genetic existence, the dualistic nature of the life and death instincts becomes apparent.

However, one question remains unanswered, and that is where exactly in the thermodynamic schema the life instinct fits. It is not the *first* law, which affirms the indestructibility of matter and/or energy. This law does not give us any hints about the necessity of life as the diametrical opposite of death, because death as the destruction of life entails the destruction of neither matter nor energy, only the transformation of one or both. It is definitely not the *third* law, which is only the furtherance of the law of entropy. The complication lies in the fact that the laws of thermodynamics are all about *closed* thermodynamic systems. An *open* thermodynamic system, on the other hand, open-ended both spatially and temporally, does not follow the law of entropy since it is not located within an *environment* to lose energy *to*. Rather, it *includes* its environment (again, spatio-temporally, in the sense that it includes its spatial externality, its past and its present), and the energy lost during the transformations within and between the closed systems it includes is inputted to it (since it is, after all, their environment). The law of an open thermodynamic system, therefore, is the reverse of entropy, and since the open thermodynamic system *precedes* any closed thermodynamic system, as in the primordial soup preceding the Big Bang, this law of reverse entropy (negentropy or syntropy) comes before the law of entropy.[22]

We are doubtlessly trying to operate at the limits of linguistic possibilities in this matter, because the expression "an open thermodynamic system" includes at least two semantic paradoxes, one involving the indefinite article *an* and the other involving the concept of the system. Once we hypothesize an "open"

---

21 Of course, life is not the only mode of existence to which entropy can be applied. For instance, the tendency of glass to break can be considered as "endeavouring to re-establish a state of things that was disturbed by the emergence of [glass structure]," that is, a return to a less organized, dispersed state of existence for silica molecules.

22 This "reverse of entropy" had already been hypothesized and conceptualized by many physicists and mathematicians; for example, as "negative entropy" by Erwin Schrödinger in 1943, as "negentropy" by Léon Brillouin in 1953, and as "syntropy" by Luigi Fantappiè in 1944 and Buckminster Fuller in 1956. In 1974, Albert Szent-Györgyi proposed to replace Brillouin's "negentropy" with "syntropy," hence indicating that the two concepts were in fact identical in content.

spatio-temporal system, this system tends to include all, and the *an* becomes a *the*. On the other hand, since an infinite (hence open) system includes an infinite number of closed *and* open systems, the use of definite and indefinite articles as such becomes problematic: any open system situated within an open system tends to include its entire environment and become identical with the system which includes it, so every indefinite article tends toward the definite. The term *system* also becomes problematic in the case of open versus closed systems: open systems are both ordered and chaotic with a tendency toward more order, while closed systems are the same with a tendency toward more chaos. Any unit within a closed system, therefore, tends toward chaos, but since the same unit is also included in the open system containing that closed system, it also tends toward order.

The paradoxical nature of the definitions of open and closed thermodynamic systems can only be resolved by the observation that no singular system can be solely open or closed. Any system is both open (from the point of view of the systems that are included within it) and closed (from the point of view of its externality). The only absolutely open system is the infinite universe, but then this entity is not observable or definable as such; it can only be hypothesized, with no possibility of verification. In the same vein, in order for us to be able to conceptualize a perfectly closed system, it is necessary to hypothesize an indivisible entity—no longer the atom, but any sub-atomic particle which is supposed to be indivisible. Any given system, then, is governed by the laws of entropy and syntropy alike, but with each containing conflicting tendencies toward indivisibility (which is infinitely entropic) and all-inclusivity (which is infinitely syntropic).

This is a possible thermodynamic re-reading of Freud's life and death instincts: every living organism situated within a closed system, for example, *here and now*, is mortal and transitory; but since these organisms are also a part of a larger system tending toward more order (that is, a more complex organization of living matter), they are also immortal and eternal. Since such an organism is in less mediated contact with the immediate closed system that includes it, it will surely die in time. But it also includes an immortal kernel that is related to the larger (and in the ultimate instance, infinite) system that includes itself and its immediate closed environment both, and so it is also eternal. The death instinct is the bodily expression of the first, immediate relationship; it is, however, related to the reproductive instinct, because the death of the single, individual organism should leave a residue (offspring) to the immediate environment which is longer-lived than itself. The life instinct, on the other hand, is related to the second, mediated relationship; it strives to duplicate or mimic the immortality it represents vis-à-vis the closed, immediate system, so it is related to the sexual drive which has no relation with reproduction but rather with individual enhancement via conjoining with and then separating from other individuals.

This understanding is already implicit in many mystical and pantheistic modes of thinking, most (but not all) of them Oriental, since the Western and rationalistic modes of thinking tend to operate only within closed systems and disregard the idea of open systems, dumping all these ideas in an all-inclusive, amorphous, and therefore chaotic concept of progress. Oriental modes of thinking, however, as represented in Daoism, Zen and *Tasavvuf*, do not operate within this chaotic concept of progress (nor with the teleological concept of an other world, of Heaven or Hell) but always hypothesize an open-ended, immortal, eternal existence beyond the limits set by language itself. Rather than trying to define this existence (which would re-route them into the traps of language), they seek to find its seeds within this closed, transitory and mortal existence, with death being the moment of truth, of both the discovery and the loss of these seeds, as suggested by P. B. Shelley in the fifty-second stanza of *Adonais*:

> The One remains, the Many change and pass
> Heaven's light forever shines, Earth's shadows fly
> Life like a dome of many-coloured glass
> Stains the white radiance of Eternity
> Until Death tramples it to fragments.

7.

Boredom, Orgasm and the Not-All/Whole

All of me, why not take all of me
Can't you see, I'm no good without you
Take my lips, I want to lose them
Take my arms, I'll never use them
Your goodbye left me with eyes that cry
How can I go on dear without you?
You took the part that once was my heart
So why not take all of me?

—"All of Me"
Gerald Marks and Seymour Simons

ANYBODY WITH AT LEAST some interest in and acquaintance with jazz will remember the song "All of Me," most probably as sung by Billie Holiday, or by Ella Fitzgerald some time later. There is another famous version (among the more than thousand) by Frank Sinatra, but it is not what comes to mind first, because it does not and *can not* sound as sincere as Holiday's. When we listen to Billie Holiday's "All of Me," we almost instinctually *know* that she is offering something impossible, something she does not have, to somebody who does not want it (although he may ask for it). So, is Billie Holiday insincere? Yes and no. She is insincere in the sense that she mischievously knows that she does not possess *all of her(self)*, and that even if she miraculously had it and willingly offered it, the other party would not know what to do with it (much less how to handle it). This is one of the reasons why Billie's life was spent in unhappiness and misery. She is, however, at the same time profoundly sincere: all her life she desperately yearned for someone who had at least some idea how to handle *all of her*, alas, in vain. Frankie, though, is completely insincere, as we can gather from his voice, that beautiful and hollow voice. He knows he is offering nothing: even if the other party agrees and reaches for him, it will be like something written in the sand. It will be washed away with the first modest wave, and the singer will already be on his way to other false and hollow promises. The woman is always *not-all*. The man is now *all-there*, now he is not, depending on when you look at him.

Boredom as the Search for Perversion

Human sexuality, as distinct from human reproduction, lacks a definite object. This absence of *definiteness*, however, is the precise nature of desire: its cause and object never overlap. Reproduction, on the other hand, which is only loosely connected to desire but operates through instinct, has a definite object. On the subcellular level this can be construed as the compulsion of a single gene (Dawkins's so-called selfish gene) to endlessly repeat and proliferate itself, and, on the more general genetic level, the same thing can be said about the species being compelled to preserve and propagate itself. In either case (each of which being only the expression of the same thing from a different perspective, or rather from the point of view of a different sphere of existence), the mechanism of these compulsions is instinct rather than desire.

The human subject, however, desires. It always knows it desires something but can never be sure of exactly what it is. Desire is always not-one (akin to Lacan's *"pas-tout"* or $\overline{V}$), directed toward that elusive "it," which constantly changes shape and form (color, gender, personality), both non-existent and more than one thing or person at once. Since the lack desire addresses is a lack *within* the subject, nothing from the outside can fill this gap. Any others which become the objects of desire, that is, candidates intended to fill the gap within the subject, almost simultaneously become *abject*, because they constantly trespass the border separating the inside from the outside. Desire can never be contented, but we can observe the *mise-en-scene* of contentment in the sexual behavior of so-called perverts, who, according to Freud, "always know exactly what they want." Since perverts are the ones who cannot, or are not willing to, cope with the non-correspondence of the cause and object of desire, they must constantly stage the act of having found the object so that they can go on "knowing exactly" what they want. In this sense, there is no basic difference between the fetishist who says, "I know exactly what I want for sexual gratification: a shoe," and the gay male who says, "I know exactly what I want for sexual gratification: a man," or the straight male who says, "I know exactly what I want for sexual gratification: a woman." In each case, the object of desire is placed halfway between its two proper loci, non-existence and everything (full presence) at the same time. Everybody who thus categorizes their desire (i.e., all of us) rightly deserves to be called a pervert.

No fetishist, however, is turned on by just any shoe, and no straight women desires just any man. The appointment of an object of desire is not a unilinear act, and it is usually realized in the actual process of looking for that object. As in Žižek's "That is not it!" anecdote,[1] the object of desire is indeed created in the process. That is, it did not exist when the search for it started: the Holy Grail is the quest itself, and as an object it is created during the quest. The case of the Yugoslav soldier is also a very good example of the promotion from abject to love object: candidates for the object of desire are always abject (the pieces of paper which are "not it" bear a distinct resemblance to Sartre's abject piece of paper in *Nausea*), but once one is selected (through a complex process involving numerous variables and unique for every human being) it gives the impression of being the answer to the cause of desire and is then promoted to being a love object. The love object is both the accumulation and the negation, that is, the *Aufhebung* of all hitherto existing objects of desire, which were or had become, every one of them, abject.[2]

The uncertainty of the object of desire is best seen in the state of mind we conventionally call boredom. Boredom is the feeling we get when we are sure we want *something* but don't have a clue about what it is. We are not bored when we actually have *nothing to do*, since it is very easy to invent or create a pastime in such instances. On the contrary, there is an abundance of things to do when we are bored, but because we cannot be sure which of these things will fill the immense emptiness we feel at the time, we cannot make a choice. Boredom, then, is only a glimpse into our primal lack, with a partial awareness (and the constant denial) that nothing will in fact be able to obviate this sense of emptiness.

That boredom is actually a precarious process in which the child is, as it were, both waiting for something and looking for something, in which hope is being secretly negotiated; and in this sense boredom is akin to free-floating attention. In the muffled, sometimes irritable confusion of

---

1   The Yugoslav soldier striving to avoid military service fakes insanity by picking up every bit of paper he sees and saying "That is not it!" until he is indeed considered insane and given his papers of discharge, at which point he says, "That is it!" (Žižek 2009, 180)

2   The well-known Turkish poet Murathan Mungan says in one of his poems ("A Lonesome Opera"), "In you I made a clean copy of all my loves." The clean copy both includes and negates and hence supersedes (in short, sublates or *aufhebt*) all rough drafts.

boredom the child is reaching to a recurrent sense of emptiness out of which his real desire can crystallize. (Phillips 2016, 69)

The relation between boredom and desire can best be observed in the bored behavior of male adolescents. When an adolescent boy is bored, he doesn't know what he wants, but he is sure he wants *something*. This something could be anything, from the most innocent activity, like going to the movies or watching a sitcom, to the most vicious, like beating somebody up or abusing drugs. The rising rate of juvenile delinquency in the late twentieth and early twenty-first centuries is the direct result of the interaction of this boredom with the changing character of the social superego. Žižek's obscene master, unlike the prohibitive master of the nineteenth and early twentieth centuries, compels the adolescent toward excessive enjoyment, which, in this case, directly or indirectly connects itself to violence. Most male adolescents, however, usually still settle for the thing in between innocent and violent acts, that is, masturbation, which is neither very innocent (it is at least frowned upon) nor very vicious (it can almost always be overlooked, even when caught in the act). Because most male adolescents fall into this category of satisfying their desires through this mildly forbidden pastime, adolescence becomes the point in their lives when they decide that desire is indeed sexual and thus directly related to their genitals.

The same is partly but not completely true for female adolescents, who feel the same uncertainty about their desires. They are, however, less easily able to settle for masturbation, because there is no tangible thing to settle upon. If they do settle for masturbation, they are practically substituting pleasure for desire,[3] an act which in itself has the potential for subversion in the long run; if they don't, however, they too remain undecided and frustrated, and this may become a source for conversion neurosis (in the late nineteenth and early twentieth centuries) or a mimicry of the male adolescent (in the late twentieth and early twenty-first centuries).

Orgasm: The Holy Grail of Sexuality

When a human being desires to be touched in a specific place in a specific way, it is never the right place and never the right way: the lack is always left untouched.

---

3   Unlike with the male adolescent, this substitution is less likely to became pathologically obsessive, lacking the singular object to be obsessed about. Female adolescents are, in this sense, closer to "[t]he rallying point for the counterattack against the deployment of sexuality," which "ought not to be sex-desire, but bodies and pleasures." (Foucault 1990, 157)

This is why human sexuality cannot be locus-oriented: it is always related to the whole body, inasmuch as the body is perceived as a whole (that is, barring a psychotic split) and cannot be ascribed to any erogenous zone. What Luce Irigaray says about female sexuality in *This Sex Which Is Not One*[4] should indeed be applicable to all human sexuality: it is always "not-one" in the sense that it lacks a single object; it is always "not it" and many things at the same time. Unfortunately, the difference between sexes is an actuality in this matter: male children, from the moment they discover that the extra piece of flesh they possess gives them a privilege over female children, and even over adult females (including their mothers) become obsessed with it. In adolescence, when they (re)discover masturbation, this obsession becomes fixed in a narcissistic frame. They settle for the poverty of the one (1) instead of the diversity of the many. The same obsession is also possible with female children, but they either become obsessed with the pleasure itself instead of an *object*, or they in fact become obsessed with the thing. Since this thing is not *of their body*, however, not a part of their bodily ego, this obsession is more of a fetishistic nature than a narcissistic one.

When talking or thinking about sex, human beings can usually be sure of one thing they desire, and that is an orgasm—although when they talk about orgasm they usually don't precisely know what they're talking about. When they only have a vague sense of what it is about, they try to quantify and hence objectify it, make scientific studies about it, share it, fake it, overrate and belittle it. Orgasm is not easily defined as an *object*, nor is it precisely an *act*: you cannot orgasm but can only have an orgasm, but you can never keep it. Therefore, it is harder still to confirm that such a thing even exists. For men it is easier to define the orgasm, or rather, *demonstrate* and mistake this demonstration for a definition, because it is usually used as a synonym for ejaculation. The presence of semen is evidence for orgasm, and at the same time it makes faking orgasm much harder for men. For women, on the other hand, no such proof exists; there is only circumstantial evidence in the form of vaginal and uterine contractions and, more rarely, the squirting of fluid from the bladder. There is, however, at least one thing we can never be sure of, which is whether women and men mean the same thing when they say they had an orgasm.

Throughout history, male orgasm has never been a problem, except maybe in Daoist erotic texts, where it is treated as something to be delayed as long as

---

4   "So woman does not have a sex organ? She has at least two of them, but they are not identifiable as ones. Indeed, she has many more. Her sexuality, always at least double, even further: it is plural." (Irigaray 1985, 28)

possible and ultimately to be done away with altogether. Even in this case the question is not about its actuality: the Daoist doctrine seems to be (probably unconsciously) aware of the dispensability of the male animal once it fulfils its species function of providing genetic material, and it proposes the postponement of ejaculation (the giving away of semen) as a way for male longevity and ultimately male immortality. Even in this doctrine, however, male orgasm—that is, a bodily function presupposing the identity of the sexual and reproductive acts, of sexual recreation and procreation—is not problematized.

Female orgasm, on the other hand, has always been problematical because its very existence, or the very acknowledgement of its existence, complicates the supposed identity of sexuality and reproduction, an identity on which the entire system of male/father domination is based. Female orgasm has never been related to reproduction since it by no means facilitates fertilization: a woman may or may not conceive regardless of whether she has had an orgasm or not. Even the supposed uterine contractions, which do not occur in every woman who claims to have an orgasm, nor even consistently in the same woman who does have an orgasm, cannot be indicated to have an effect on the probability of conception. This means that the orgasm, as the indicator of sexual pleasure, is always already separated from the reproductive function as regards the female body.

Once the basic difference between the male orgasm and female orgasm is established, that is, once we acknowledge that the former is inseparably linked to the reproductive function while the latter has nothing to do with it, the first question to be addressed becomes why we are unreasonably, almost hysterically, insistent on using the same name for two fundamentally different bodily functions.

The first possible answer seems to be that we are trying to contain, determine and delimit female sexuality within the male sexual/reproductive function by ignoring the basic difference(s) between the two sexualities, all for the purpose of maintaining male domination. If male and female orgasms are one and the same thing, women are again assigned to submissiveness, because most of them do not even manage to have an orgasm most of the time. Although they seem to be taking the female side in the sense that they establish a basic inequality and hence an injustice between sexes as regards sexual pleasure, the studies on female sexuality, from Kinsey in the 1950s to Masters and Johnson in the 1960s, only reaffirm the concept of the female as a kind of faulty, incomplete male. Shere Hite's study of female sexuality in 1974 (*The Hite Report on Female Sexuality*) and its emphasis on the clitoris and female masturbation seems to somewhat change this tendency toward inclusion. However, none of these studies base their arguments on the basic differentiation between sexuality and reproduction. Freud, who had failed to make this differentiation in both his early writings and his later metapsychological studies, could only comprehend female orgasm as a by-product of the reproduction process, branding "clitoral" orgasm "infantile," i.e., pre-reproductive:

> First of all, there can be no doubt that the bisexuality, which is present, as we believe, in the innate disposition of human beings, comes to the fore much more clearly in women than in men. A man, after all, has only one leading sexual zone, one sexual organ, whereas a woman has two: the vagina—the female organ proper—and the clitoris, which is analogous to the male organ. We believe we are justified in assuming that for many years the vagina is virtually non-existent and possibly does not produce sensations until puberty. It is true that recently an increasing number of observers report that vaginal impulses are present even in these early years. In women, therefore, the main genital occurrences of childhood must take place in relation to the clitoris. Their sexual life is regularly divided into two phases, of which the first has a masculine character, while only the second is specifically feminine. Thus in female development there is a process of transition from the one phase to the other, to which there is nothing analogous in the male. A further complication arises from the fact that the clitoris, with its virile character, continues to function in later female sexual life in a manner which is very variable and which is certainly not yet satisfactorily understood. We do not, of course, know the biological basis of these peculiarities in women; and still less are we able to assign them any teleological purpose. (Freud 2010, 4592)

As in the case of instincts we have argued earlier, Freud once again concludes his argument (here about female sexuality) on a note of uncertainty, employing the modest Enlightenment attitude[5] of "we do not know enough—yet." For him, the clitoral focus of pleasure in women is both infantile and masculine, but he admits that he fails to explain the fact that the clitoris remains a focus for pleasure in adult women. He would probably have been very much surprised by the

---

5   I use the term *modest Enlightenment attitude* in contrast with *arrogant Enlightenment attitude*, the latter of which denotes overgeneralization, conjecture, and inability to admit ignorance, even temporarily.

findings of Kinsey, Masters and Johnson and, finally, Shere Hite, which all con-
clude that the clitoris not only remains a focal point for pleasure but that it does so
for *more* women than those who "matured" into the "femininity" of vaginal orgasm.

Apart from the fact that Freud does not make the distinction between
sexuality and reproduction, which is understandable given the sociosexual circumstances of his time, he also fails to acknowledge the true significance of the
clitoris, since he regards it an "atrophied penis" (Freud 2010, 4674). According to
Luce Irigaray,

> In these terms, woman's erogenous zones never amount to anything
> but a clitoris-sex that is not comparable to the noble phallic organ,
> or a hole-envelope that serves to sheathe and massage the penis in
> intercourse: a non-sex, or a masculine organ turned back upon itself,
> self-embracing. (Irigaray 1985, 23)

The definition of the clitoris as an atrophied penis creates an evolutionary
paradox because it implies that all species with a male penis also had a female one
which has atrophied during the course of evolution. This is a Lamarckian rather
than Darwinian hypothesis and far from being the case. The clitoris is a fairly new
organ to evolution, only found in higher mammals, and it does not at all show
any indication of atrophying. Quite on the contrary, it seems to be developing
and gaining function. As early as 1954 this unique significance of the clitoris was
acknowledged by some researchers:

> Most significant of all, however, are histological studies in females of
> the sensory cells known as the genital corpuscles, which "are highly
> specialized end-organs for the perception of this particular sensation
> (i.e. orgasm) just as the retina is adapted for the sense of sight and the
> neuro-epithelium of the nose is adapted for the sense of smell" [Kelly,
> G. L. Sex *Manual* (ed. 5). Augusta, Georgia, Southern Medical Supply
> Co., 1950, pp. 30 et seq.]. These histological studies indicate that gen-
> ital corpuscles do not occur in the vaginal mucosa and are confined
> predominantly to the *glans clitoridis* (*ibid*). Some are also found in the
> areas directly adjacent to the clitoris, notably the *labia minora*. (Mar-
> mor 1956, 241)

And further;

The meaning of these findings is that the chief sensory area for erogenous sensation in women is localized in the *glans clitoridis*, just as in men it is localized in the homologous *glans penis*. (The shaft of the penis, like the vagina, is lacking in genital corpuscles.) (Marmor, 241)

As we can see, the clitoris is not an analog of the penis itself but only of the *penis gland*, and in that sense it is not inferior to its analog but, because it has developed into an independent organ in itself whereas the penis gland remains only an adjunct of the penis, much superior.

We find a supposedly fully developed (that is, penis-like) clitoris in some female canines (the spotted hyena to be precise); but this clitoris, just like the penis, is attached to the urinary tract and the reproductive organ(s), and in this sense it is the only true analog of the penis in the entire animal kingdom. The clitoris as we know it becomes an independent organ as soon as it is separated from the urinary tract and the reproductive organ(s), and, not surprisingly, the higher primates are the first animals on the evolutionary ladder to possess an independent and fully developed and functional clitoris. It is only based on the existence of such a clitoris that the bonobos, as almost-human primates, were able to "invent" face-to-face copulation. With the sole exception of the bonobos (and of course *Homo sapiens sapiens*), mammals copulate using so-called doggy-style, which does not physically involve the clitoris in the reproductive act, thus distancing it from, or not fully involving it in, the sexual.

Once we stop considering the clitoris as an atrophied and much smaller, dysfunctional penis, a kind of cute but impotent little sister, so to speak, we can glimpse into the unique significance of the female orgasm. Female orgasm, just like the clitoris, is purely for pleasure itself. It is not in any way linked to an instinctual function and has no place in the biologically rooted (i.e., pre-symbolic) reproduction process. Therefore, female orgasm and male orgasm have very little in common, almost nothing but their name. One is multiple, goal- and center-free, and not linked to the moment, the other is goal- and moment-oriented, singular and final. Human sexuality, having been incrementally divorced from the reproductive act beginning with the higher primates, is not object-oriented; male sexuality, on the other hand, not yet rid of its biological and anatomic ties with reproduction, still seeks a central object to build its desire around. The only object to be found in this respect is of the male body, the locus of the yet unbroken tie with reproduction, namely the penis. Therefore, male desire can only turn on itself, on its sole center of pleasure, becoming exclusively masturbatory and ending in a closure.

The Not-All of Female Sexuality

There are numerous instances where female sexuality looks and sounds like male sexuality and, although in many fewer instances, vice versa. This is because female sexuality is not solely biological; it is a symbolic construction. Symbolic structures, however, do not rise up from the mind like Athena from Zeus's head; they have roots in biology and anthropology among other things. Sexuality, then, is a symbolic construction built upon a biological difference throughout the immensely slow formation of what we call culture, intertwined with it, inseparable from it and in its turn also shaping it. The historical positioning of sexuality within culture has taken the form of what we call male domination, and it is the contention of most of us that this is the source of much injustice, corruption and wasting of physical and psychical potential.

As long as a symbolic structure functions in actuality—however irrational, unjust, corrupt, and exploitative it may seem—its roots remain unquestioned because the material circumstances for its transformation are not yet symbolized: "Mankind always sets itself only such tasks as it can solve; looking at the matter more closely, it will always be found that the task itself arises only when the material conditions for its solution already exist or are at least in the process of formation" (Marx 1968, 183). However, once that structure ceases to function, or once it gives definite signals that it will in the near future cease to function—that is, in Foucault's terms, once "words and things do not hold together"—we must go back to the roots and perform an archaeological operation in order to discover the potentialities for change, hopefully for the better.

The change for the better in our case is not a utopia of glorious female sexuality as the ideal locus for all of us. To continue with Foucault, the utopian urge, in cases when words and things do not hold together, can only offer consolation: in such cases we have to turn to "heterotopias," to "the other loci" (plural) rather than the "non-existent good locus" (singular):

> Utopias afford consolation... Heterotopias are disturbing, probably because they secretly undermine language, because they make it impossible to name this and that, because they shatter or tangle common names, because they destroy "syntax" in advance, and not only the syntax with which we construct sentences but also that less apparent syntax which causes words and things (next to and also opposite one another) to "hold together." (Foucault 1970, xviii)

We have tried to establish that male sexuality is biologically linked to the reproductive (and therefore death) instinct, whereas female sexuality is not necessarily so (even though this is only so as a potential). The female body is bio-logically capable of experiencing sex as distinct from the reproductive act; even when there is no possibility of reproduction, as with homosexual sex and planned birth control, the male body can only experience it as a by-product of what is usually a futile reproductive act. Of course, male domination has shaped female sexuality in its own image for thousands of years, not allowing its potentiality to be fully (or even noticeably partly) actualized. But now that biological-genetic technology provides the means to separate the last threads connecting reproduc-tion to sex—that is, to the pursuit of pleasure for its own sake—and now that "the material conditions for [the] solution [to the problem of the predominance of the phallus] already exist or are at least in the process of formation," we can set ourselves the task of solving this problem.

The potential solution we can turn to is inherent in feminine sexuality but does not solely consist of it. Of course, feminine sexuality itself is inseminated (metaphor intended) by the leftovers, crossovers and even basic structures of male sexuality, and, in order to carry out its subversive function, it should purge itself of these things through a conscious, intentional act. This is no mean feat because these structures have not merely passed into the female sexual sphere as a result of naked coercive power or simple ideology (as false consciousness, so to speak): it is language itself that facilitates this takeover, and if there is going to be a change, it will involve a change in the entire symbolic order. The problem is that women, lesbians, transvestites and transgender people, as the apparent subalterns of a male/father-dominant order, cannot do it alone and entrenched in their sepa-rate identities. This is not because they are inherently unable or unwilling to do so but because the delimited identities of woman, lesbian, transvestite, transgender (or whatever you like) are necessarily exclusive *qua* identities and thus predicate their existence on the presence of a mutually exclusive other. They cannot create "their own language," as Irigaray would have it, because once they accept the ini-tial subaltern position vis-à-vis the symbolic order, the male-dominated language, they are "unable to speak" (Spivak), nor can they be content with simply exclud-ing male sexuality, since it is always already inside as the Other (in this case the dominant or big Other), as the predominant constitutive element.

In order to seek a radical transformation rather than merely being transgres-sive, we should rather let it in to let it out; allow the penis in in order to let the phallus out. This implies the acceptance of the penis not as the sign of the male one (1) but as one of the many parts of the body, thus stripping it of its central position and its surplus meaning as the imaginary residing place of the phallus and demoting it to its original and actual position—an organ like any other which can be used for urination and an erogenous zone consisting of a concentration of sensitive nerve-endings. Some people have it and some don't, just like a clitoris and breasts, or, more accurately, a sixth finger, and its existence or non-existence should not have any hierarchical effect on human relations. One may choose to remove it surgically or obtain one surgically or artificially, but its presence and function will no longer be a determining factor in the formation of our language and our psyche. In other words, we should take the penis away from the phallus so that it will not have a material leg to stand on and its merely symbolic character would become apparent. Once it ceases to be the leg that the phallus, the central signifier of the existing symbolic order, stands on, what is the penis other than an oversized, clumsy clitoris, anyway?

This act of going over to the sphere of female sexuality, regardless of biological sex, seems to be an act of ultimate transgression in the sense that it not only subverts but also cancels out one of the most important dualities our civilization stands on, but in actuality it is not. For an act to be transgressive, you must have a desire along with certain limits imposed upon it by an other. To transgress is to reach for the other (the *objet petit a*), going over the limits of the other (the Name-of-the-Father). In the present case, the going over is not the result of a desire for an object but rather an urge to *become* that object, akin to the "transgression" of *straight* male-to-female transvestites who both desire the female body and at the same time want to share in the female performance. This is a two-way transgression, threatening the *reality* of male-female and straight-gay performative dichotomies while itself remaining within the same binary structure and usually retaining its most conservative elements. This is why straight male-to-female transvestitism is the least tolerable transgender act within the existing symbolic order, often treated either as an abomination or as pure performance. Most straight male-to-female transvestites are thus forced into prostitution, with a very (lucky?) few forced onto the stage. To be sure, this does not mean that such transvestitism represents an actual *Aufhebung* in the Hegelian sense. Rather, it is the overlapping of desire and identification, of wanting to have and wanting to become, that *shows us* the way out of the existing deadlock of multiple (and rapidly increasing) gender *identities*—but which cannot go there itself. A revolutionary transgression, on the other hand, would strip these gender *identities* of their identificatory character and leave them as merely genders, which can be as many as there are people with desires.

In actuality, transgression is very rarely revolutionary. It assumes a desire (for enjoyment) and an intervening agent, most likely the Name-of-the-Father, blocking realization of the desire. But as Žižek has pointed out, this is not usually the case: our problem today is with the obscene master, who makes enjoyment itself a must (*Enjoy Coke!* as a command). When the Name-of-the-Father invades the sphere of enjoyment and takes it into its domain, there emerges a possibility that refusing to enjoy becomes the really transgressive, or rather revolutionary, act; for example, giving up a compulsory, momentary desire for the sake of friendship, the cause, the nation or humanity may actually be revolutionary. It is only when this giving up becomes permanent or institutionalized that it becomes an act of the superego. But imagine if the compulsion behind the momentary desire was the work of the obscene master himself. What if the moment of transgression was missed long ago when this compulsion was accepted as something genuine coming from within? Judith Butler indicates a moment when transvestitism ceases to be transgressive, starts to bifurcate and partially reproduces the hitherto existing performances when she says, "Parody by itself is not subversive, and there must be a way to understand what makes certain kinds of parodic repetitions effectively disruptive, truly troubling, and which repetitions become domesticated and recirculated as instruments of cultural hegemony" (Butler 1999, 177). The transvestite then becomes a slave to the obscene master, and the transvestite act only serves to re-emphasize the limit rather than blurring or subverting it. "Control your desire!" Lacan had said. Not in the name of the father, not in order to secure a place in the gaze of the father, but in order to gain insight into it, to deconstruct it (in order to reconstruct it later), to reflect upon the subject who is presumed to desire that desire. Victorian morality had a point: don't be a slave to your desire. To this directive we can now add: because it may not be yours.

In order to begin acting against the central significance of the penis in male sexuality (as the agent of the reproductive act) on the one hand and against the central significance of the phallus in the symbolic order (as the signifier of an omnipresent lack) on the other, we will have to move from transgression to cancellation.

Irigaray's positing of the not-one against the phallic one was an act of conceptualization rather than subversion: she was either restating the obvious or presenting us with yet another dichotomy.[6] In order to conceptualize a multifocal

---

6   Although she is the first person to familiarize us with the concept of "not-one" (Irigaray 1985), Irigaray stops short of dialectically transcending the male/female dichotomy. Rather than direct-

language, one which is structurally polyglot and not constructed around a single, omnipotent master signifier, it is not enough to simply posit an alternative locus for it to exist in alongside the existing symbolic order. In order to be liberated from the 1, the phallic signifier must itself be cancelled out and *dispersed*, so to speak. To be sure, the act of cancellation we refer to here is in itself a phallic act, the bar crossing the 1 being another phallic sign. Since the phallus is a signifier and not something tangible residing in a Winter Palace or *Hôtel de Ville* (or in a single penis), the act of cancellation must be carried out in the realm of signification, in the realm of language—that is, discursively (at least in the beginning). This act may appear to be a fight between two phallic acts struggling for domination, and from a certain perspective it indeed is. In another sense, however, it also represents an attempt to go beyond the phallic, crossing over to the non-phallic.

By creating two apparent paradoxes and resolving them, Lacan's formulae for sexuation will be of great help for getting over this seemingly paradoxical situation. His contradicting statements that both $\forall x \Phi x$ and $\exists x \overline{\Phi x}$ ("All men are subject to the phallic function. There is at least one man who is not subject to the phallic function") can only be understood as positing the existence of a single (phantasmatic) male figure (the primordial, seminal father, Ouranos/Kronos, so to speak) who single-handedly creates the entire symbolic order in which all men are subject to the phallic function. This primordial father becomes the perpetrator of what we call civilization, not by his existence, his acts and his laws, but only by his giving birth to the first really civilized act: patricide. Rather than being an objective account of what happened in history, this is a tale Freud tells us in *Totem and Taboo*, which he concocted by combining mythological narratives with anthropological and present-day psychic facts (Freud 2010f, 2782). In this tale, the primal father stands as a figure which is responsible for, but not subject to, the entire symbolic order. He is the lawmaker who is not subject to his own laws, and therefore the order he upholds cannot yet be called civilization: it barely differs from the order established by alpha male gorillas or orangutans. On the contrary, it is the revolt of the brothers which follows that sets what we call civilization into motion. In the act of killing and devouring the father, they both retain and supersede this primordial order; the Name-of-the-Father is still there, devoured and hence internalized by the brothers, becoming the kernel of male-domination, but now each perpetrator of the *nouveau régime* is subject to

---

ly addressing non-straight sexuality, which always already entails the potential for a subversion of the concept of the phallus as the sole facilitator of love or sexuality, she seeks to find ways to restructure the not-one within what Judith Butler will call the heterosexual matrix. (Butler 1999)

their own law, that is, to the phallic function. All the same, each of them carries inside a part of the primal father who was not subject to this law, to the phallic function. This is how what seems like a Lacanian paradox makes sense through the re-reading of a Freudian tale.

If, however, we take the Xs to signify not persons but acts, the formulae can thus be read as: "All male acts are subject to the phallic function. There exists at least one male act that is not subject to the phallic function." Just like the one exception which set the whole symbolic order in motion, this rendering of the formulae gives us an exception which will radically transform or sublate it. The brothers, in the act of revolting against, killing and devouring the father, were for a fleeting moment not subject to the phallic function, although in the end they re-established the function with a twist: a system of checks and balances and a dispersed state. To be sure, this new order is not for the sisters and wives but only for the brothers; nor does it allow for any freedom for children, the (physically and/or psychically) sick or the old. It is a democratic order providing equality and fraternity based on a particular definition of the *demos* as the community of mature, productive males, providing for *their* equality, and *their* fraternity. Classical Athenian democracy (which is the predecessor of the existing Western white, straight, male order on a global scale) is only a variation of this primal order, including non-Greek-speaking adult males outside the democratic community as slaves. Although we can be as critical as we want about this democratic system, the passage to this new order nevertheless represents a moment when a crack in the symbolic order and the phallic/castrating function becomes apparent, allowing for the reshuffling of existing signifiers and corresponding upheaval in the existing state of affairs.

The attempt to bar the 1 and cross out the phallic signifier will represent another such moment, when a similar crack in the symbolic order will appear and another reshuffling of existing signifiers will take place. This sublation can only take the form of a crossing over to the female side of Lacan's equation, $\overline{\exists x \Phi x}$ *and* $\overline{\forall x \Phi x}$: "There does not exist any woman who is not subject to the phallic function," and "Not-all (of) woma/en is/are subject to the phallic function," to which Lacan himself has already allowed passage for any speaking being:

> Opposite, you have the inscription of the woman share of speaking beings. It is expressly stated in Freudian theory, that all speaking beings, whoever they be and whether or not they are provided with the attributes of masculinity—attributes which have yet to be

determined—are allowed to inscribe themselves on this side. (Lacan 1985, 150)

Although at first sight the female side of the equation seems to be constructed on the same paradox as the male side, the resolution of the paradox must be through another means, since there is no corresponding mythic tale for women.[7] Of course, we may remind ourselves of the fertility goddesses of all sorts here, but these goddesses are not exempt from the phallic function: they are either antecedent to the male-dominant (symbolic) order, in which case there will be no exemption, or they exist within it as remnants of the primordial earth-mother, this time submitting to the phallus either completely (Gaea, who can only rebel against male dominance in order to save her sons, or Hera, who is resigned to the position of the jealous wife) or at least partially (Kybele, who as universal mother submits to the primal division of labor between men and women).

The resolution to this apparent paradox is the acknowledgement of a pre-symbolic kernel in each woman, a kernel which is also present in male infants but is most of the time nearly annihilated in the process of growing up, of becoming men—that is, in securing them a place in the symbolic order which designates them as masters. Female infants, on the other hand, also grow up into the symbolic order, but the place reserved for them in this order is that of a knave. In both cases they lose the exclusively pre-symbolic mental faculties they have as infants, however, in the process of growing up the female infant keeps a part of this infantile or pre-symbolic faculty as a hard, impenetrable kernel—so impenetrable that men fail to understand women most of the time and Freud refers to them as the "dark continent," an unmistakable metaphor for the Real. This kernel is usually referred to as the empathic faculty and assigned (by both scientific and popular discourses) to women most of the time.

---

7 There is no corresponding tale of a conspiracy of sisters taking down the father (or, for that matter, the mother) in mythology. Elektra comes close to matricide, but she does it to revenge her father and, regardless, ultimately lets her brother Orestes to do the actual killing, submitting to the phallic order. A conspiracy of sisters does kill and mutilate a king (Pentheus), but the king's mother herself is among the conspirators, and the killing is done in the name of Dionysus, a male god. Lastly, Orpheus was killed in exactly the same way as Pentheus, again in the name of Dionysus.

8.

The Empathic
and the Semiotic

Two additional qualifications are in order. First, distinct levels of processing—mind, conscious mind, and conscious mind capable of producing culture—emerged in sequence. That should not leave the impression, however, that when minds acquired selves, they stopped evolving as minds or that selves eventually stopped evolving. On the contrary, the evolutionary process continued (and continues), possibly enriched and accelerated by the pressures created by self-knowledge, and there is no end in sight. The ongoing digital revolution, the globalization of cultural information, and the coming of the age of empathy are pressures likely to lead to structural modifications of mind and self, by which I mean modifications of the very brain processes that shape the mind and self.

—Antonio Damasio
Self Comes to Mind

ASIDE FROM BEING THE root of one of the most important human traits, compassion,[1] empathy is also what makes communication between pre-linguistic infants and their caregivers (mostly their mothers) possible. Every infant loses this faculty, if not entirely then to a large extent, as it is co-opted into the symbolic order, that is, as it learns language. Female children, however, need to retain this faculty at least partially, since they themselves are supposed to become mothers at a future date and will need it for communication with their own infants. A contemporary trend in neuroscience tentatively assigns the empathic faculty to the existence of mirror neurons, or the *mirror network* in the brain, which make *mimesis* (both in

---

1   On closer inspection, we will discover that *empathy* and *compassion* come from Greek and Latin versions of the same basic root, παθοσ and *passio*, that is, "strong feeling," sometimes even "pain" or "agony," with the prefixes both pointing to sharing.

the sense of mimicry and representation) possible and are, not surprisingly, to be found in greater abundance in women.

Empathic Women vs. Rational Men? No Way!

This observation can be interpreted with two different and mostly conflicting frames of reference, one from an *essentialist* and the other from an *evolutionary* point of view. The essentialist interpretation begins with the observation and treats as an essential quality the abundance of mirror neurons in women, proceeding to build upon this supposedly essential difference all manner of cognitive and behavioristic assumptions that separate men from women. The social division of labor, therefore, becomes the direct outcome of this biological axiom based on the fact that childcare is historically assigned to women, which in turn becomes the "scientific explanation"—that is, the excuse—for male domination. Marx and Engels had suggested, as we have already noted, that the division of labor (first "natural" and eventually "social") is identical with private property and institutionalizes a family structure in which the "wife and children are the slaves of the husband" (Marx and Engels 2010c, 46).

The "natural division of labour in the family" seems to be, first and foremost, a division based on bearing and caring for children, even before the division between hunting (mostly male) and gathering (mostly female) came into being. Anthropologist and evolutionary biologist Jared Diamond argues that:

> Men are much better able than women to track and kill big animals, for the obvious reasons that men don't have to carry infants around to nurse them and that men are on the average more muscular than women. In the view of anthropologists, men hunt in order to provide meat to their wives and children. [...]
>
> Meat provisioning by traditional hunters is considered a distinctive function of human males, shared with only a few of our fellow mammal species such as wolves and African hunting dogs. It is commonly assumed to be linked to other universal features of human societies that distinguish us from our fellow mammals. In particular, it is linked to the fact that men and women remain associated in nuclear families after copulation, and that human children (unlike young apes) remain unable to obtain their own food for many years after weaning. (Diamond 1997, 92–93)

However, he adds, this is a view accepted too hastily by anthropologists. He then directs our attention to a study by Kristen Hawkes among Paraguay's Northern Ache Indians (he also points out that it was significant that this study was made by a *woman*):

> An Ache man's hunting bag varies greatly from day to day: he brings home food enough for many people if he kills a peccary or finds a beehive, but he gets nothing at all on one-quarter of the days he spends hunting. In contrast, women's returns are predictable and vary little from day to day because palms are abundant; how much starch a woman gets is mainly a function of just how much time she spends pounding it. A woman can always count on getting enough for herself and her children, but she can never reap a bonanza big enough to feed many others. (Diamond 1997, 94)

This means that even in the early hunter-gatherer communities, women were potentially able to procure sufficient food, although they were also caring for children almost full-time. Men were not fathers in the contemporary sense of the term, and they shared the spoils of their hunt with the community not for the greater good but for power (he who controls the main *protein* supply controls the community) and the increased opportunity to seduce other women (the bond of monogamy being much looser at the time), and hence better guarantee their genetic continuity.

> Thus, it is not the case that men hunters and women gatherers constitute a division of labor whereby the nuclear family as a unit most effectively promotes its joint interests, and whereby the work force is selectively deployed for the good of the group. Instead, the hunter-gatherer lifestyle involves a classic conflict of interest. (Diamond 1997, 100)

This last observation clinches the case against the naturality of the social division of labor and for Marx's argument that class struggle and private property were already implicit in the primitive family structure itself.

A recent dig in the Andes found a female body buried along with implements associated with hunting, and this has caused a flood of celebration (perhaps slightly exaggerated) in the popular scientific community (Haas 2020).

The anthropological study itself (Haas et al. 2020) points out the existence of female hunters in pre-Neolithic hunter-gatherer communities and warns against gender-specific prejudices (*Males hunt, females gather*). One swallow, however, does not a summer make. There were female physicians in Ancient Egypt and Greece, but this fact does not change the general rule that medicine in these societies was fundamentally a male occupation. This and similar finds do indicate that the gender-based division of labor is not set in stone and that gender roles almost immediately preceding the Neolithic age were in fact fluid and definitely not as strict as proponents of women's natural subordination would have us believe. It demonstrates that women without children (due to natural causes or perhaps by choice) could participate in the hunt.

This recent revelation, however, is more significant for the imagining of the future than for trying to rewrite the past: the natural/biological foundation of the gender-based division of labor remains basically intact. Women were biologically assigned to childcare, not only because the patriarchal order coerced them to be but also because the males lacked the necessary biological and instinctual compulsion to care for the young, and the males' assumption of this role would have ended their genetic line, as it had most likely already done in communities which no longer exist. This means that females who did undertake this function and limited their habitat to the home and its immediate surroundings could not have participated in the hunt *en masse*. They would, however, still have been primary food providers for the community in addition to their role as primary caregivers for children, since hunting is a capricious activity, affected by even minor changes in the climate and the ecosystem. One species of prey changes its migration route, and lo and behold, you are without meat for years while the entire community depends on women's gathering for survival. Thus, rather than trying to invalidate the hitherto imagined basic structure of pre-Neolithic communities, it would be better to imagine a future in which women will not be coercively assigned to childcare and therefore to the home, instead sharing in the productive and creative activities of the community as equals. True, at a certain point in history this was less likely, if still possible; but with the recent technologies in fertilization and fetal development as well as the many cultural factors that make it possible and desirable for women to seek life paths other than merely being mothers and homemakers, this is more than possible and increasingly likely. Women are not empathic *by nature*: they became so at a definite period in history, or rather, they retained this faculty while men lost it, and they now have the potentiality to also master the semiotic sphere, that is, language, under today's circumstances without losing their access to the empathic. Likewise, men only lost their connection to the empathic at a definite point in history, a price they paid as they developed a symbolic order, a language. Again, under today's circumstances they can reconnect with the empathic to escape the prison that language became for them, not sacrificing but enhancing it by this reconnection.

If we proceed a little further forward in history, we find that the *coerced* monogamy of women is only a recent (that is, Neolithic) development, and hence what we know as so-called fatherhood is also a recent position. In the absence of fatherhood, childcare *naturally* becomes the lot of women. However, the historical fact, which is that it led to the subjection of women to the patriarchal order, is *not* a natural outcome but a *social* one already determined by relations of power. The so-called evolutionary (but in fact essentialist) interpretation, which treats this difference itself as a natural outcome, therefore only tries to justify the subservient role assigned to women in the *social* division of labor, something particular to human communities.

Distinct from other mammalian infants, the human infant is born helpless. It is true that as we go up the evolutionary ladder, the time needed for neural maturation (sensory and motor, not to mention the higher mental functions) increases, and in human beings this maturation period reaches such a length as to render the human infant completely helpless and dependent ("motor incapacity and nursling dependence") in its first two to three years. Lacan points out that:

> This jubilant assumption of his specular image by the child at the *infans* stage, still sunk in his motor incapacity and nursling dependence, would seem to exhibit in an exemplary situation the symbolic matrix in which the *I* is precipitated in a primordial form, before it is objectified in the dialectic of identification with the other, and before language restores to it, in the universal, its function as subject. (Lacan 1997, 2)

This dependency is almost always on the genetic mother who is the primary caregiver (as in most mammalians), and it requires an instinctual counterpart, often referred to as the maternal instinct. As long as there is no language, that is, insofar as we are operating outside the symbolic, human sphere, this does not lead to a discernible social and/or hierarchic discrimination between the male and female members of the species. The females have their instincts, the males have theirs, and that does not lead to any significant differentiation beyond the instinctual realm. With the advent of language, however, it all starts to change:

language—that is, the symbolic order—is structured around a lack and, unlike empathetic communication which seeks unity, strives for an impossible fulfilment, the fantastic repossession of something which was never there. This inane but endless search starts to waste a great amount of libidinal energy, spending it for the obscure purposes of desires. As a result, the maternal instinct, the overpowering, single-minded urge of females to "mother" whenever they have young, is constantly challenged by desire; they seem to have other needs which compete with this primal instinct. They thus start to lose their empathic abilities, because language tends to expand and invade the ground formerly occupied by empathy in almost all matters of intraspecies communication. This, in fact, is the exact point where an evolutionary Y junction presents itself.

If women follow men's lead and give up their empathic ability altogether, or, in other words, if empathic communication is repressed by the semiotic so as to make the former practically impossible, the empathic bond between mother and infant, which is an important part of the child's maturation process, also breaks down. Although both language and empathic communication are rooted in the same mirror network within the entire neural structure, language tends to expand and invade the ground formerly occupied by empathy in almost all matters of intraspecies communication, and in one sense cannibalizes its twin. As a result, the young do not get the required care and do not carry their mothers' genes onto the next generation. The genes which actually manage to survive belong to women who to some degree retain the empathic function, allowing them to mother their offspring into maturation. It is not surprising, then, to find that the female genes with a higher chance of survival are the ones which provide for a higher concentration of mirror neurons, neurons which make mimicry of the other(s) and empathy possible. Iacoboni argues that mirror neurons may play a very significant role in mothering:

> The role of mirror neurons in maternal empathy is still largely unknown, although it is probable that these cells are important for this crucial function. [...] In a collaborative project with a group of Italian neuroscientists and psychologists in Rome, I have recently studied the neural responses of moms looking at pictures and imitating the expressions of their own and another baby (whose mother they did not know). The babies are six to twelve months old, and they are expressing joy, distress, and no particular emotion. The data were conclusive: strong responses in mirror neuron areas, in the insula and in limbic

areas. Mothers are highly empathic subjects, and we were pleased to see such robust responses in this circuit, which [...] connects mirror neurons with the emotional brain centers and, in this instance, allows the empathic understanding of the babies' emotional states by virtue of simulating the observed facial expressions. (Iacoboni 2009, 127)

Maybe it is necessary at this point to dwell a little bit more (and speculate rather freely) upon the true nature and function of the so-called mirror neurons: Discovered in 1996 by Giacomo Rizzolatti and his team at the University of Parma, mirror neurons are neurons that "fire up," that is, become activated, while one performs a certain act, as well as while one observes others performing it. These neurons are believed by some in the neuroscientific community to be responsible for mimicry (leading to learning) and empathy (leading to non-symbolic emotional communication). Rizzolatti's initial study was of macaque monkeys, and the neurons he studied were few in number, hence being easy to identify, isolate and observe individually. We should keep in mind, though, that while they've been reinforced on a theoretically more extensive and substantial plane, the set of beliefs triggered by Rizzolatti's work are challenged (if not refuted outright) by the very recent understanding that no specific location or neuron type is solely responsible for any given behavioral characteristic.

This challenge, however, is not limited to a theoretical questioning alone: there is a wide spectrum of critics, ranging from those who call the mirror neurons "a myth" and talk about the "real" neuroscience of communication and cognition (Hickok 2014)—in response to which I lose all interest—to those who very aptly question the sudden, widespread and haphazard popularization of the term *empathy* (Bloom 2016)—with which I can readily "empathize." The argument about the mirror network cannot be easily dismissed as a mere fad, nor is it something to build a whole narrative around. Likewise, when popularized as an expression of "love, kindness and compassion," the term *empathy* loses all of its semantic significance and becomes a part of the recent wave of extra- or pseudo-scientific (and pseudo-mystical) narratives that are starting to dominate this new age of so-called post-truth.

A more reasonable approach asserts that it is rather the *network* of different types of neurons and specialized locations that are responsible for empathy and mimicry. Pro-mirror-neuron studies also relate this network to the anticipation and perception of others' intentions (Iacoboni et al. 2005):

[T]here is a special class of nerve cells called mirror neurons. These neurons fire not only when you perform an action, but also when you watch someone else perform the same action. This sounds so simple that its huge implications are easy to miss. What these cells do is effectively allow you to empathize with the other person and "read" her intentions and figure out what she is really up to. You do this by running a simulation of her actions using your own body image. (Ramachandran 2011, 22)

These neurons are mostly dysfunctional in persons in the autistic spectrum, who "are largely characterised by deficits in imitation, pragmatic language, theory of mind, and empathy" (Oberman et al. 2005, 190–198), and several studies indicate that female subjects show a larger gray matter volume in those areas of the brain chiefly connected with mirror neurons (Cheng et al. 2009, 713–720; Cheng et al. 2006, 1115–1119; and Cheng et al. 2008, 113).[2] This difference, however, should be ascribed to the historical and evolutionary step I commented on above, of men having no viable instinctual compulsion for the care of the young, rather than being attributed to an *essential, immutable* and *absolute* structure—a lesson we should have learned from Stephanie Shields's pathbreaking comments regarding the essentialist interpretation of evolution being "science play[ing] handmaiden to social values" (Shields 1975, 751).

Of course, all of this data only provides us with observable facts (thanks primarily to the rapidly developing technologies of observation and measurement in contemporary cognitive neuroscience) but says little about the whys. Sensible speculation regarding the existence and function of mirror neurons could benefit from Freud's theoretical account of the formation and function of the ego.

The Ego and the "Self"

The ego, Freud maintains, is what holds the (human) mind and body together and separates it from all externality by filtering, interpreting and buffering against external stimuli. If we try to construct an analogy with unicellular organisms, the ego is almost identical with the ectoderm:

---

2   A more popular version of similar findings can be found in Baron-Cohen (2003). Baron-Cohen's approach seems to be essentialist rather than evolutionist, but most of his empirical evidence about the difference itself nevertheless appears to be quite convincing.

Let us picture a living organism in its most simplified possible form as an undifferentiated vesicle of a substance that is susceptible to stimulation. Then the surface turned towards the external world will from its very situation be differentiated and will serve as an organ for receiving stimuli. Indeed embryology, in its capacity as a recapitulation of developmental history, actually shows us that the central nervous system originates from the ectoderm; the grey matter of the cortex remains a derivative of the primitive superficial layer of the organism and may have inherited some of its essential properties. It would be easy to suppose, then, that as a result of the ceaseless impact of external stimuli on the surface of the vesicle, its substance to a certain depth may have become permanently modified, so that excitatory processes run a different course in it from what they run in the deeper layers. A crust would thus be formed which would at last have been so thoroughly "baked through" by stimulation that it would present the most favourable possible conditions for the reception of stimuli and become incapable of any further modification. (Freud 1961, 20)

Freud goes on to argue that this "baked through" portion of the unicellular organism is specialized in protection against stimuli as much as (and even more than) in receiving it:

Protection against stimuli is an almost more important function for the living organism than reception of stimuli. The protective shield is supplied with its own store of energy and must above all endeavour to preserve the special modes of transformation of energy operating in it against the effects threatened by the enormous energies at work in the external world—effects which tend towards a levelling out of them and hence towards destruction. (Freud 1961, 21)

In *The Ego and the Id*, he defines the ego with almost the same terms as he defines the ectoderm:

It is easy to see that the ego is that part of the id which has been modified by the direct influence of the external world through the medium of the Pcpt.-Cs. [Perception- Consciousness]; in a sense it is an extension of the surface-differentiation. Moreover, the ego seems to bring

the influence of the external world to bear upon the id and its tendencies, and endeavours to substitute the reality principle for the pleasure
principle which reigns unrestrictedly in the id. (Freud 1989, 18–19)

The ectoderm in the unicellular organism and the ego in human beings are
both the interface of the self with the external world, filtering, interpreting and
buffering against stimuli, protecting against excess, shaping themselves accordingly in doing so, getting "baked through," to use Freud's metaphor, and becoming
(in human beings) the conveyor between perception and consciousness, including parts from both but identical with neither. The ego, therefore, has nothing
to do with some kind of an "inner self," because it is not internal as such; it is
the broad boundary between the internal and the external, practically *defining* the
internal (and of course, in doing so defining what is *external* as well) but not identical with it:

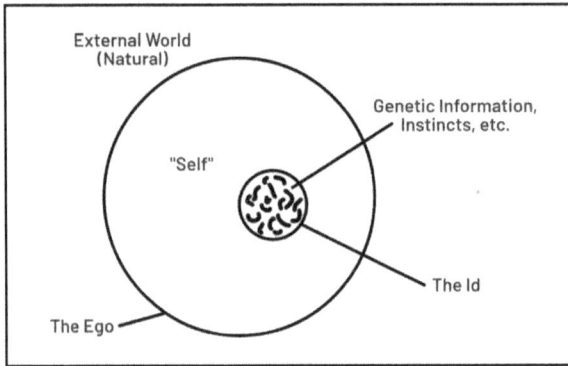

Although the ectoderm is a metaphor for the ego, the *skin* in more complex
organisms is not, since the ego is not simply a surface but only a "projection of
a surface":

The ego is first and foremost a bodily ego; it is not merely a surface
entity, but is itself the projection of a surface. If we wish to find an
anatomical analogy for it we can best identify it with the "cortical
homunculus" of the anatomists, which stands on its head in the cortex,
sticks up its heels, faces backwards and, as we know, has its speech-area
on the left-hand side. (Freud 2010a, 3960)

Going a step further, as the self and the ego develop and come into a more sophisticated intercourse with the external world, that is, as the external world perceived by the self becomes a *social and cultural* (meaning human-made) world as well as a natural one, the outer layer of the ego is baked through a second time to give birth to a more specialized interface, the superego:

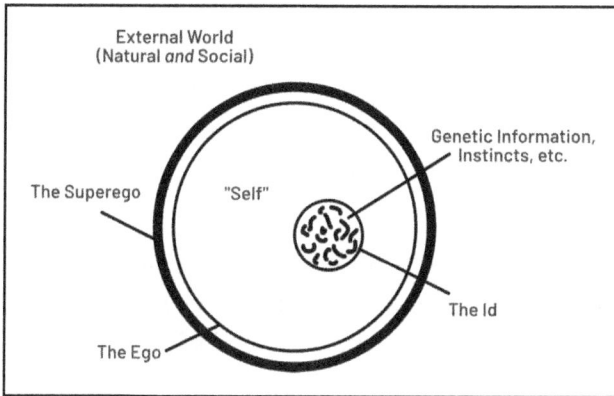

To reiterate the same thing in Lacanian terms, the ego (and its more specialized offspring, the superego) encircles and encapsulates the Symbolic universe and shelters it from the constant threat of invasion by the Real, which encompasses all externality. The Real can only seep into the Symbolic as buffered, filtered and interpreted by the ego and the superego. The superego is the outermost layer of the self, since it is the more baked (this time by the cultural and social externality) outer portion of the ego. The ego and the superego together act as the imaginary mode of the self, endlessly constructing images from perceptions, some of which will then be translated into symbols. There is, however, another Real *inside* the self, the biological, genetic identity representing the species, which cannot be integrated into the Symbolic.[3] This Real is, in turn, encapsulated by the id, which both filters and transmits the life and reproduction instinct of the species which are as alien to the self as externality:

---

3   This is just another way of expressing Jacques-Alain Miller's argument about extimacy: "Exti-macy is not the contrary of intimacy. Extimacy says that the intimate is Other—like a foreign body, a parasite." (Miller)

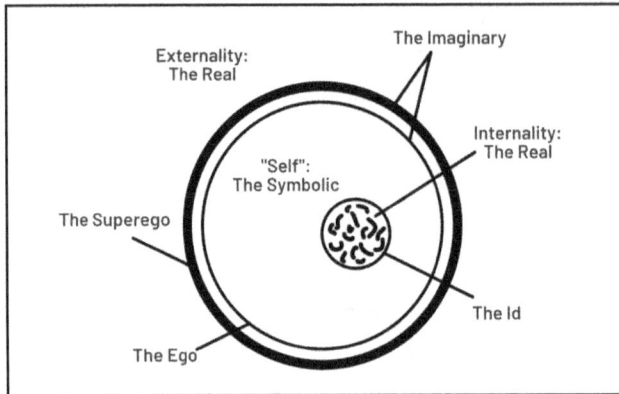

The newborn infant, once thrown from the safety and protection of the uterus, comes face to face with a myriad of stimuli against which it is helpless. The ego begins to form at the moment of birth (actually even earlier, considering that the uterus is also an environment for the fetus) in order to filter out excess stimuli and reduce it to a level manageable for the entire nervous system, itself in the first stages of formation and differentiation. In doing so it (1) limits input from the senses from perception to the conscious level (the pcpt-cs system in Freud's abbreviations) and (2) at a later stage of development puts restrictions on perceived stimuli, filtering out those which do not make sense, lest they challenge the integrity of the symbolic order. In this way we only perceive certain wavelengths of light or sound, and later on we even ignore some stimuli that are within the perceptible spectrum but semantically useless, what we call white noise. We do, however, still perceive these, although they can only be registered on the unconscious level: this is how some sounds beneath the threshold of our hearing spectrum may give us a feeling of terror and how subliminal visual messages can create feelings of thirst or hunger even when we are not originally hungry or thirsty.

The Ego and Language

The ego which senses, filters, buffers against, and interprets the outside world becomes a structure specific to human beings as soon as it starts to ascribe symbols to its interpretations, which then become meanings. Animals, which have a rudimentary ego, do have information about the outside world, and some even pass this information on to other members of their species, but they lack the paradigmatic expanse and the syntagmatic structure to assign meaning to this information. It is only with *speaking beings* that the outside world loses its homogeneity and is divided between an outside world and homologues. For animals, there are no homologues; there are only the members of the same species which they "know" (in the sense of *recognizing, connaître*) through instinct. In order to be able to speak, there must be somebody to be spoken *to* and something to be spoken *about*: speech necessitates a *trinary* structure, which is lacking in animals, who *communicate* to the entire species at once rather than to *other individuals*, beings like them. For language to develop and function, then, it is necessary for the speaking subject to possess what contemporary neuroscientists call a theory of the mind.[4] Once this trinary structure is established, however, human beings (as speaking entities) temporarily lose, if not their individuality, then at least their uniqueness. There are many homologues, beings like themselves wandering about; each one is just one of the many identical entities. In order for them to be able to start speaking, they must admit that they are not unique. And only through the use of speech, through addressing these homologues, is individuality won back again, but this time with a twist. Now this individuality can be *named* (hence determined). That is, there is a *self* in opposition to, first, bodily equivalents (other selves) and only then the external world.

Any language is initially made up of two distinguishable sets of utterances, those of demands and those of prohibitions. An ape (let's say a chimpanzee) "tries to take" by reaching for, and another ape may "refuse to give" by pulling back; in human terms, we demand and we refuse. In the primate world demanding and refusing are not yet *symbolized acts*. We have started with apes (and not animals in general) to understand the acts of *taking* and *giving*. These acts can only become possible with *grabbing*, which again presupposes the existence of a hand, an appendage on the forelimb defined by the existence of an opposable thumb. A feline may take something using its mouth in order to bring it to a more secure place to eat, and give by dropping it, especially when feeding its young, but cannot demand other than through threatening behavior. All of these acts are the direct outcomes of and instinctual responses to a need. In domesticated felines

---

4 The term was first coined by Premack and Woodruff in 1978. It refers to the ability of a subject to empathize with and sense or recognize the intentions of its homologues, identifying them as such. Among other things, it is the ability to ascribe a *mind* (similar to the subject's own) to another being. It can go wrong in opposing directions, for instance, in the assigning of a conscious mind to a non-human primate based on bodily and behavioral similarities or in the unwillingness to do so to *Homo sapiens sapiens* of different races or skin colors based on trivial differences. Admittedly, the term *theory of the mind* is scarcely capable of carrying that much semantic weight, but until somebody discovers or invents a better one (preferably a single-word term [*enskepsia?*]), it is all we have.

and canines especially, we observe these same acts repeated with things which are not edible, a confused instinctual behavior due to their being away from the natural environment in which they can hunt and scavenge.

Already in apes, however, we start to observe demands which do not have unmediated links to a natural need: a chimp may try to take something it doesn't immediately need, which is the crudest form of desire at work. It may try to grab a piece of fruit another has in hand, although it is not hungry. This may result in a fight in chimps and gorillas and in sexual intercourse in bonobos. This latter result is something unprecedented in the animal world, because bonobos are one of the very few species other than human beings who can copulate at will, meaning that they are not bound by the periodicity of sexual function. They are, just like human beings, always in heat, always ready to have sexual intercourse.

Whether it ends up in a fight or in copulation, this demanding and grab-bing behavior of apes does not necessarily spring from a need. Like children who always want things regardless of need (whether, for instance, they are hungry or not), apes have already begun to be motivated by desire, that is, driven by a pri-mordial lack which haunts them from the moment of their birth. Since this lack cannot be determined, defined, described or even named, it can never be obvi-ated. It is always disguised as an indeterminate need, but the moment that need appears to be satisfied, it finds itself another object.

When an animal needs something, it instinctually and immediately seeks satisfaction by eating, drinking, copulating, defecating, urinating, scratching or covering itself. When an animal is disturbed and driven by a feeling of lack, how-ever, it may do one, any combination or none of these, but the expected outcome, satisfaction, does not appear. The more complex and developed their nervous systems are, the more pronounced, compelling and exigent this feeling of lack becomes, and hence the ways in which the (now almost human) animal seeks satisfaction become accordingly complex, ritualized. However, it is not only the level of development of the nervous system that plays a key role in the acknowl-edgement of the feeling of lack; it is also sight. Let us take a Turkish proverb and an almost universal phrase to demonstrate this point. In Turkey, when a person desires anything they *see*, we say, "Sees a horse and limps, sees water and thirsts." The almost universal phrase is, of course, "love at first sight." In both cases desire is triggered by the sense of sight, but we know in both cases that the consequential "need" is not genuine. The person who "sees water and thirsts" is not driven by a genuine, bodily need for water but only by the sight of it. Without a doubt, that desire becomes as *bodily* as the genuine need almost immediately, so there is no way to distinguish between the two. Love at first sight is not love by any definition but desire. In both cases, any of the other four senses would not do: nobody can touch water and thirst, nor can anybody fall in love at first smell, not even the congenitally blind, who are supposed to have a more developed olfactory sense. The sense of sight becomes the key factor in perceiving and conceiving of the things around us as objects, and thus metamorphosing our shapeless feeling of lack into desire and then projecting it onto objects.

When a need is not identical with an unmediated bodily stimulus but springs from the ego seeking an imaginary completion, it can only express itself as desire. But for desire to come into being there has to be (1) a hand which can grab, hold onto and keep things; (2) an eye which can sense both the self and the external objects *qua* objects (that is, be capable of going through the mirror stage and identifying "I" as "I"); and (3) a nervous system that can combine these two faculties into manipulation. The needs arising from bodily stimuli are few, definite and satisfiable. The needs arising from the feeling of lack, on the other hand, are limitless, indefinite and non-satisfiable: they are in fact everything the eye can see and the hand can reach. The problem arises when there is an incongruity between the things the eye can see and the hand can reach.[5] When we see something and want it, regardless of whether we really need it or not, but it is in the possession (in the grasp) of somebody else, the only thing we can do is to demand (request, ask for) it. In order to demand, we need a language, because the very act of demanding, the utterance "Give me *that*," not only turns the demanded object into an object of desire but also turns the entity we demand it from into an individual that is our semiotic equivalent:

> Demand constitutes the Other as already possessing the "privilege" of satisfying needs, that is to say, the power of depriving them of that alone by which they are satisfied. The privilege of the Other thus outlines the radical form of the gift of that which the Other does not have, namely, its love. (Lacan 1997, 286)

---

5   In later stages of human development, this incongruity will be named after Tantalus, whose punishment in Hades was that, although standing up to his chin in water, the pool dried up whenever he reached for it, and although boughs heavy with fruit hung over his head, they lifted out of reach when he tried to pick one. Tantalus, who was a son of Zeus and committed a series of crimes, stealing Ambrosia from Olympus and butchering his own son and serving the flesh to gods, thus becomes the epitome of having the object of desire placed in our sight but just beyond our reach, and therefore the root of the verb *tantalize*.

The three necessary requirements that are the *sine qua non* of language—the speaking subject, the addressee object or subject, and the subject matter, which is, as yet, nothing more than an object of desire—are thus fulfilled. In this sense, language emerges as a substitute for both violence (in chimpanzees) and sexuality (in bonobos), and as such it is embedded in both.

In the human world a demand is always already symbolized, discursified, so to speak, while refusing to give may be an act not yet symbolized, or a simple utterance of "No!," which may or may not be a linguistic sign. Language is complete when refusals also become fully symbolic acts, which means that they are organized into categorical prohibitions or bars. A linguistic or bodily equivalent (that is, another individual) may refuse to give something to us, but this does not prevent us from asking for that something again from another individual, or from the same individual under different circumstances. However, when the tribe declares something— endogamy, for instance—*taboo*, it's not only sex with a fellow member of the tribe but also the *demanding* itself (that is, the linguistic act) that becomes prohibited. Again, it is not a surprise to find that the second commandment prohibits the utterance of God's name before murder, theft and adultery, stating, "Thou shalt not take the name of the Lord your God in vain," barring not an act but an utterance, limiting the use of language *as such*. Barring a linguistic act with another linguistic act is what makes language a form of social organization.

Needless to say, such organization becomes possible only with a certain level of communal intercourse (*Verkehr*) and production. Bakhtin (as Vološinov)[6] writes:

> Classification of the forms of utterance must rely upon classification of the forms of verbal communication. The latter are entirely determined by production relations and the socio-political order. (Vološinov 1973, 20–21)

Let us take the case of traffic signs as an example. In order for the system of traffic signs (which is a kind of a language in itself) to appear, there has to be *traffic* (*Verkehr*), that is, a considerable number of *motor vehicles* (a definite state of technology), each trying to follow its own course on a limited network of roads (a definite organization of urban topology). So, upon arriving at our destination, if we see this sign, we immediately recognize our object cause of desire there, that

---

6   I'm not going to contribute to the controversy surrounding the authorship of *Marxism and the Philosophy of Language*. I will just take at face value Michael Holquist's contention that Bakhtin was indeed the author while keeping an open mind about any evidence otherwise.

is, the desire to park and get rid of this car so that we can get on with our business. At the same time, however, we also recognize the bar crossing it, which says we can do nothing of the sort. The no parking sign is a linguistic sign complete with desire (the P), prohibition (the bar) and a syntactic structure which connects these two (the P framed by a circle and the bar running through it). Desire requires a certain level of development of the human hand, eye, brain and psyche. Prohibition, on the other hand, requires a certain level of development of the same, but now within a sociocultural matrix. Desire and the prohibition thereof, rooted in specific physiological, neurological and societal structures, are what make a bunch of *Homo sapiens sapiens* into individuals organized as a society.

The passage from a group of gregarious animals (whose members are not yet individuals *as such*) into society requires the use of the hand, not only as a forelimb with an opposable thumb to facilitate grabbing but also as a tool-making organ. In order to make tools, however, the hand must be backed up by a brain capable of designing them:

> [M]any a human architect is put to shame by the skill with which a bee constructs her cell. But what from the very first distinguishes the most incompetent architect from the best of bees, is that the architect has built a cell in his head before he constructs it in wax. (Marx 1976, 129–130)

The same passage also requires a certain stage of development of the sense of sight and the ability to distinguish individual members as homologues. The precondition for this ability, however, is not only the neurological development of a specialized "face recognition" center in the brain (the fusiform gyrus) but also the mirror stage in which the subject itself sees and recognizes itself as self in a reflecting surface.

It is true that:

> Since he comes into the world neither with a looking glass in his hand, nor as a Fichtian philosopher, to whom "I am I" is sufficient, man first sees and recognises himself in other men. Peter only establishes his

own identity as a man by first comparing himself with Paul as being of like kind. And thereby Paul, just as he stands in his Pauline personality, becomes to Peter the type of the *genus homo*. (Marx 1976, 19ff.)

It is obvious, however, that this is another case of reciprocal causality: In order for Peter to "establish his own identity as a man by first comparing himself with Paul as being of like kind," he must first have the means of comparison, that is, the knowledge of what he himself is like. On the other hand, as long as he is incapable of recognizing Paul as a bodily equivalent, an other which is alike but not quite, Peter's recognition of himself as self in a reflecting surface does not establish an identity as such. Marx's statement and Lacan's concept of the mirror stage seem to be conflicting, because we tend to conceptualize as a single event a transition which may have taken tens of thousands of years. This transition is only complete through language, when Peter is able to utter "I, Peter, you, Paul" and (to a third person) "He, Paul." Tarzan becomes an individual not only when he utters "Me, Tarzan, you, Jane," but also when he identifies Cheetah as Cheetah (as something alike but not quite human) and names it so.

To sum up, the statement that human beings are individually oriented rather than species-oriented (or genetically driven) affirms rather than precludes their social character, because individuality (as different from the *indivisibility* of the unicellular organism) can only exist and develop dependent on the existence of other individuals, other speaking beings which are more or less our bodily equivalents:

The human being is in the most literal sense a *Zoon politikon* [city-dwelling animal], not merely a gregarious animal, but an animal which can individuate itself only in the midst of society. (Marx 1973)

As a matter of fact, the less species-oriented human beings are, the more social they become: socialization and individuation become, in Marx's sense, more or less identical. Desire, then, assumes a social as well as an individual character and becomes embedded in the basic social relationships human beings establish. For their *needs*, human beings *cooperate*, just as most of the higher mammals do; for their *desires*, on the other hand, they have to *speak*. The family, and especially the nuclear family in proto- and proper bourgeois societies, where the offspring are born and formed into the likeness of others, becomes the main institution in which desire emerges and is shaped. The tensions desire builds up and later partially discharges are thus mainly relational, since they presuppose speech (either one's own or others') and every desiring being is born into the symbolic order (or, conversely, the symbolic order can only exist as the common ground of desiring beings).

Although it is possible to ascertain that desire is essentially different from need—that it springs from a *sense* of lack rather than an unmediated bodily stimulus and, lacking the means for immediate satisfaction (in fact, satisfaction *at all*), can only be located in the symbolic order—the body's responses to both remain basically the same. However, the source of energy tapped by desire in order to build up the tensions later partially resolved to create a likeness of pleasure is still the same source instinct utilizes; that source is the libido. In this sense only, desire and instinct still occupy the same position vis-à-vis the body's energy economy. This is why the body cannot usually differentiate instinct from desire, often mistaking one for the other, and usually forces the mind or psyche into the same misrecognition.

Thus, for example, when popular culture tries to explain a case of rape by invoking "animal instinct," it cannot be more wrong, because although it utilizes the same muscles and bodily motion patterns, rape has nothing at all in common with instinctual copulation. If it were born out of pure instinct, rape would be more easily forgivable because the rapist, being a slave to instinct, could be considered *non compos mentis*, albeit temporarily. The actual motivating force behind rape, however, is not instinct but desire: a desire to dominate the female (or in some instances male or child) body by sheer force, to literalize the metaphor and escape the symbolic threat of castration by turning the penis into the phallus, albeit temporarily. This is why a rapist can never achieve satisfaction (for which reason every rapist is a potential serial rapist) other than the pathetic pseudo-satisfaction of ejaculation. If there is anything bestial in rape, it is not that it springs from instinct but that the rapist, unable to cope with (or indeed, *control*) desire, regresses into a pre-symbolic form of expression and chooses the "chimpanzee way"[7] out of this inability to cope, which is something definitely not forgivable.

---

7   It is important to note that although bonobos seem to be more sexually oriented animals than chimps do, rape is a chimpanzee rather than bonobo mode of behavior—in bonobo communities, rape is punishable by collective female violence. This is precisely because rape is not a sexual act after all; it is one of the main pathways for violence to enter into the socialized symbolic network as a means of domination (in this case male over female).

The Mirror Network and "The Mystical"

So, we know for sure that we can perceive things beyond the simple and extremely limited signals from our senses. When we try to locate these perceptions in the symbolic order, however, we can only file them under the umbrella term *extra-sensory perception*, abbreviate it as ESP, and either place the phenomena in the realm of metaphysics or leave it to science fiction writers (who have a very pronounced affinity for such occurrences). At best, we place them at the far limits of science, where some weird "scientists" carry out wacko experiments on telepathy, clairvoyance or telekinesis. Although not yet tested to its full potential, the mirror network as it relates to connecting with others outside the limits of our senses, as the wellspring of empathy and what neuroscientists today call the theory of the mind, may well give us an insight into these poorly observed, inadequately tested and metaphysically obscured facts.

For instance, it's quite possible that human beings, like most animals, can anticipate an approaching earthquake, but do not register it on the conscious level since they are unable to make sense of this anticipation,[8] and that they later, after having experienced the quake, repress the earlier perception in the terror of the experience, since they are not able to assign any meaning to it. This, of course, is sheer speculation, for we are not likely to test it under laboratory conditions, being unable to create in a laboratory an artificial analog for an approaching earthquake with all its implications.

Aside from making intelligent and experienced guesses about your future and managing to startle you every once in a while (because we tend to forget the guesses which do not come true), a palmist (or any kind of fortune teller) also makes some remarks about your present state or your past which are uncannily close to the truth. Due to their accuracy, these remarks cannot be mere guesses, and they make you more susceptible to believing in the speculations about your future. We can again speculate that these things happen not because the fortune teller has direct access to our memories or minds, or to the truths of the universe, but because they are more open (albeit unconsciously or even involuntarily) to the stimuli emanating from us in the form of body language, word selection, vocal inflection, eye movement, etc. That is to say, stimuli not readily perceptible by

---

8   This is because, unlike animals, human beings are driven by the need to make sense of phenomena, that is, to place them in a semantic framework. Whenever they are unable to do so, defense mechanisms are employed to either explain away or ignore such phenomena, and first and foremost among these mechanisms is *denial*.

ordinary people under everyday circumstances can hold meaning for the pseu-do-mystic who manages to temporarily suspend the prohibitions of the ego through bizarre rituals and actually communicate with us by translating into a kind of mystical (that is, semi-garbled) narrative what we communicate uncon-sciously. Again, we have no way of testing this speculation, since we have no way of stuffing a palmist and their client into a functional MRI, ritual and all.

Ritual is always, first and foremost, a way to temporarily override ego direc-tives (that is, *the reality principle* in Freudian terminology). It either facilitates the expression and/or formation of a community spirit through the temporary suspension of individual egos or, in more developed spiritualistic structures, uses the same suspension to create the likeness of direct communication with a higher being (gods or demons), with the sacred, the spiritual sphere. In the most primitive religions, this communication (or the illusion of communication) was achieved by the mediation of a shaman or a witch doctor, who was either psychotic, with an underdeveloped or punctured ego which could not uphold the reality principle consistently, or who tried to achieve the same effect through the use of halluci-nogenic or ego-suppressing substances. In such communities, psychosis (usually paranoid schizophrenia or hebephrenia, or in some cases even simple epilepsy) was not considered an abnormal state of mind but rather an integral part of the communal structure, with the psychotic placed in a special, privileged and taboo niche. These people were either the *burakumin* or *dalit* (untouchables in Japanese and Indian cultural structures, respectively) or the shaman or witch, but in any case deemed *sacer*, and the use of hallucinogenic or ego-suppressing drugs was not abnormal or illegal but reserved for only this minority. Modernity, not only in the temporal sense but also in the politico-geographic sense of global Western European domination, has deprived these people of their *sacer* status and placed them outside society, as a kind of externality, an excess stimulus rejected by the social ego. But since "the Real always comes back to its place," as Lacan suggests, they insistently come back to disturb the social structure in the shape of the Gre-co-Roman (later European) Bacchanalia, Saturnalias and carnivals and later as merely "the carnivalesque" (Bakhtin 1984).

Since the superego is nothing but a more specialized portion of the ego, however, ritual tends to suspend the superego as well, and this is precisely what happens during the carnival: the ritualistic temporary suspension of the ego is supposed to connect us with the sacred; the ritualistic temporary suspension of the superego, on the other hand, connects us with the mundane, the taboo of the unmediated flesh, and unreasoned violence. In both cases, we become more susceptible to the stimuli we tend to censor, block or cancel out in our everyday lives. In some cases, the two become intermingled, and the ostensible communication with a higher being becomes inseparable from an orgy of violence. The earliest literary examples of this are in Euripides's *Bacchae*, where King Pentheus is torn to pieces by women of the Dionysiac cult (including his mother and wife), and the mythological account of Orpheus's killing by women. Real life examples range from the purge of the Knights Templar in the early fourteenth century and the *auto-da-fé* to the Salem witch trials of the seventeenth century and the *Nacht der langen Messer* in 1934 (although suspension of the ego leads to a nationalistic rather than religious possession in this last example).

Freud had already foreseen the relevance of so-called Extrasensory Perception to psychoanalysis in his 1933 *New Introductory Lectures on Psychoanalysis* (the chapter "Dreams and Occultism") but was unable to assign a physical mediator to the seemingly unmediated form of psychical communication:

> The telepathic process is supposed to consist in a mental act in one person instigating the same mental act in another person. What lies between these two mental acts may easily be a physical process into which the mental one is transformed at one end and which is transformed back once more into the same mental one at the other end. The analogy with other transformations, such as occur in speaking and hearing by telephone, would then be unmistakable. And only think if one could get hold of this physical equivalent of the psychical act! (Freud 2010b, 4664)

We can say that we might have gotten hold of (or at least have an insight into) this physical equivalent with the discovery of the mirror network.

The upshot of my argument here is simply this: although still at the stage of early discovery, mirror neurons—along with the much broader concept of the mirror network being developed around the data gathered through their study—provide insight into not only the empathic connection between human beings but into all kinds of extra-semiotic connections between human beings and their environments more generally; connections normally hindered or even made entirely impossible by the defensive shield of the ego. The delimitation of our communication with the world around us separates us from the rest of the cosmos (and from each other) but at the same time makes it possible for language to come into being. Language seems to appear at the expense of the empathic faculty but is at the same time entirely dependent on it, since an infant can only learn language through mimicry of the sounds and lip movements of adults, which means extensive utilization of the mirror neurons. By the same token, the mirror stage posited by Lacanian psychoanalytic theory—where possible sense of the self is from the very start both attained and confused, where the infant *mimics itself mimicking itself*—can only be comprehended neuroscientifically through the function of the mirror network (Lacan 1997, 1–6).

The moment language comes into being, however, it turns on its perpetrator, empathy, and starts to incessantly claim ground from it. The empathic faculty is chaotic and boundless and as such is semantically void: it perceives everything at once and does not order, categorize, sequentialize or hierarchically organize its perceptions. As such, it could never give birth to civilization as we know it: It would make war, torture, lying, exploitation, oppression and evil in general entirely impossible, along with fine arts, philosophy, science and all notions of the good life. The Holocaust and Einstein, the auto-da-fé and Shakespeare, and Ancient Greek Slavery and Plato would all be incomprehensible within the auspices of the empathic function. Language, on the other hand, is *order* and makes civilization (in both its aspects) possible: in order to be able to attain this order, however, and create meaning out of it, it has to filter and limit perceptions. Order can only be created by the things that are left out of itself in this process; in Lacanian psychoanalytic thought this is called *the Real*. In order to be able to catch even a glimpse of the Real, however, some part of the empathic faculty must be left intact. As a matter of fact, the Real is the hard kernel within the symbolic order left out by the shield of the ego but leaking in through the remnants of the empathic faculty. In Hegelian terms, language is the self-alienation and hence the negation of empathy; but since empathy still exists and functions within the limitations of the symbolic order, the negation is not final. All mystical narratives, all tales of extrasensory perception and ability (never fully believed but at the same time never entirely refuted), witches, witch doctors, shamans, premonitions, out-of-body experiences, transcendental meditation, communication with spirits, yoga, the mystical aspect of Oriental martial arts: any and all of these are either futile or, at most, half-baked attempts at representing the empathic within the symbolic.

If we consider human history as a constant struggle between empathy and language,[9] with language gradually and constantly gaining ground without

---

9 This, by the way, is another way of referring to class struggle, for Marx has already told us class struggle begins with the social division of labor within the family, between man, woman and child. From this we can deduce other dichotomies—between woman and man, child and adult,

being able to annihilate empathy entirely, the final outcome that lies in our future should be in the form of an *Aufhebung*[10] rather than in the semiotic completely obliterating the empathic. The symbolic cosmos (language) will be subverted by the penetration of the empathic, which is non- linear, non-causal, non-discursive and synchronic (the Real quasi-represented in the imaginary), and the empathic chaos will be ordered by the intervention of the semiotic, which is linear, causal, discursive and sequential (the symbolic diffused in the imaginary).[11] The subverting drive in this *Aufhebung* should almost certainly come from the empathic side—creating a "discourse (semiotic) which is not a discourse (empathic)"—the side assigned the subaltern position from the beginning of what we call civilization, which is the history of male domination over female, reproductive domination over the sexual, and organizational and relational domination over the creative and emergent.

---

insane and sane, infirm and healthy, queer and straight—all connecting to (if not in a causal relationship with) the dichotomy between empathic and semiotic.

10 *Aufhebung*, in Hegelian terminology, is barely translatable into English as *sublation*. In our case, it will be the sublation of the dichotomy between language and empathy, with the outcome containing and negating both.

11 Using a musical metaphor, the empathic is a single chord, with all the sounds in synchronous resonance, while the semiotic is a simple melody, with the sounds following each other in a given sequence. The ensuing *Aufhebung*, on the other hand, should take the form of a Wagnerian polyphony, creating perfect resonances in any temporal cross section but also consisting of multiple contrapuntal sequences and harmonically intertwined melodies.

A Provisional Conclusion

Rather than concentrating the female principle into a "private" retreat, into which men periodically duck for relief, we want to rediffuse it— for the first time creating society from the bottom up. Man's difficult triumph over Nature has made it possible to restore the truly natural: he could undo Adam's and Eve's curse both, to reestablish the earthly Garden of Eden. But in his long toil his imagination has been stilled: he fears an enlargement of his drudgery, through the incorporation of Eve's curse into his own.

—Shulamith Firestone
The Dialectic of Sex

From Identity to Entirety

As EARLY AS 1983, John D'Emilio had heralded that in the near future gay and lesbian identity politics would cease to be a minority movement and become truly universal. In 2021, we can confidently add trans and gender fluid politics to this, as LGBTQ+ people continually become bolder, more visible and more outspoken in the present century. The passage from the struggle of a minority for recognition, from identity politics, to a political stance for *everyone* signifies one of the most important revolutionary steps since the invention of the term *sexual politics*.

This is quite congruent with what has been happening within feminism since the beginning of the last century, especially with the advent of the global crisis of neoliberalism: as masculinity (and its domination) becomes more and more fragile, insecure and indeed pointless, the masculine reaction to women's liberation becomes all the more desperate and violent. Some nation-states, riding this wave, seek to prohibit abortion and LGBTQ+ movements while some others turn a blind eye to these grievances and abandon women and children against the fragile masculine outrage.

This, in turn, ignites several different reactions. First, against this crude but imminent threat, some women, maybe not a majority but still a considerable minority, have become entrenched in identity positions and blame men in general rather than male/father domination for the recent atrocities, that is, the swiftly rising wave of femicide, rape, violence and child molestation. Other women, however, have begun to make a smooth transition from identity politics to a more universal political stance, involving everyone in their demands for liberty and equality. This can be observed in protests ranging from the first, massive US Women's March against Donald Trump's presidency in 2017 to the Polish demonstrations (nearly as massive) against the government's attempt to ban abortion in 2020 and the ongoing, persistent women's demonstrations in Turkey, which have remained almost the only mode of opposition on the streets.

Many men, desperately endeavoring to separate themselves from the instigators of this upsurge of violence, attempt, however clumsily, to side with women, although most of them are quite unwilling to give up their less apparent male privileges. In so doing, they try to shape and mold the movement by "mansplaining" (as is their habit) and only end up helping water it down, so to speak, restraining and cramping its radicalism. Other men, as yet only a minority, show signs of acknowledging women's pioneering position and try to restructure their agenda for liberation accordingly, albeit as clumsily.[1]

In all these cases, we can observe a certain transition from identity politics to universal politics, or to a politics of entirety, accompanied by a resistance to it. Some women, gays, lesbians, and trans and gender fluid people may be more or less satisfied with or hopeful for the existing state of affairs and expect it to go on indefinitely, with themselves in a better, more respectable and more equal position within it, as is their right. They may see patriarchy as something not structural and immanent in this phase of capitalism and may dream of a capitalism, or some regime akin to it, without patriarchy, becoming entrenched in their identity positions as a part of the free competition between identities. Others, however, thankfully a gradually increasing proportion of them, see patriarchy as an inseparable and integral part of class societies and their last instalment, late capitalism, seek alliances and consensuses with other movements struggling against it and acquiring, more often than not, a pioneering role in this fight.

---

1 The author of this book, as a straight, white male, must also confess, however unwillingly, that his style is also cramped by the same clumsiness, marred by, if nothing else, the constant self-conscious endeavor to make it prejudice-proof, and failing as often as not.

The *Oikos* and the *Polis*

Although the struggle against patriarchy goes on and expands in the public sphere, the same struggle in the privacy of our homes does not exactly follow suit, at least not as enthusiastically and efficiently. The 1960s slogan "The personal is political!" is back with a vengeance,[2] but there seems to be a secret pact to apply it to *others'* personal lives, not ours. Most of us, indeed an overwhelming majority, belong to families and have a lot of ideological, psychological and unspoken frailties pertaining to our own kinfolk and ancestors: many of those who have no qualms about exposing sexual molestation and violence in the public sphere (in their workplaces, schools or interpersonal relations) become curiously silent when it comes to their homes. We should, of course, qualify this statement: women *do* speak out against their husbands and lovers and face violence, threats, and even murder as a consequence. However, very few women (or children) speak out against their fathers, grandfathers, uncles and brothers. According to the 2020 Report of the *We Will End Femicide Platform* in Turkey:

> Of the 300 women killed in 2020, 97 were by the men they were married to, 54 were by the men they were with, 38 were by acquaintances, 21 were by the men they were married to previously, 18 were by their sons, 17 were by their fathers, 16 were by their relatives, 8 were by the men they were with previously, 5 were by their brothers, 3 were by someone they did not know. It could not be determined the degree of [closeness of the] people who killed 23 women. (We Will End Femicide Platform. 2020)

This report tells us that 180 (60%) of the 300 murders by known perpetrators were committed by the husband, ex-husband, partner, or ex-partner and 56 (18.7%) were committed by family (fathers, sons, brothers and relatives). If you add 38 (12.7%), representing undefined acquaintances, to the latter figure, the role of the close circle of the family becomes clearer.

---

2   The slogan, "The personal is political," was first used in print by Carol Hanisch, as the title of a 1970 essay published in *Notes from the Second Year: Women's Liberation* (Hanisch 2000). Hanisch later stated, however, that the title was not her invention but given by the editors, Shulamith Firestone and Anne Koedt. It is more reasonable to assume that although the slogan seems to belong to Hanisch (and through her, to Firestone and Koedt), it was already in much wider use within the feminist movement of the '60s.

We may remember from chapter 3 the unexpectedly high rate of sexual molestation of children within the family (about one in five), not forgetting the fact that this figure represents only the *reported* cases. Most cases are only reported as the result of a series of coincidences, such as Fritzl's daughter miraculously escaping after two decades or the Turkish five-year-old complaining to the psychiatrist, "My father's milk is too bitter!"[3] However popular the slogan "The personal is political!" (or, alternatively, "The private is political!") may have become, the *home* seems to have some kind of immunity, especially the home we grew up in rather than the one we build. The fathers and, along with them, the mothers who are usually unwilling accomplices are frequently protected by their victims themselves. The more we go back into our personal histories, the more exponentially the weight of feelings of guilt, self-blame and severe repression increase, and *this* is how the family safeguards itself against scrutiny and change: through our desperate attempts to exempt our childhood memories (many of them false ones) from critical inquiry.

So, what is this home that keeps us hostage in our most fragile, irrational and vulnerable moment? The English language makes a very significant distinction (maybe more than any other language) between *home* and *house*, almost the same distinction as the one between *soul* and *body*: a house without a home is simply an empty shell, an unmoving, unanimated torso, a mere architectural edifice in an uninhabited wasteland. The main difference, however, is not simply the fact of human habitation. Put any person or unrelated persons in a house and they will not make it home: the Classical Greek word for home, *οἶκος*, does not only mean both home and house, but also *family* (*οἰκονομικός*: pertaining to household or family). So, in order to make a house a *home*, you have to implant a *family* in it. The natural opposite of home, then, is the public sphere, where people interact not as families (or members of families) but as individuals and discuss and decide about the affairs of the community as a whole. This is the Greek *πόλις*, not only a city or a state but also a communal structure organized around an *agora* (a market), not only a focus for buying and selling but also as the locus of everything that happens outside the home.

---

3   As a matter of fact, in this particular case as well, the psychiatrist had at first missed the child's meaning and thought that she was referring to the spoiled milk given to her by the father. Her real meaning only became clear when they asked the child to draw a picture of her father and she clumsily sketched a penis. https://www.hurriyet.com.tr/cocuk-istismarinda-biz-cocugun-soyledigi-her-seyi-dogru-kabul-ederiz-24496232.

The seeming oxymoron, *political economy*, therefore acquires another meaning when we try to explore the etymology of *home*: *economy* comes from οἶκος (home or house), while *politics* is directly related to πόλις (the city or public sphere), its direct opposite. So how can we talk about political economy, which can also be translated as "the communality of home," or, better still, "the publicity of the private"? As we can see, we are back at the slogan "The private is political!"—but now with an added paradox: it is not only a feminist slogan but it is also at the root of the critique of all class societies. In trying to explain that exploitation is not located merely in the sphere of economics, but rather in the convergence of the economic and the political, Marx says, "It is only the domination of accumulated, past, materialised labour over direct, living labour that turns accumulated labour into capital." (Marx 2010g, 213) What makes accumulated wealth (an economic category) *capital*, is *domination* (a political category).

We can rewrite the same statement for sexual politics with only minor alterations: "It is only the domination of the *penis* (male sexuality) over direct, living sexual expression that turns penis into *phallus*." Just as we don't need to destroy accumulated wealth itself in order to abolish capitalism, we don't need to destroy the penis altogether in order to cancel out the phallus, to abolish male/father-dominated society. Once the dominion of past, accumulated, and materialized labor over immediate living labor is abolished, it ceases to be capital and is reduced to simple wealth in the service of living labor. In the same vein, once male/father domination—that is, the central character of the phallus in language, (re)production and human relationships; the domination of reproduction over sexuality—is abolished, the phallus ceases to be the phallus and is reduced to a simple organ, the penis, only one among many in the human body, only useful for urination and for one of the many ways of sexual expression.

Although male/father domination covers and hovers over the entire expanse of private and public spheres, the entire domain of politics and economics, it is first and foremost located in the home, in the actuality of the family, where the father exists as a symbol and a name and is nourished and sustained as the bearer of the phallus, the still-central signifier of the symbolic order. The family is where the ghost of the father continually returns for rejuvenation and re-animation, and *this* is the secret of his uncanny longevity.

This is why the phallic order that is represented as male/father domination in sociosexual relations and as the power of money in socioeconomic relations can only be subverted by a combined effort, a simultaneous act of desertion on the male side and of subversion on the female side. The exceptional act of crossing

over from the male to the female side of the sexuation matrix involves a self-de-
nial for men, which means giving up the privileged position of determining what
signifies what within the symbolic order, a privilege already non-existent for individual men as well as women and which only existed in the symbolic presence of
the Name-of-the-Father. If men—who are without exception subject to the phallic function, to the law of castration, but at the same time all descendants of the
phantasm of the primordial father who was not subject to his own law—manage
to pass over to the realm of the women—who cannot escape the phallic function
and appear as always already castrated, but at the same time each possess a kernel
which cannot be penetrated by the law of castration—then the act (or threat) of
castration itself and the phallus which signifies it will be stripped of all surplus
meaning and be reduced to the status of mere signs.

The Next Step

In 1989, Ursula Le Guin, a radical feminist who was worlds wiser than I am,
described her goal in life as being "to subvert as much as possible without hurting anybody's feelings" (Le Guin 1989, vii). The family is one area where it is
extremely hard to follow her example: whatever you do or say, it will definitely
hurt *somebody's* feelings. You can mention Josef Frizl, the father and serial rapist
who victimized his daughter for two decades, or the father and rapist Noah Cross
in Polanski's *Chinatown*, but there is somebody, somewhere (including myself)
who is an avid fan of Atticus Finch in *To Kill a Mockingbird*, the loving single father
who is a mentor, caretaker and friend for his children as well as a rare upholder of
justice. Medea murdered her innocent sons for revenge, but then there is Marmee,
the unbelievably "good" mother in Louisa May Alcott's *Little Women*. If you are
not convinced by her exaggerated goodness, there is always Brecht's Grusha Vashnadze, who lets go of her (non-genetic) son so that he will not get hurt. We can
conjure up the ghosts of Goneril and Regan, Lear's evil daughters who victimized
their father as well as their sister, Cordelia, but then there are the happy sororities
of (again) *Little Women* and *The Little House on the Prairie*. It may be hard to find
good brothers in fiction and in history, starting with the story of Oedipus's sons,
Eteocles and Polyneices, who kill each other, not to mention Remus and Romu-
lus or the serial fratricides of the Ottoman and Persian courts, but then somebody,
somewhere definitely had a good elder brother, such as Jem in (again) *To Kill a
Mockingbird*, who was the ideal elder brother to Scout.

Popular literature and cinema try very, very hard to convince us that a good family exists somewhere, and there are undoubtedly some among us, not a very small minority, who actually had good (at least tolerably fair) families. It is impossible to decide how many of these good families are real exceptions and how many seem so due to our false or selective memories, but the exercise is not really necessary anyway.

My entire argument is based on the dual reckoning that (1) the family as we know it is structurally collapsing, independent of our criticism and struggle, and the search for alternative ways of organizing our reproductive lives, kinship and sexuality has already started; (2) the family was and still is the fundamental locus of male/father domination, and while this domination permeates the political and social domains, it's only replenished within its locus. A new regime of reproduction, sexuality and kinship will not, however, come into existence on its own as an emergence, nor as a result of our utopian imagination or our philosophical and critical considerations, but only on the ruins of the old, using building blocks (sometimes cornerstones and keystones) that are remainders of the old, defunct family. Unfortunately, we are not free to pick and choose, deciding what to use and what to discard, although we can still make an effort in that direction, if for nothing else than the sake of posterity.

We can, for instance, try to retain Grusha's non-genetic motherhood, her altruism and caring, and extend it to every one of us regardless of gender. We can try to keep the spirit of solidarity, cooperation, and complicity already practiced by siblings in most families and extend it throughout the consciously-chosen kinship structures we strive to form in the future. And finally, we can try to keep the mentorship and protective presence of Gandalf and combine it with the sense of justice and caring company of Atticus as the sensible remainders of fatherhood. In all these cases, we can try to extract the looming presence of the phallus, and the resultant existence of the ownership of women and children alike, and leave it behind.

Today's struggles against male/father domination have grown (and grown *up*), not only repeating the 1960s call for sexual freedom and lifestyles not hampered by the ancient regime(s) of morality and the family but also adding to these a new call for the liberation and abolition of childhood and of old age. This is another ongoing process rather than a wishful utopian demand. In 2020, amid the worldwide angst of the COVID-19 pandemic, Andreas Chatzidakis, Jamie Hakim, Jo Litter, Catherine Rottenberg and Lynne Segal (as The Care Collective) published *The Care Manifesto* (The Care Collective 2020). It is one of the very strong indications that the concept of care has been extremely politicized and, as a viable alternative for the family *as we know it*, has already become one of the outstanding items on the agenda in the struggle against neoliberal capitalism.

Edgar Allan Poe had already seen the impending downfall of the family back in 1839 and told us about it in a story, using one of the most disturbing and blood-chilling metaphors ever penned:

> The radiance was that of the full, setting, and blood-red moon which now shone vividly through that once barely-discernible fissure of which I have before spoken as extending from the roof of the building, in a zigzag direction, to the base. While I gazed, this fissure rapidly widened—there came a fierce breath of the whirlwind—the entire orb of the satellite burst at once upon my sight—my brain reeled as I saw the mighty walls rushing asunder—there was a long tumultuous shouting sound like the voice of a thousand waters—and the deep and dank tarn at my feet closed sullenly and silently over the fragments of the "House of Usher." (Poe 1903, 119)

The "once barely-discernible fissure" from the roof to the base has already become an enormous crack. Fortunately, that crack is also "how the light comes in" (Leonard Cohen, "Anthem").

Returning to what we *can* do, in order to facilitate the demotion of the phallus from the central signifier of the symbolic order to a mere organ, to close the door on its renewed promotion in the foreseeable future and thereby expedite the long overdue demise of male/father domination, we can:

- Problematize, if not desert altogether, our identity positions as regards gender, age, and sexual orientation and preference. For this purpose, we should start anew from the initial hypothesis that male/father domination is not merely domination by males but rather domination by the phallic, castrating position which could be occupied by almost anyone, regardless of gender and sexual orientation and preference. Unfortunately (in all but one sense), the only beings excluded from this position are children, which makes them the absolute subalterns of male/father domination.
- Commence wherever and whenever possible the radical social and communal application of the recent technologies of fertilization, fetal development and child bearing. This step will help

advance these technologies beyond endorsing the existing dominant family system and making it possible for infertile couples to own more children. It will instead help promote the freedom of women from painful childbirth and wet-nursing (at least for those who demand and welcome this change) and, more importantly, the freedom of children from ownership by their parents.

- Commence wherever and whenever possible the communalization of childbirth, wet-nursing and childcare, demanding societal support for this process. The same applies to the communalization of care for the elderly, physically and/or psychically different people, and those temporarily ailing and indisposed. Needless to say, the ideological and material apparatuses of the existing and persisting nation-states should be kept as far away as possible from this process.

- Commence wherever and whenever possible a non-doctrinaire way of teaching language and other semiotic skills for infants, starting from the assumption that existing languages are only *one of the possible modes of human communication*. With this step, it will become apparent that another mode of communication and interaction with other human beings and eventually with the rest of life on our planet is possible. It will also make it possible to combine the semiotic with the empathic rather than the former totally repressing the latter.

- Problematize, if not desert altogether, the use of language and linguistic skills as a means of domination over those less skilled in such usage, especially children. For this purpose, it is perfectly possible to start applying the Wittgensteinian dictum, "One should keep quiet on the things one cannot talk about," as practical advice rather than an obscure theoretical statement and keep silent every once in a while.

- Complement the ongoing dissolution of the nuclear family by seeking out other communal lifestyles, transforming premodern communal modes and nodes of existence (be they religious, ethnic, local, neighborhood or extended familial) into political ones (another already ongoing process), and endeavoring to discover new ones.

- Communalize and politicize so-called private life so that the private crimes against women and children now hidden behind the illusion of the sanctity of family and home will come out into the open and be accessible to communal intervention. This intervention, which may initially be limited to the immediate community, will eventually and incrementally be taken over by the global community as a whole.

- Extend *ad infinitum*, and therefore obliterate, the existing conception of the family as a union of two genetically non-connected individuals and their offspring, where, paradoxically, sexuality is prohibited so that it can be practiced legitimately. This step will make it possible to create an open, consciously chosen communality, an open-ended kinship network where, as the free connection of individuals overriding the barriers of the ego and the superego (however temporarily), sexuality is neither prohibited nor permitted but simply *is*.

References

Abel, Gene G., Alan Jordan, Nora Harlow, and Yu-Sheng Hsu. 2019. "Preventing Child Sexual Abuse: Screening for Hidden Child Molesters Seeking Jobs in Organizations That Care for Children." *Sexual Abuse* 31, no. 6 (September 2019): 662-683.

Abel, Gene G., and Nora Harlow. 2001. *The Stop Child Molestation Book: What Ordinary People Can Do in Their Everyday Lives to Save Three Million Children.* Bloomington: Xlibris Corporation.

Arantes-Oliveira, Nuno, Javier Apfeld, Andrew Dillin, Cynthia Kenyon. 2002. "Regulation of Life-Span by Germ-Line Stem Cells in *Caenorhabditis elegans*." *Science* 295, no. 5554 (January 18): 502–505.

Bailey, Nathan W. and Marlene Zuk. 2009. "Same-sex Sexual Behavior and Evolution." *Trends in Ecology and Evolution* 24, no. 8 (August 2009): 439-46.

Bakhtin, M. M. 1984. *Rabelais and His World.* Translated by Hélène Iswolsky. Bloomington and Indianapolis: Indiana University Press.

Baron-Cohen, Simon. 2003. *The Essential Difference: Men, Women and the Extreme Male Brain.* London: Penguin/Basic Books.

Berglund, Hans, Per Lindstrom, and Ivanka Savič. 2006. "Brain response to putative pheromones in lesbian women." *PNAS* 103, no. 21: 8269–8274.

Berman, Jennifer R. and Cynthia Kenyon. 2006. "Germ-Cell Loss Extends *C. elegans* Life Span through Regulation of DAF-16 by kri-1 and Lipophilic-Hormone Signaling." *Cell* 124, no. 5 (March 10, 2006): 1055.

Bloom, Paul. 2016. *Against Empathy: The Case for Rational Compassion.* New York: HarperCollins.

Brecht, Bertolt. 1963. *Die Kaukasische Kreidekreis.* Frankfurt: Suhrkamp Verlag.

Brecht, Bertolt. 1966. *The Caucasian Chalk Circle.* Translated by E. Bentley. New York, NY: Grove Press.

Brecht, Bertolt. 2015. "The Augsburg Chalk Circle." In *The Collected Short Stories of Bertolt Brecht*, edited by J. Willett and R. Mannheim. London: Bloomsbury.

Brecht, Bertolt. 1983. *The Good Woman of Setzuan.* In *Two Plays by Bertolt Brecht.* Revised English versions by Eric Bentley. New York: Meridian Classic.

Brennan, Patricia L.R., Jonathan R. Cowart, and Dara N. Orbach. 2021. "Evidence of a functional clitoris in dolphins." *Current Biology* 32, no. 1 (January 10, 2021), PR24-R26.

Buss, David. 1995. *The Evolution of Desire: Strategies of Human Mating*. New York: Basic Books.

Butler, Judith. 1999. *Gender Trouble: Feminism and the Subversion of Identity*. NY and London: Routledge.

Cady Stanton, Elizabeth et al. 1848. "The Declaration of Sentiments." https://www.womensrightsfriends.org/pdfs/1848_declaration_of_sentiments.pdf.

Care Collective, The. 2020. *The Care Manifesto: The Politics of Interdependence*. London: Verso.

Chalmers, David. 1996. *The Conscious Mind: In Search of a Theory of Conscious Experience*. NY: Oxford University Press.

Cheng, Y. et al. 2006. "Gender Differences in the Human Mirror System: a Magnetoencephalography Study." *Neuroreport* 17, no. 11: 1115–1119.

Cheng, Y. et al. 2008. "Gender Differences in the Mu Rhythm of the Human Mirror-Neuron System." *PLoS ONE* 3, no. 5, e2113.

Cheng, Y. et al. 2009. "Sex Differences in the Neuroanatomy of Human Mirror-Neuron System: a Voxel-based Morphometric Investigation." *Neuroscience* 158, no. 2: 713–720.

Collier, Jane, Michelle Z. Rosaldo, and Sylvia Yanagisako. 1997. "Is There a Family: New Anthropological Views." In *The Gender/Sexuality Reader*, edited by R. Lancaster and M. di Leonardo. London and NY: Routledge.

Cunha, Gerald R. et al. 2014. "Development of the External Genitalia: Perspectives from the Spotted Hyena (Crocuta crocuta)." *Differentiation*, 87 no. 1–2 (January–February 2014): 4–22. doi:10.1016/j.diff.2013.12.003.

D'Emilio, John. 1983. "Capitalism and Gay Identity." In *Powers of Desire: The Politics of Sexuality*, edited by Ann Snitow, Christine Stansell, and Sharon Thompson. New York: Monthly Review Press.

D'Emilio, John. 2006. "The Marriage Fight Is Setting Us Back." *Gay & Lesbian Review Worldwide*, November–December 2006.

D'Emilio, John. 2014. *In a New Century: Essays on Queer History, Politics, and Community Life*. Madison: The University of Wisconsin Press.

De Gouges, Olympe. 1996 (1791). "The Declaration of the Rights of Woman." In *The French Revolution and Human Rights: A Brief Documentary History*, edited and translated by Lynn Hunt, 124–129. Boston and NY: Bedford/St. Martin's.

De Gouges, Olympe. 1979 (1791). "The Declaration of the Rights of Woman and the Female Citizen." In *Women in Revolutionary Paris 1789–1795*, 87–96. Translated by Daline Gay Levy, Harriet Branson Applewhite, and Mary Durham Johnson. Urbana: University of Illinois Press,

De Waal, Frans. 2009. *The Age of Empathy: Nature's Lessons for a Kinder Society*. New York: Harmony Books.

De Waal, Frans. 2005. *Our Inner Ape*. New York: Riverhead Books.

Diamond, Jared. 1997. *Why is Sex Fun? The Evolution of Human Sexuality*. New York: Basic Books.

Diamond, Jared. 1999. *Guns, Germs and Steel: The Fates of Human Societies*. New York and London: W. W. Norton & Company.

Donahue, Chad J., Matthew F. Glasser, Todd M. Preuss, James K. Rilling, and David C. Van Essen. 2018. "Quantitative assessment of prefrontal cortex in humans relative to nonhuman primates." *PNAS*, 115, no. 22: E5183–E5192.

Ellis, Havelock. 1915. *Studies in the Psychology of Sex; Volume II: Sexual Inversion*. Philadelphia: F. A. Davis Company, Publishers.

Estren, Mark J. 2012. "The Neoteny Barrier: Seeking Respect for the Non-Cute." *Journal of Animal Ethics*, 2, no. 1 (Spring 2012): 6–11.

Firestone, Shulamith. 1979. *The Dialectic of Sex*. New York: The Women's Press.

Foucault, Michel. 1970. *The Order of Things*. London: Tavistock.

Foucault, Michel. 1978. *The History of Sexuality Volume 1: An Introduction*. Translated by Robert Hurley. New York: Pantheon Books.

Freud, Sigmund. 1951. "Letter to an American Mother" (April 9, 1935). *American Journal of Psychiatry*, 107 (1951).

Freud, Sigmund. 1995. "Three Contributions to the Theory of Sex." In *The Basic Writings of Sigmund Freud*, edited and translated by A. A. Brill. New York: The Modern Library.

Freud, Sigmund. 1953. *Three Essays on Sexuality*. In *The Standard Edition of the Complete Psychological Works of Sigmund Freud, Vol. VII*. Translated by James Stratchey. London: The Hogarth Press.

Freud, Sigmund. 2010a. *Beyond the Pleasure Principle*. In *Complete Works*, edited by Ivan Smith (online).

Freud, Sigmund. 2010b. *The Ego and the Id*. In *Complete Works*, edited by Ivan Smith (online).

Freud, Sigmund. 2010c. *New Introductory Lectures on Psycho-Analysis*. In *Complete Works*, edited by Ivan Smith (online).

Freud, Sigmund. 2010d. "Female Sexuality." In *Complete Works*, edited by Ivan Smith (online).

Freud, Sigmund. 2010e. *New Introductory Lectures on Psycho-Analysis*. In *Complete Works*, edited by Ivan Smith (online).

Freud, Sigmund. 2010f. *Totem and Taboo*. In *Complete Works*, edited by Ivan Smith (online).

Fritzon, Katarina, Nathan Brooks, and Simon Croom. 2020. *Corporate Psychopathy: Investigating Destructive Personalities in the Workplace*. London: Palgrave Macmillan.

Fuster, Joaquín. 2008. *The Prefrontal Cortex* (Fourth Edition). London: Elsevier.

Goode, Sarah D. 2010. *Understanding and Addressing Adult Sexual Attraction to Children: A Study of Paedophiles in Contemporary Society.* London and NY: Routledge.

Goodstein, Laurie. 2013. "Pope Says Church Is 'Obsessed' With Gays, Abortion and Birth Control." *New York Times,* September 19, 2013. http://www.nytimes.com/2013/09/20/world/europe/pope-bluntly-faults-churchs-focus-on-gays-and-abortion.html.

Graves, Robert. 1960. *The Greek Myths.* Harmondsworth: Penguin.

Haas, Randall, James Watson, Tammy Buonasera, John Southon, Jennifer C. Chen, Sarah Noe, Kevin Smith, Carlos Viviano Llave, Jelmer Eerkens, and Glendon Parker. 2020. *Female hunters of the early Americas. Science Advances, 6 no. 45, eabd0310–.* doi:10.1126/sciadv.abd0310

Haas, Maya Wei. 2020. "Prehistoric female hunter discovery upends gender role assumptions." *National Geographic,* November 4, 2020. https://www.nationalgeographic.com/science/article/prehistoric-female-hunter-discovery-upends-gender-role-assumptions.

Hanisch, Carol. 2000. "The Personal is Political." In *Radical Feminism: A Documentary Reader,* edited by Barbara A. Crow, 113–117. New York: NYU Press. 2000.

Haraway, Donna J. 2016. *Staying with the Trouble: Making Kin in the Chthulucene.* Durham and London: Duke University Press.

Hegel, G. W. F. 2001. *Philosophy of Right.* Translated by S. W. Dyde. Kitchener, Ontario: Batoche Books.

Hegel, G. W. F. 1991. *Part I of the Encyclopedia of Philosophical Sciences with the Zusatze.* Translated by T. E. Geraets, W. A. Suchting, and H. S. Harris. Indianapolis and Cambridge: Hackett Publishing Company, Inc.

Hickok, Gregory. 2014. *The Myth of Mirror Neurons. The Real Neuroscience of Communication and Cognition.* NY and London: W. W. Norton & Company.

Hua, Cai. 2001. *A Society without Fathers or Husbands: The Na of China.* Translated by Asti Hustvedt. New York: Zone Books.

Ian, Marcia. 1997. "Freud, Lacan, and Imaginary Secularity." In *American Imago* 54, no. 2 (1997): 123–147.

Iacoboni, Marco. 2009. *Mirroring People.* New York: Picador.

Iacoboni, Marco et al. 2005. "Grasping the Intentions of Others with One's Own Mirror Neuron System." *PLoS Biology,* 3, no. 3 (March 2005): 0529–0535. www.plosbiology.org

Irigaray, Luce. 1985. *This Sex Which Is Not One.* Translated by Catherine Porter and Carolyn Burke. Ithica, NY: Cornell University Press.

Jaeger, Gustav. 1884. *Entdeckung der Seele.* Leipzig: Ernst Günthers Verlag.

Jataka, The, vol. VI. 1907. "Mahaushadha" in *The Maha-Ummagga Jataka* (546/5). Translated by E. B. Cowell and W. H. D. Rouse. Cambridge: The Cambridge University Press

Jones, Ernest. 1976. *Hamlet and Oedipus.* New York: The Norton Library.

Kant, Immanuel. 1887. *The Philosophy of Law: An Exposition of the Fundamental Principles of Jurisprudence as the Science of Right*. Translated by William Hastie. Edinburgh: T&T Clark.

Kant, Immanuel. 2003 (1784). "Idea for a Universal History with a Cosmopolitan Purpose." In *Kant: Political Writings*, edited by Hans Reiss. Translated by H. B. Nisbet. Cambridge: Cambridge University Press.

Katz, Jonathan Ned. 2007. *The Invention of Heterosexuality*. Chicago: Chicago University Press.

Krafft-Ebing, R. v. 1906. *Psychopatia Sexualis*. Translated by J. F. Rebman. New York, NY: Rebman Company.

Lacan, Jacques. 1985. *Feminine Sexuality*, edited by Juliet Mitchell and Jacqueline Rose. Translated by Jacqueline Rose. New York: Norton.

Lacan, Jacques. 1991. "The Two Narcissisms." In *The Seminar of Jacques Lacan; Book 1, Freud's Papers on Technique 1953–1954*, edited by Jacques-Alain Miller, 118–128. Translated by John Forrester. NY and London: W. W. Norton & Company.

Lacan, Jacques. 1997. *The Seminar of Jacques Lacan; Book 7, The Ethics of Psychoanalysis 1959–1960*, edited by Jacques-Alain Miller. Translated by Dennis Porter. NY and London: W. W. Norton & Company.

Lacan, Jacques. 1998. The Seminar of Jacques Lacan. *On Feminine Sexuality: The Limits of Love and Knowledge. Book 20: Encore 1972–1973*, edited by Jacques-Alain Miller. Translated by Bruce Fink. NY and London: W.W. Norton & Company.

Lacan, Jacques. 1998. *The Seminar of Jacques Lacan: Book 5, Formations of the Unconscious 1957–1958*, edited by Jacques-Alain Miller. Translated by Russell Grigg. Madden, MA: Polity Press.

Lacan, Jacques. 1997. Écrits: A Selection. Translated by Alan Sheridan. London: Routledge.

Lacan, Jacques. 2013. *On the Names-of-the-Father*. Translated by Bruce Fink. Madden, MA: Polity Press.

Le Guin, Ursula K. 1974. "The Day Before the Revolution." *Galaxy*, August 1974.

Le Guin, Ursula K. 1989. *Dancing at the Edge of the World*. NY: Grove Press.

Lewis, Sophie. 2019. *Full Surrogacy Now: Feminism Against Family*. London and NY: Verso.

Malinowski, Bronislaw. 2001. *Sex and Repression in Savage Society*. London: Routledge Classics.

Malinowski, Bronislaw. 2002. *Argonauts of the Western Pacific: An Account of Native Enterprise and Adventure in the Archipelagoes of Melanesian New Guinea*. London: Routledge.

Marcus, David K. and Michael R. Cunningham. 2003. "Do Child Molesters Have Aberrant Perceptions of Adult Female Facial Attractiveness?" *Journal of Applied Social Psychology*, 33, no. 3, (March 2003): 499–512.

Marmor, Judd. 1954. "Some Considerations Concerning Orgasm in the Female" *Psychosomatic Medicine*, XVI, No. 3.

Marx, Karl. 1973. *Grundrisse*. Translated by Martin Nicolaus. http://www.marxists.org/archive/marx/works/1857-gru/g1.htm.

Marx, Karl. 2010a. *Capital Volume I*. In *Marx & Engels Collected Works, Vol. 35*. London: Lawrence & Wishart.

Marx, Karl. 2010b. *Economic and Philosophical Manuscripts of 1844*. In *Marx & Engels Collected Works, Vol. 3*. London: Lawrence & Wishart.

Marx, Karl and Frederick Engels. 2010c. *The German Ideology*. In *Marx & Engels Collected Works, Vol. 5*. London: Lawrence and Wishart.

Marx, Karl and Frederick Engels. 2010d. *Manifesto of the Communist Party*. In *Marx & Engels Collected Works, Vol. 6*. London: Lawrence and Wishart.

Marx, Karl. 2010e (1845). "Theses on Feuerbach." In *Marx & Engels Collected Works, Vol. 5*, London: Lawrence and Wishart.

Marx, Karl. 2010f (1888). "Theses on Feuerbach." In *Marx & Engels Collected Works, Vol. 26*. London: Lawrence and Wishart.

Marx, Karl. 2010g. *Wage Labour and Capital*. In *Marx & Engels Collected Works, Vol. 9*. London: Lawrence and Wishart.

Marx, Karl. 1978. "Thesen über Feuerbach." In *Marx and Engels Werke, Band 3*. Berlin: Dietz Verlag.

Marx, Karl. 1968. Preface to *A Contribution to the Critique of Political Economy*. In *Marx and Engels, Selected Works*. Moscow: Progress Publishers.

Miller, Jacques-Alain. 2009. "Extimity." *The Symptom* 9, Fall 2009. https://www.lacan.com/symptom/extimity.html.

Missing Children Europe. http://miniila.org/childsexualabuse

Mitchell, Juliet. 2000. *Psychoanalysis and Feminism*. NY: Basic Books.

Oberman, Lindsay M. et al. 2005. "EEG Evidence for Mirror Neuron Dysfunction in Autism Spectrum Disorders." *Cognitive Brain Research* 24 (2005): 190–198.

O'Brien, Mary. 1983. *The Politics of Reproduction*. Boston, London and Henley: Routledge & Kegan Paul.

Phillips, Adam. 1995. *Terrors and Experts*. London: Faber & Faber.

Phillips, Adam. 1996. *Monogamy*. London and Boston: Faber and Faber.

Phillips, Adam. 2016. *On Kissing, Tickling and Being Bored: Psychoanalytic Essays on the Unexamined Life*. London: Faber and Faber.

Poe, Edgar Allan. 1903. "The Fall of the House of Usher." In *Tales of Mystery and Imagination*. London, Edinburgh, Glasgow, NY and Toronto: Henry Frowde.

Premack, David and Guy Woodruff. 1978. "Does the Chimpanzee Have Theory of Mind?" *The Behavioral and Brain Sciences*, 4: 515–526.

Qianfu, Li. 2001. *The Chalk Circle*. Translated by Ethel van der Veer. Cambridge: In Parentheses Publications.

Ramachandran, V. S. 2011. *The Tell-Tale Brain: Unlocking the Mystery of Human Nature*. NY and London: W. W. Norton & Co.

Ratzinger, Joseph A. (Pope Benedict XVI). 2012. *Address of His Holiness Benedict XVI on The Occasion of Christmas Greetings to the Roman Curia;* Friday, December 21, 2012. http://www.vatican.va/holy_father/benedict_xvi/speeches/2012/december/documents/hf_ben-xvi_spe_20121221_auguri-curia_en.html.

Ratzinger, Joseph A. with Vittorio Messori. 1985. *Ratzinger Report on the State of the Church*. San Francisco, Ignatius Press.

Recalcati, M. 2019. *The Mother's Hands: Desire, Fantasy and the Inheritance of the Maternal*. Translated by A. Kilgariff. Cambridge: Polity Press.

Roselli, Charles E., Radhika C. Reddy, and Katherine R. Kaufman. 2011. "The Development of Male-oriented Behavior in Rams." *Frontiers in Neuroendocrinology* 32, no. 2: 164–169.

Roselli, Charles E. and F. Stormshak. 2010. "The ovine sexually dimorphic nucleus, aromatase, and sexual partner preferences in sheep." *Journal of Steroid Biochemistry and Molecular Biology* 118: 252–256.

Roselli, Charles E., Kay Larkin, John A. Resko, John N. Stellflug and Fred Stormshak. 2004. "The Volume of a Sexually Dimorphic Nucleus in the Ovine Medial Preoptic Area/Anterior Hypothalamus Varies with Sexual Partner Preference." *Endocrinology* 145, no. 2: 478–483.

Savič, Ivanka, Hans Berglund, and Per Lindstrom. 2005. "Brain response to putative pheromones in homosexual men." *PNAS* 102, no. 20: 7356–7361.

Schrefer, Eliot. 2022. *Queer Ducks (and Other Animals): The Natural World of Animal Sexuality*. Katherine Tegen Books.

Schwartz, John. 2007. "Of Gay Sheep, Modern Science and Bad Publicity." *The New York Times,* January 25, 2007.

Segal, Lynne. 1994. *Straight Sex*. Berkeley and Los Angeles: University of California Press.

Shields, Stephanie. 1975. "Functionalism, Darwinism, and the Psychology of Women: A Study in Social Myth." *American Psychologist* 30 (1975): 739–754.

Somay, Bülent. 2014. *The Psychopolitics of the Oriental Father: Between Omnipotence and Emasculation*. London: Palgrave Macmillan.

Sokal, Alan and Jean Bricmont. 1998. *Fashionable Nonsense: Postmodern Intellectuals' Abuse of Science*. New York: Picador.

Vološinov, V. N. 1973. *Marxism and the Philosophy of Language*. Translated by Ladislav Matejka and I. R. Titunik. NY and London: Seminar Press.

We Will End Femicide Platform. 2020. *2020 Report of We Will End Femicide Platform*. Accessed July 5, 2022. http://kadincinayetlerinidurduracagiz.net/veriler/2949/2020-report-of-we-will-end-femicide-platform.

Wollstonecraft, Mary. 1796. *A Vindication of the Right of Women* (Third Edition). London: Printed for J. Johnson, No: 72, St. Paul's Churchyard

Young, Lindsay C., Brenda J. Zaun, and Eric A. Van der Werf. 2008. "Successful same-sex pairing in Laysan albatross." *Biol. Lett.* *2008* 4: 323–325.

Žižek, Slavoj. 2009. "My Own Private Austria." *The Symptom,* *10* (Spring 2009).

Žižek, Slavoj. 2009. *The Sublime Object of Ideology.* London: Verso.

www.ingramcontent.com/pod-product-compliance
Lightning Source LLC
Chambersburg PA
CBHW022050020426
42335CB00012B/629